Georges Ohnet

The Ironmaster or

Love and Pride (Edition 3)

Georges Ohnet

The Ironmaster or
Love and Pride (Edition 3)

ISBN/EAN: 9783337006099

Printed in Europe, USA, Canada, Australia, Japan

Cover: Foto ©Thomas Meinert / pixelio.de

More available books at **www.hansebooks.com**

Vizetelly's One Volume Novels.

I.

THE IRONMASTER;

OR,

LOVE AND PRIDE.

By GEORGES OHNET.

TRANSLATED FROM THE 146TH FRENCH EDITION.

THIRD EDITION.

LONDON:
VIZETELLY & CO., 42, *CATHERINE STREET, STRAND.*
1884.

GEORGES OHNET.

TRANSLATOR'S PREFACE.

A LITERARY work which in its double form of novel and drama has yielded its author nearly £12,000 in a couple of years, is one to awaken both curiosity and interest. Such has been the pecuniary result of M. Georges Ohnet's "Le Maître de Forges," here presented to the English reader under the title of "The Ironmaster." A few years ago a young Frenchman, unknown to fame, wrote a play, which he called "Les Mariages d'Argent," or, as we might say in English, "Marrying for Money." The manuscript was submitted in turn to several of the more noted theatrical managers of Paris, and "declined with thanks" by one and all of them. After such a decided rebuff many a young man, doubtful of his own talent, would probably have abandoned literature for good; but M. Ohnet was aware that fame was only to be achieved by dint of unflagging energy and perseverance in this toilsome nineteenth century. He took back the manuscript of "Marrying for Money," and turned to a different form of literary labour. He wrote a novel called "Serge Panine," and not only succeeded in getting it published, but in bringing it under the notice of the French Academy, which, although often derided, is none the less the foremost literary corporation in the world.

"Serge Panine" was highly commended by such writers as Emile Augier, Octave Feuillet, Jules Sandeau, Victorien Sardou, and Alexandre Dumas *fils*, and guided by the approbation of some of the most eminent of its members, the Academy did not hesitate to award "Serge Panine" a crown of honour.

This well-deserved distinction brought M. Georges Ohnet into prominent notice. "Serge Panine" was transferred to the stage, and met with remarkable success at the Gymnase Theatre in Paris. Thus encouraged, the young novelist and playwright suddenly bethought himself of his earlier venture, "Les Mariages d'Argent." The play had been rejected in the days when he was a nonentity, but now that he had become some one, the very managers who had carelessly tossed it aside unread would no doubt have gladly accepted it. However, M. Ohnet preferred to adopt the course he had followed in the case of "Serge Panine." He transformed "Les Mariages d'Argent" into a novel, which he called "Le Maître de Forges," and the enterprising manager of the Paris *Figaro* eagerly secured the right of publishing it as a *feuilleton*.

"Le Maître de Forges" at once proved a success. The circulation of the *Figaro*—the widest in France, if the halfpenny journals are excepted—immediately increased, and its *feuilleton*, identical in plot and dialogue with the contemptuously rejected drama, became the talk of the town. Reconverted into a play, it was ultimately produced, like "Serge Panine," at the Gymnase. The first performance proved a perfect triumph, and, with M. Jacques Damala, the husband of Madame Sarah Bernhardt, in the title-rôle, the piece is even yet drawing crowded houses. To give some idea of its success, it may be mentioned that as M. Ohnet was entitled to 12 per cent. on the amount of each night's receipts, he derived £3,000 from the first hundred performances alone. In England the play has been adapted on two occasions—by Mr. Robert Buchanan under the title of "Lady Clare," and more recently by Mr. A. W. Pinero as "The Ironmaster."

At the present date the receipts from "Le Maître de Forges" at the Gymnase have exceeded one million francs, while no fewer than 146,000 copies of the work in its form as a novel have already been sold in France, so that, even making due allowance for M. Emile Zola's literary triumphs, this success is altogether the most remarkable that has been achieved of recent years in the domain of fiction across the Channel. "The Ironmaster" is a story of admirably sustained interest, skilfully told in graceful yet forcible language. The strongly marked characters develop themselves naturally, both in their language and their actions. The book, moreover, unlike the general run of French novels, conveys a sound moral. It chastises the malice which is born of envy, and establishes the folly of that selfish pride which blinds its possessor to all consideration for the commoner clay of humanity. It shows anew how needful it is that husbands and wives alike should study each other's characters before marriage, and it enforces in convincing language the oft-repeated lesson that a woman should never trifle with the affection of the man to whom she is mated for life.

LONDON, *May*, 1884.

THE IRONMASTER;

OR,

LOVE AND PRIDE.

I.

On a clear day of the month of October, 1880, a young man, clad in an elegant shooting costume, was seated at the outskirts of one of those pleasant oak-woods which deck with their refreshing shade the lower slopes of the Jura. A big brown spaniel stretched on the heather a few paces off gazed attentively at his master, as if anxious to ascertain whether they would not soon be setting off again. But the sportsman did not seem disposed to resume his ramble yet awhile. He had leant his gun against a tree, thrown his empty game-bag on to the bank of a ditch, and, with his back to the sun and his chin resting on his hand, he let his eyes roam over the admirable panorama displayed before him.

Across the road beside which he had halted, and fringing a thick wood, there stretched a plantation of two years' growth, with its scattered foliage rising amid ferns and yellow grass. The wooded ground sloped gently down into the valley, so as to allow, among the meadows, a view of the large village of Pont-Avesnes, with the conical, slate-covered steeple of its old church rising high above the red-roofed houses. On the right hand was the château, girt round with a broad dried-up moat planted with fruit-trees. The Avesnes, a narrow little streamlet ambitiously called a "river" by the people round about, sparkled like a silver ribbon between the pollard willows with quivering foliage inclined upon its banks.

The ironworks—with their tall chimneys emitting ruddy smoke, swept away by the wind—stretched their blackened walls farther on at the foot of the hill, the rocky basement of which was pierced with large openings serving for the extraction of the ore. Above these excavations were rows of green vines, yielding a flinty-flavoured, poor white wine, commonly sold as Moselle. The pale blue sky was full of sunshine; a transparent haze hung like a light veil over the heights; peacefulness pervaded the smiling scene; and the atmosphere was so pure that the dull thuds of the forge-hammers mounted through space from the valley to the forest.

Lulled by the calmness that surrounded him, the young sportsman remained motionless. By degrees the landscape had ceased to attract his gaze. A feeling of intense content had fallen over him, and he smilingly followed his thoughts, which rambled through the distant past. The sun turning in its course at last gilded the ruddy tree-tops, a heavy heat rose from the heather, and the silence of the woods became more profound. Suddenly, however, the sportsman was aroused from his meditation, for a cold nose rubbed against his knees, while two eyes, human-like in their expression, addressed to him a mute prayer.

"Ah, ah!" said the young man to his dog, "so you are weary of this, my good old fellow? Come, don't be impatient. We'll start off."

And rising with a sigh, he hung his game-bag at his side,

took up his gun, and, crossing the road, sprang over the little ditch bordering the plantation.

The spaniel was already sniffing in the tall grass, and on reaching a bramble he suddenly stopped short with raised paw and bent neck, as motionless as if he had been changed to stone. His tail wagged gently, while with his eyes he seemed to call his master. The latter hastily made several steps forward, and at the same moment a fine hare bounded from the cover, showing his yellow hindquarters and speeding along like a bullet. The young man raised his gun and fired precipitately, but as the smoke cleared away he perceived with vexation, if not with astonishment, that the hare was still scampering towards the wood.

"Another miss!" he muttered, and turning towards the spaniel, who was waiting resignedly, he added, "What a pity, eh? You pointed him out so cleverly."

At the same moment the report of a gun resounded among the foliage a hundred yards or so from the young sportsman, and after a minute's silence the noise of footsteps was heard proceeding through the underbrush, the branches parted, and a vigorous-looking fellow wearing a blue linen shooting blouse, a pair of high boots, and an old hat, appeared at the edge of the wood. In one hand he carried his gun, while with the other he held by its hind paws the hare which the spaniel had started.

"It would seem you have been more lucky than I," said the young sportsman with a smile, as he approached the newcomer.

"Ah! so it was you who fired, monsieur?" rejoined the man in the blouse.

"Yes, and clumsily, too, for the animal started up at my feet and was only twenty paces off when I took aim."

"That certainly wasn't brilliant," resumed the man in the blouse, with a touch of irony in his voice. "But how does it happen, monsieur, that you are shooting over this part of the forest?"

"Why," said the young sportsman, somewhat astonished, "I shoot here because I've a right to——"

"I don't think so. These woods belong to Monsieur Derblay, who does not allow any one to set foot in them."

"Ah, ah! the ironmaster of Pont-Avesnes," rejoined the young sportsman rather haughtily. "If I'm on his land it is without knowing it, and I'm really sorry it should have occurred. You are no doubt Monsieur Derblay's keeper?"

"And you, who are you?" retorted the man in the blouse without answering the question asked of him.

"I am the Marquis de Beaulieu, and I beg you to believe that I am not in the habit of poaching."

On hearing this the man in the blouse flushed crimson, and bowing most deferentially exclaimed, "Pray excuse me, Monsieur le Marquis. If I had known whom I had to deal with I should not have approached you nor asked you for any explanations. Pray continue shooting; I will withdraw."

Whilst listening the young Marquis attentively scanned the man in the blue blouse. He seemed to be above his rustic costume. His face, framed by a black beard, was handsome and intelligent. His hands were well shaped and well cared for. Moreover, the gun he had just hung over his shoulder was one of those admirable weapons, handsome in their simplicity, such as English gunsmiths alone know how to produce.

"Thank you," returned the Marquis coldly, "but I have not the honour of knowing Monsieur Derblay. I am only aware that he is a troublesome neighbour, with whom we are on bad terms. I should therefore regret firing another shot on his land. I only reached Beaulieu yesterday. I am imperfectly acquainted with the ground, and my love of sport has led me to overstep our limit. However, it shall not occur again."

"As you please, Monsieur le Marquis," answered the man in the blouse softly; "but I can guarantee that Monsieur Derblay would have been happy to prove to you in this circumstance that if he be a troublesome neighbour it is in spite of himself. He has encroached on the Beaulieu estate in laying down a mining railroad; but rest assured that he regrets it, and that he is ready to indemnify you as you may please. The boundary of two neighbouring estates is sometimes uncertain," he added with a smile. "You have just experienced this yourself. So do not judge Monsieur Derblay without knowing him. Later on you would certainly regret your severity."

"You are no doubt one of the ironmaster's friends?" observed the Marquis, looking at the man in the blouse. "One of his people, perhaps; for the warmth you show in defending him——"

"Is quite natural, believe me, Monsieur le Marquis." And abruptly changing the conversation, the man with the black beard added, "But you don't seem to have been very lucky either over Beaulieu or Pont-Avesnes. Monsieur Derblay prides himself on his preserves, and he would be annoyed to hear it said that you left his land emptyhanded. Pray, therefore, accept this hare which you so obligingly started, together with these four partridges."

"I cannot accept them," hastily replied the Marquis. "Keep them, pray; you would disoblige me by insisting——"

"And yet I *must* insist, even at the risk of displeasing you," answered the man in the blouse. "I will lay the game on the bank here. You are free to leave it if you choose, but it will only be for the benefit of the foxes. I have the honour of saluting you, Monsieur le Marquis." And, leaping back into the wood, he strode rapidly away.

"Monsieur! monsieur!" called the Marquis; but the man in the blouse was already out of sight. "What a strange adventure!" muttered M. de Beaulieu. "What shall I do?"

An unexpected intervention put an end to his perplexity, for the brown spaniel had approached the bank, and taking one of the partridges in his mouth with all due precaution, he now brought it to his master. The latter began to laugh, and stroking the dog exclaimed, "So you don't want us to go back with nothing." Thereupon, placing the hare and the four partridges in his game-bag, the young Marquis turned homewards, trudging somewhat heavily along with this unwonted burden.

The Château de Beaulieu, in the Louis XIII. style, and comprising a central building and two wings, is built of white stone with red brick dressings. The pointed roofs of the wings are surmounted by tall sculptured chimney-stacks of highly characteristic aspect. A broad terrace, more than five hundred yards long, with a balustrade in red granite and decked with parterres of flowers, extends in front of the château, being reached by a flight of eight steps arranged as a grotto underneath, whilst up the wrought-iron railings flowers and creeping plants climb in profusion, offering a perfumed support to those who mount or descend. The terrace, which has a southern aspect, becomes a delightful walk in the autumn. The view is charming, for the château, built on the heights which face the vineyards and quarries of Pont-Avesnes, is surrounded by a park of fifty acres sloping gently down into the valley. M. Derblay's ironworks may have somewhat spoiled the beauty of the landscape and have troubled the rural calm, but Beaulieu nevertheless remains a highly covetable estate.

And yet for long years it remained deserted. In 1845, when the Marquis de Beaulieu—father of the young man who has already been introduced to the reader—attained his majority, he found himself in possession of a superb fortune, and began to lead an extravagant life in Paris. Still, every year, during the shooting season, he spent three months or so at Beaulieu. It was then fête-time for the aristocracy of the district, and the Marquis's lavish prodigality enriched the neighbourhood for the whole winter.

When the Revolution of 1848 burst forth, the vinegrowers of Pont-Avesnes, electrified by the socialistic speeches of a few ringleaders, took it into their heads to requite the Marquis's generosity by sacking his château. Armed with guns, scythes, and pitchforks, with the red flag waving in their midst, they climbed up to Beaulieu, yelling the "Marseillaise." They broke down the park-gates, which the porter obstinately refused to open, and scattering themselves through the château, they began to pillage it, destroying whatever they could not carry off. The brightest of the band at last lighted upon the cellar-door, and thereupon revelry followed theft. The Marquis's wines were choice, and the vinegrowers appreciated them like true connoisseurs. With inebriety their violent instincts returned. Spreading through the conservatories, which were tended with especial care, the brutes began to tread the flowers underfoot and break the marble vases.

In a verdant bower there stood an admirable statue of Flora, the work of Pradier, beneath the pedestal of which a cascade fell murmuring into a stone basin. One madman was on the point of slashing the charming figure with his scythe, when the most drunken of the band suddenly became sentimental, darted in front of the masterpiece, declaring that he was a friend of art, and would plunge his pitchfork into the stomach of any one who dared to touch the statue. Thus the Flora was saved. However, to console themselves, the good people of Pont-Avesnes thought of planting a tree of liberty. They uprooted a young poplar in the park, and after decorating it with red rags, came with joyful howls to replant it in the middle of the terrace. Then they returned to the town and continued their revolutionary orgie, yelling until midnight. On the following morning a brigade of gendarmerie arrived at Pont-Avesnes, and order was speedily restored.

When the Marquis was apprised of this outbreak he began by laughing. Having always behaved so munificently towards the folks of Pont-Avesnes, it seemed to him only natural that they should try to harm him. But when he learnt that a so-called tree of liberty had been planted on the terrace, his wrath was kindled. This, he considered, was carrying the joke too far. He sent orders to his gardener to uproot the young poplar, saw it into logs of the customary size, and despatch these logs to him in Paris, to be used as firewood. He moreover sent five hundred francs to the drunkard who, declaring himself the friend of art, had saved the statue of Flora; and he caused the good people of Pont-Avesnes to be informed that, by way of retaliating against their revolutionary farce, he would never again set foot at Beaulieu as long as he lived.

As this decision implied a loss of at least twenty thousand francs a year, the village made an effort at reconciliation through the medium of its mayor, and even tried the effect of a petition signed by the municipal council. All of no avail. The Marquis did not forgive the tree of liberty, and the château of Beaulieu remained closed. To tell the truth, the Marquis was considerably influenced in his resolution by the attractions of the capital. Club and greenroom life, sport and gallant adventures, kept him away from Beaulieu even more forcibly than his rancour against the peasants. However, after leading for several years a life of pleasure and excitement, he wearied somewhat of his follies, and took advantage of a rational moment to marry.

His young wife, the daughter of the Duc de Bligny, had a tender heart and a calm mind. She worshipped the Marquis, and knew how to close her eyes to his weaknesses. He was one of those delightful prodigals for whom pleasure is the quintessence of life, whose hands and heart are always open; he did not know how to resist a wish of his wife, and yet he was capable of killing her with sorrow, to mourn her bitterly afterwards. When the Marchioness began to scold him in a maternal way after some excessive folly, he would kiss her hands, with tears in his eyes, and say, "You are a saint." But on the morrow he began again.

The young couple's honeymoon had lasted three years, and this was praiseworthy on the part of such a man as the Marquis. Two children were born of the marriage, a son and a daughter. Octave and Claire grew up, reared by their mother—the heir in serious fashion, so that he might become a useful man; the daughter delicately, so that she might charm the life of the suitor she selected. By a freak of nature, however, the son was the living image of his mother, sweet-tempered, tender-hearted, and gay, while the daughter inherited her father's impetuous and ardent character. Education may soften nature but it cannot change it. As Octave grew older he became the amiable young fellow he had promised to be, while Claire proved the superb and haughty damsel already foreshadowed in infancy.

However there soon came to them a companion, brought by misfortune and mourning. The Marchioness's brother—the Duc de Bligny—left a widower when very young with a little son, perished miserably as a gentleman-rider on a racecourse, having his ribs broken by his horse's hoofs. This descendant of the Crusaders, who died like a jockey, left scarcely any fortune behind him, and after the funeral little Gaston, his son, was led, clad in black, to the house of his aunt the Marchioness, where he remained. Treated like a third child, he grew up with Octave and Claire. Older than they were, he possessed innately the power of fascination and the elegant instincts pertaining to the refined race he sprang from. Still, he had been but little cared for by his father, whose dissipated life was hardly conducive to paternal watchfulness. At times abandoned to the servants, who suffered him to witness their low intrigues; at others taken by the Duke, his father, to some *partie fine*, and excited by the highly-spiced fare of restaurants, the innocence of this child, betwixt the debauchery of varlets and the gallant adventures of his father, was put to a sore trial.

When he was brought to the Beaulieu mansion he was of weakly constitution, sad-minded, and somewhat corrupted from a moral point of view. But in the healthier atmosphere of family life he regained all the graces and all the freshness of youth. At nineteen, when his studies were finished, he promised to become a charming cavalier and an accomplished gentleman. It was at this moment he perceived that his cousin Claire, by four years his junior, was no longer a little girl.

She had been suddenly transformed. Like a lovely butterfly emerging from a chrysalis, Claire had just blossomed forth in all the splendour of her radiant beauty. She was of fair complexion. Her black eyes gleamed with soft refulgency, and her admirably developed figure was of matchless elegance. Gaston adored her madly. His love came upon him like a thunderbolt; still, for two years he kept his secret deep in the recesses of his heart.

A great misfortune induced him to speak. Confession comes more readily from the heart in moments of grief. The Marquis de Beaulieu suddenly died. This brilliant *viveur* passed away discreetly in the English fashion.* He was not taken ill; he simply ceased to live. He was found stretched on the carpet in his study. He had wished to examine the documents connected with a lawsuit in which he was engaged against some distant relatives in England, and this unwonted task had proved too much for him.

Medical men, who are bent on determining everything with precision, and who do not admit that any one can dispense with their opinion, especially when it is a matter of death, declared in this instance that the Marquis's demise was due to the rupture of an artery. Club friends shook their heads, however, and said among themselves that poor dear Beaulieu had finished like Morny—used up, burnt to a cinder by "high life." It is certain that no one could lead such an existence as the Marquis had led for five-and-twenty years with impu-

---

* In the above expression the translator has scrupulously respected M. Ohnet's phraseology. "To depart in the English fashion," as is commonly said in France, means to go off without saying "good-bye." Had M. de Beaulieu been an Englishman, we should probably have said of him that "he took French leave." Cordial as may be their neighbourly intercourse, Frenchmen and Englishmen seldom let a favourable opportunity pass without having a fling at each other; and the present is only one instance out of many.

nity. Others were of opinion that the revelation made by the business man of this superb prodigal, that his entire fortune was exhausted, had killed him as surely as if a bullet had been lodged in his heart.

The Marquis's family, however, did not seek to ascertain the causes of his sudden demise: it only thought of weeping. M. de Beaulieu was loved and respected as if he had been a model husband and father. The Marchioness put all her household into mourning, and ordered princely obsequies for the man whom she had so dearly loved despite his faults, and whom she bitterly regretted. Octave, now Marquis de Beaulieu, and the Duc de Bligny, his adopted brother, officiated as chief mourners, surrounded by the oldest nobility of France; and in the evening, when they returned to the gloomy, silent mansion, they found the Marchioness and Claire, clad in black, waiting to console them and thank them for having fulfilled this sad and painful duty. Then the Marchioness retired into her own room with her son to speak to him of the future, and Gaston went out into the garden with Claire.

The shades of night were spreading under the tall trees. It was a beautiful summer evening; the air was balmy with the scent of flowers. The young couple walked slowly round the lawn without exchanging a word. They were both following their thoughts. By a mutual impulse they paused together and sat down on a stone bench. A fountain played in the marble basin at their feet, and its monotonous murmur lulled their reverie. Suddenly, however, Gaston broke the silence, and, speaking precipitately, like a person who has restrained himself too long, he told Claire in touching terms how bitterly he regretted the excellent man who had filled his father's place. The young Duke was powerless to moderate his feelings. His nerves had been too cruelly overstrung all day long, and now, in his utter weakness, he succumbed to his acute emotion. Unable to restrain his tears, he began to sob, and then letting his heavy head fall on to Claire's burning hands, he cried—

"Ah! I shall never forget what you and yours have been for me. No matter what may happen to me in life, you will always find me near you—I love you so." And between his sobs he repeated, "I love you! I love you!"

He coloured deeply and seemed almost ashamed of his weakness, as Claire gently raised his head and looking earnestly at him said, with a soft smile, "And I, too; I love you."

Transported, Gaston raised a cry: "Claire!"

She placed her hands upon his lips, however, and with the solemnity befitting an engagement, imprinted a kiss upon his forehead. Then they slowly rose to their feet again, and, leaning on each other, resumed in silence their walk around the lawn. They no longer thought of speaking: they were listening to their hearts.

On the morrow Octave de Beaulieu began to study law, and Gaston entered the diplomatic service. The Republican Government was at that time seeking for the support of aristocratic names, with the view of reassuring the foreign powers, who watched the triumph of democracy with anxious eyes. The young Duke was attached to the *cabinet* of M. Decazes, and a brilliant diplomatic future seemed reserved for him. Eagerly received into society, he had created a great sensation by his elegant bearing, his graceful features, and his charming conversational powers. Sought after by mothers with marriageable daughters, he had remained indifferent to all advances. He had only eyes for Claire, and his most pleasant evenings were those he spent in his aunt's little drawing-room, watching his cousin as she worked, bending her head over her embroidery. The wayward hair curling over her neck sparkled in the lamplight, and Gaston remained grave and silent, devouring with his eyes, as it were, those golden locks which he longed to kiss devoutly. At ten o'clock he took leave of the Marchioness, shook hands in brother-like fashion with Claire, and went off into society to dance till dawn. In summer-time the whole household hied away to Normandy, where the Marchioness had some property. In memory of her husband's rancour, she had not yet returned to Beaulieu. Gaston was supremely happy in the country: he galloped on horseback through the woods with Octave and Claire, whilst the Marchioness dived into the family records in search of fresh documents for the English lawsuit.

A very large sum had been bequeathed by will to M. de Beaulieu; but the legacy had been contested in England, and the solicitors of the adverse parties, entering into the suit like so many rats into a cheese, were making money by prolonging the hostilities. The action, which the Marquis had brought mainly out of vanity, was carried on by his widow out of interest, for M. de Beaulieu's fortune had been grievously compromised by his follies, and the great English legacy represented by far the larger part of the two children's patrimony. The Marchioness had a handsome fortune of her own perfectly secured, but it only sufficed to defray the heavy expenses of everyday life. So, although Madame de Beaulieu held legal quibbling in horror, she had become a pleader in view of defending Claire's and Octave's interests. Immersed in documents, constantly in correspondence with her lawyers, she had really become most proficient in legal knowledge. She had perfect confidence in the result of the suit. The opinion of her relatives strengthened her sense of security, and it was generally considered that Claire would bring a dowry of a couple of millions of francs (£80,000) to the man who was fortunate enough to please her. Her hand had already been asked for in marriage by suitors of high birth and great fortune. But she had refused them all, and when at last the Marchioness anxiously questioned her, she unhesitatingly replied that she was engaged to the Duc de Bligny.

Madame de Beaulieu was by no means overjoyed on hearing of this engagement. She not only had very strong preconceived ideas on marriages between cousins, but she also judged Gaston with singular penetration. She considered him light-headed, passionate, and inconstant, quite capable of ardent love, but incapable of loving faithfully. Still, she did not try to influence her daughter. She was acquainted with Claire's wonderfully firm character, and knew that nothing would induce her to set aside a freely contracted engagement. Moreover, in the depths of her heart she was perhaps flattered by the idea of an alliance which would restore to her family the grand name of Bligny, which she herself had relinquished on marrying. So she received her nephew graciously, and, as she could not treat him better than she had done so far, she continued to regard him as her son.

Precisely at this period the Duke was appointed secretary to the French embassy at St. Petersburg, and it was agreed on both sides that the marriage should take place as soon as the young diplomatist obtained his first leave of absence. This first leave was given six months later. Gaston arrived in Paris, but only for a week. He was entrusted with a confidential mission which the ambassador had not chosen to expose to the risks attendant upon the exchange of ciphered despatches.

A week! Could the wedding in all conscience take place in so short a time? There was not even time for the banns to be properly published. During his brief visit the young Duke showed himself affectionate towards Claire, but his manner was tinged with a shade of levity which contrasted with his pious adoration of former times. Since his departure he had mixed in Russian society, the most corrupt that exists in the world, and he returned to Paris with very singular ideas on love. The expression of his face had changed like the feelings of his heart. His features were harder and more marked; it seemed as if a trace of debauchery now lingered on his once unsullied brow. However, Claire did not or would not see the alteration. Her tenderness was unsusceptible of change, and besides, she had confidence in her noble lover, and waited. But if Gaston's letters were at first frequent, they gradually became few and far between, although always full of passionate protestations. To believe him, the postponement of his happiness made him suffer cruelly. But he no longer spoke of returning, and two years had elapsed since his departure.

At her daughter's request, Madame de Beaulieu had closed her drawing-rooms during the past two winters. Claire wished to live in seclusion, so as to avoid the solicitations of undiscouraged suitors. Meanwhile, Octave continued studying jurisprudence, and the Marchioness became more and more immersed in the documents of her interminable lawsuit.

When spring returned, Claire, capricious as usual, expressed a wish to visit the Beaulieu estate, which she had never seen, her father having placed it under interdict prior to his marriage. The Marchioness, who was incapable of resisting her daughter, and who considered moreover that a change would do her good, consented to undertake the journey. And thus it happened that one fine October day the young Marquis, who had just taken his degree, was met, gun in hand and accompanied by his brown spaniel, in the woods belonging to M. Derblay, the ironmaster.

II.

Whilst the young Marquis was trudging back, heavily laden, towards the château, Madame de Beaulieu and Claire sat in the drawing-room enjoying the close of this fine day. The large glass doors stood open, and the sun's rays streamed into the room, brightening the faded gold of the frames enclosing the portraits of the family ancestors, smiling or solemn in their ceremonial costumes. The Louis XVI. furniture in carved wood, painted white and picked out with sea-green, was upholstered in tapestry representing Ovid's "Metamorphosis." A broad screen, hung with Genoa velvet, encompassed the low, cosy arm-chair in which the Marchioness sat, attentively knitting some woollen hoods for the little children of the village.

Madame de Beaulieu was then over forty years of age. The hair crowning her grave gentle face was almost white, and gave her a noble appearance. Her black melancholy eyes seemed still moist with the tears she had shed in secret. Of slender frame and delicate health, she took every kind of precaution. Even on this warm afternoon a shawl was stretched over her knees, sheltering her tiny feet, encased with persistent coquetry in low black satin shoes, from the fresh air.

Ensconced in a large arm-chair, with her head resting against the tapestry at the back, and her hands hanging down inert,

Claire, whose gaze was lost in the sky, contemplated without seeing it the admirable horizon stretched out before her. For an hour she had remained thus, motionless and silent, enveloped in the sunlight, which, illuminating her fair hair, gave it the gleam of an aureole around the Virgin's head.

The Marchioness had been anxiously watching her daughter for some minutes. A sad smile had strayed over her lips, and to attract Claire's attention she now stirred the basket containing her balls of wool, a significant "Hem! hem!" accompanying the movement. But the young girl, quite insensible to this indirect appeal, still remained motionless, and tenaciously followed her train of thought. The disappointed Marchioness thereupon laid her work on the table, and, drawing herself up in her chair, exclaimed in a slightly scolding tone, "Claire! Claire!"

For a moment Mademoiselle Beaulieu closed her eyes as if to bid her dream good-bye, and then, without moving her head, but merely raising her beautiful white hands to the arms of the chair, she answered, "Mother."

"What are you thinking about?"

Claire remained for a moment silent, and a wrinkle creased her forehead. But at last, making an effort, she calmly replied, "I was thinking of nothing, mother. The warm air had made me feel drowsy. Why did you call me?"

"For you to speak to me," said the Marchioness, with a shade of affectionate reproach in her voice. "To prevent your remaining so silent and absorbed."

There came another brief pause, and Claire resumed her listless attitude, while the Marchioness, leaning forward, and careless of the fresh air, threw aside her shawl. At last, turning slowly towards her mother, Mademoiselle de Beaulieu displayed her beautiful sad face, and resuming aloud the train of thought she had been silently following, she asked, "How long is it since we have had any letters from St. Petersburg?"

The Marchioness nodded her head, as if to say, "I knew what it was all about," and then, trying to speak as calmly as possible, she answered, "It must be about two months."

"Two months, yes!" repeated Claire, with a painful sigh.

The Marchioness's patience was now quite gone, and, abruptly rising, she came and sat down near the window in front of her daughter. "Come," said she, taking hold of Claire's hands, "come, why do you always think about that and torture your mind so?"

"What can I think of," answered Claire bitterly, "but of my betrothed? And how can I avoid torturing my mind, as you say, in trying to divine the reason of his silence?"

"I own that it is difficult to explain," rejoined the Marchioness. "After spending a week with us last year, my nephew, the Duc de Bligny, started off, promising to return to Paris during the winter. He next began by writing that political complications detained him at his post. Then he pretended that as the winter season was over, he should wait for the summer before returning to France. Summer came but not the Duke. Here, now, is autumn, and Gaston no longer even favours us with pretences. He does not even take the trouble to write to us. If this be only mere negligence, it is already too much. My dear girl, everything is degenerating. Even the men of our station no longer know how to be polite."

As she spoke, the Marchioness raised her white head, which made her look like one of the great ladies with powdered hair who smiled all round the drawing-room from their handsome frames.

"But supposing he were ill," Claire ventured to say, already impelled to defend the man she loved. "Supposing he were altogether unable to communicate with us?"

"That is out of the question," replied the Marchioness pitilessly. "The Embassy would have informed us of it. You may be sure that he is in perfect health, quite fresh and gay, and that he led the *cotillon* all last winter in the ball-rooms of St. Petersburg."

A nervous twitch contracted Claire's features, and she turned pale as though all the blood in her veins had rushed to her heart. Then forcing herself to smile, she said, "He promised me so often that he would come and spend the winter in Paris, and I was eagerly looking forward to the time when I should find myself with him in society. His successes would have been triumphs for me, and he would perhaps have noticed mine. It must be confessed, mother, he is not jealous, and yet there might be reason for jealousy. I have been courted wherever we have gone, and I am scarcely allowed to remain in peace even in this desert of Beaulieu. It would seem that I have attracted the attention of our neighbour the ironmaster."

"Monsieur Derblay?"

"Yes, mother, Monsieur Derblay. On Sunday, at mass—you did not notice it, you are too pious—I was reading my prayers beside you, and without knowing why, I felt ill at ease. Something stronger than my will attracted my attention, and in spite of myself I turned, raised my eyes, and perceived Monsieur Derblay."

"He was praying?"

"No, mother; he was looking at me. Our eyes met, and I could distinguish in his a kind of mute invocation, as it were. I lowered my head, and during the rest of the service

I strove not to look again in his direction. However, as we left the church I found him waiting under the porch. He did not dare to offer me holy water, but he made a deep bow, and as we passed out I felt that his eyes were following me. It appears this was the first time he had been seen at mass this year."

As Claire finished speaking the Marchioness returned to her old place, and having comfortably settled herself in her arm-chair, she exclaimed, "Well, his presence at church will perhaps increase his chances of salvation. But at all events, instead of making soft eyes at you, he would do much better if he indemnified us for his encroachments on our land. I consider him rather ridiculous with his mute invocations, indeed. And you must really have little to think of, Claire, to occupy yourself with the sighs of this iron-smelter, who one of these fine mornings will end by making us deaf with his hammering."

"But, mother, Monsieur Derblay's homage is respectful, and I have no cause to complain of him. Besides, I only mentioned him as an example—as one out of many. However, people say that women's hearts are changeable. The Duke stays away, and I am here, like Penelope, awaiting a return which never takes place. Hasn't Gaston ever thought that I might perhaps grow weary of waiting? He ought to have done so, but I fear he has not. And so I remain here alone, patient and faithful——"

"And you act very wrongly," exclaimed the Marchioness, vivaciously, "If I were in your place——"

"No, mother," interrupted Mademoiselle de Beaulieu, with solemn firmness, "I don't act wrongly. Besides, my conduct is only natural and quite undeserving of praise, for I love the Duc de Bligny."

"You love him!" rejoined the Marchioness, who was unable to hide her irritation. "How you do exaggerate! The idea of transforming a childish friendship into deep love, of assimilating a tie of relationship to a bond for life. You and Gaston grew up together. You thought you would always live on, side by side, and you imagined you would never be happy unless the Duke became your husband. But all that is folly, child."

"Mother!" cried Claire.

But the Marchioness was fairly started, and the opportunity of easing her mind which now presented itself was too favourable a one for her to allow it to escape. "You greatly deceive yourself respecting the Duke," she resumed. "In point of fact he is light-headed and frivolous. As you know yourself, he has certain independent habits which he would never be able to shake off; and I foresee a great many deceptions for you in the future. Shall I tell you what I really think? Why, that there will be cause to regret this marriage should it ever take place."

Claire had started to her feet, and a crimson flush was rising to her cheeks. For a moment the mother and the daughter remained looking at each other without speaking. It seemed as if the first words they exchanged would have exceptional gravity. Mademoiselle de Beaulieu was at last unable to restrain herself any longer, and in a quivering voice she exclaimed, "This is the first time you have spoken to me like that, mother. Do you want to prepare me for some bad news? Has the Duke's absence a serious motive that you have hidden from me? Have you learned——"

The Marchioness felt frightened on observing her daughter's violent emotion. She realised more forcibly than ever how deeply and firmly Claire was attached to the Duc de Bligny.

She perceived that she had gone too far, and so, promptly retreating, she rejoined, "No, child, I know nothing; nothing has been told me. I even consider that I am not told enough. I am astonished by this long silence on my nephew's part, and it seems to me that Gaston really carries diplomacy too far."

A weight was lifted from Claire's heart; she felt reassured, and attributed her mother's strong language to a feeling of displeasure which she herself could not help thinking was justified. Accordingly she strove to recover her serenity, and exclaimed, "Come, mother, let us have a little more patience. The Duke is thinking about us, I'm sure of it; and he will surprise us by arriving here unexpectedly."

"I hope so, dear, since it is your wish. At all events, my nephew De Préfont and his wife arrive to-day from Paris. Perhaps they will be better informed than we are."

"Ah!" interrupted Mademoiselle de Beaulieu at this moment, "here is Octave coming along the terrace with Monsieur Bachelin, the notary." And availing herself of this opportunity to bring her painful conversation with her mother to a close, she eagerly rose to her feet.

She passed from the drawing-room on to the flight of steps which conducted to the terrace, thus advancing into the full sunlight. Twenty-two years of age, Claire was now in all the radiance of her beauty. Her tall figure was exquisitely proportioned, and her arms, springing from a superb bust, terminated in a pair of hands worthy of a queen. Her golden hair was knotted on the summit of her head, so as to allow a full view of her round white neck. Leaning slightly forward, with her hands resting on the iron balustrade, listlessly fingering one of the creeping plants which twined around the bars, she looked the living incarnation of youth in all its grace and vigour.

For a moment Madame de Beaulieu gazed at her admiringly; then she shook her head in silence and heaved a final sigh. The gravel on the terrace was grating under the tread of the new arrivals, whose voices were already wafted confusedly to the drawing-room.

Maître Bachelin, the notary, was a little man of sixty or thereabouts, somewhat corpulent owing to the sedentary office life he had led. With his white hair and his clean-shaven red face, his solemn black clothes and just a glimpse of wristbands falling over his hands, he was a perfect type of the *tabellion** of the old *régime*. Strongly attached to his noble clients, invariably repeating the formula, "Madame la Marquise" in a devoutly unctuous voice, he busied himself with the interests of the Beaulieu family by hereditary right. In fact the Bachelins were by birth the notaries of the lords of Beaulieu; and the worthy man whom we have now to introduce prided himself on possessing in his office various charters dating from the reign of Louis XI., and whereon figured the rough feudal signature of Marquis Honoré-Onfroy-Jacques-Octave de Beaulieu, and the ornamental flourish of Maître Joseph-Antoine Bachelin, royal notary.

The worthy man was delighted when the Beaulieu family came back to their château, for naturally enough he hoped for his own return into favour. He had long fretted over the absence of his noble clients, and now that they had visited their fine estate he trusted they would resume the practice of spending the summer there. Desirous of displaying his

---

* This term "tabellion," which nowadays is so often applied to French notaries in a sneering fashion, really has no insulting meaning at all. Indeed, "tabellion" was simply the *official* title of the legal functionaries who, prior to the Great Revolution, discharged notarial duties in subordinate jurisdictions, notably on those demesnes where the *seigneurs* administered justice.—*Trans.*

knowledge and acumen, he had placed himself at Madame de Beaulieu's disposal to unravel the entangled skein of the English lawsuit. For six weeks or so he had been actively corresponding with the solicitors in London, and had wonderfully accelerated matters. In fact, in that month and a half Maître Bachelin had done more work than all the other legal advisers of the Beaulieu family in ten years; and despite the unfavourable opinion which he had expressed regarding the result of the suit, the Marchioness was delighted with his help and stupefied by the ardour he displayed. She realised that he was one of those devoted advisers worthy of being raised to the rank of friend, and she treated him accordingly.

Bound for the château, Maître Bachelin had met the young Marquis at the park gate, and, perceiving that Octave was heavily laden, he had perforce taken charge of his gun, which he carried under his left arm, whilst under his right appeared a bulky black leather portfolio stuffed full of papers.

"Why, how hampered you are in your movements, poor Monsieur Bachelin!" gaily cried Claire to the notary, who, whilst hastening up the steps, was vainly trying to bow and take off his hat.

"Pay accept the assurance of my profound respect, mademoiselle," answered the notary. "As you perceive, I unite in my person the symbols of right and might: the code under one arm and a gun under the other. But the gun is under the left one. *Cedant arma togæ!* Excuse me; no doubt you don't understand Latin. I am only a vulgar pedant."

"Oh, my sister knows enough Latin to understand that," exclaimed the Marquis, laughing. "And as for your being a pedant, well no, I prefer to think you the best fellow in the world. Now, pray return me my gun. Thanks." And taking his weapon, Octave mounted the steps behind the notary.

"You have had good sport, it seems," said Mademoiselle de Beaulieu, waylaying her brother on the threshold of the drawing-room, and feeling the weight of his game-bag.

"Oh, I'll be modest! I don't care to strut about in borrowed plumes. To tell the truth, this game was not killed by me."

"Who killed it, then?"

"I don't know," answered the Marquis; and as his sister made a gesture of astonishment, he added, "really, I don't. The fact is, I had lost my way on the Pont-Avesnes land, when I met another sportsman, who accosted me and asked me who I was. He was rather haughty at first, and did not mince matters in speaking to me, but as soon as I told him my name he became not merely polite, but very amiable, and almost forced me to accept what he had in his own game-bag."

"How singular," exclaimed Mademoiselle de Beaulieu. "Perhaps this man wanted to play you some joke."

"Well, no, I hardly think so. He rather seemed desirous of pleasing me; and, in fact, as soon as he had deposited the game on the bank of a ditch for me to take it, he hurried off as fast as his legs could carry him, so as to prevent my refusing the gift."

"Will Monsieur le Marquis allow me to ask him a question?" said Maître Bachelin, who had been listening attentively.

"Certainly, by all means, my dear sir."

"Well, what was this person like?"

"Oh! he was a tall fellow, very dark, wearing a blue blouse and an old grey felt hat."

"Ah, ah! I was not mistaken," muttered the notary to himself; and he added in a louder key, "Well, I can tell you whom you are indebted to for your mysterious gift, Monsieur le Marquis. The person you met was simply Monsieur Derblay."

"Monsieur Derblay!" exclaimed the Marquis. "What, rigged out in a blouse like a peasant, and wearing a slouched hat like a poacher? Come, that isn't possible."

"Don't forget, Monsieur le Marquis," rejoined Maître Bachelin with a smile, "that we are all rustic sportsmen hereabouts. Why, take myself, for instance; I like to be decently dressed under ordinary circumstances, but I should very likely frighten you if you met me at the edge of a wood when I'm out shooting. The person you spoke with was Monsieur Derblay, you may be sure of it. And even if I didn't recognise him by the striking portrait you sketched of him, that amiable gift of his would suffice to dispel all my doubts. Oh, it was certainly he."

"Well, if that be the case, I *was* polite. In speaking about him I told him he was a troublesome neighbour, and I added all sorts of other unpleasant things. Why, I shall have to go and apologise to him."

"You won't need to take that trouble, Monsieur le Marquis. If you will kindly inform Madame de Beaulieu of my arrival I will acquaint you in her presence with various matters which I am sure will modify the opinion you had formed of Monsieur Derblay."

"Upon my word, I don't ask anything better," replied Octave, ridding himself of his shooting paraphernalia. "This ironmaster seemed to be an amiable fellow." With these words the Marquis entered the drawing-room, approached his mother, and respectfully kissed her hand. "Maître Bachelin is here, mother, and would like to see you," he said.

"Why doesn't he come in?" eagerly replied the Marchioness. "Why, for the last ten minutes I have heard you chattering on the steps. Good afternoon, my dear Bachelin." And as the notary bowed as deeply as his corpulence would admit of, the Marchioness added, "Have you brought me some good news?"

The expression of Bachelin's features changed, and in lieu of a smile a look of concern spread over them. Eluding his noble client's question, he answered in a serious tone, "I have brought you some news, yes, Madame la Marquise."

Then, as if desirous of passing to a more pleasant topic, he resumed, "I went this morning to Pont-Avesnes, and I saw Monsieur Derblay there. All the questions at issue between you and him in reference to the boundaries of your estates are as good as settled, for my worthy friend accepts whatever conditions you may lay down. He is happy to be able to place himself at your good pleasure."

"But if that is the case," said Madame de Beaulieu with a shade of embarrassment, "we have no conditions to lay down at all. As there is to be no battle, there can neither be victor nor vanquished. The matter shall be submitted to your arbitration, my dear Bachelin, and whatever you decide will be equable, I'm sure."

"Your decision delights me, and I'm really happy to see peace re-established between the château and the ironworks. The only point now is to sign the preliminaries, and with this object Monsieur Derblay proposes to call at Beaulieu with his sister, Mademoiselle Suzanne, so as to offer you his respects, Madame la Marquise; that is, if you are pleased to authorise him."

"Oh, certainly. Let him come by all means. I shall be glad to see this Cyclops who is blackening the whole valley. But come, I don't suppose it is merely the treaty of peace that makes your portfolio so bulky," said Madame de Beaulieu, pointing to the notary's letter-case. "You have, no doubt, brought me some fresh documents in reference to our English lawsuit."

"Yes, Madame la Marquise, yes," rejoined Bachelin, with evident perturbation; "we will talk business if you desire it."

As the notary spoke he gave the Marchioness an appealing glance, as if to call her attention to the presence of her son and daughter. Madame de Beaulieu understood him, and a vague dread made her heart sink. What bad news could her confidential adviser have to tell her that absolute privacy seemed requisite? However, she was a resolute woman, and so turning towards her son she exclaimed, "Octave, pray see if orders have been given for the carriage to be sent to the station to fetch our cousins who arrive at five o'clock."

On hearing this Claire raised her head, and her brother started. The Marchioness's desire was plain. She had devised a pretext to induce her son to leave the room. These three beings who loved each other so dearly had a mysterious common preoccupation which they mutually endeavoured to hide from one another. However, without asking any questions, Claire and the Marquis gave their mother a smile, and left the drawing-room in opposite directions.

Mademoiselle de Beaulieu slowly descended the steps leading to the terrace. An idea that Bachelin might have brought some news of the Duc de Bligny had suddenly occurred to her, and greatly agitated, with her head whirling so that she could not fix her mind on any precise thought, she walked along under the tall trees, unconscious of the passing time, so deep was her emotion.

The Marchioness and Bachelin had remained together in the drawing-room. The notary no longer made any effort to retain a smiling countenance; his expression was serious and thoughtful. For a moment Madame de Beaulieu remained silent, as if anxious to enjoy her tranquillity of mind as long as was possible, but at last coming to a resolution she exclaimed, "Well, my dear Bachelin, what have you to tell me?"

The notary sorrowfully shook his white head. "Nothing pleasant, Madame la Marquise," he replied; "and it is a source of great affliction for an old retainer of your family like myself. I fear that the success of the action which the late Marquis de Beaulieu, your husband, brought against his collateral relatives in England is seriously compromised——"

"You don't tell me the whole truth, Bachelin," interrupted the Marchioness. "You would not be so downcast if there were still a ray of hope. Come, speak; I am strong and prepared for the worst. Have the English courts decided? Is the action lost?"

The notary lacked the courage to reply in words, but his gesture was equivalent to the most complete confession. The Marchioness bit her lips, and a tear glittered under her eyelashes, speedily dried, however, by the burning flush which mantled over her face.

As for Bachelin, in his consternation he began to pace hurriedly up and down the drawing-room. He had forgotten his usual respectful manner, and no longer remembered in what a hallowed spot he found himself. Carried away by his emotion, and gesticulating as was his wont when he studied a case in his office, he rattled on in this desultory fashion: "The action was not properly launched! Those English solicitors are donkeys! And rapacious, too! They write you a letter; it's so much. You answer them, they read your reply; it's so much more! If the Marquis had even only asked me for advice! But he was in Paris, and his solicitor there gave him bad counsel! Another set of donkeys, those Paris solicitors!—fellows who only know how to increase the consumption of stamped paper!"

At this point the notary paused abruptly, and then striking his hands together added, "Ah! it is a terrible blow for the house of Beaulieu!"

"Terrible, indeed," said the Marchioness, "for it implies my son's and my daughter's ruin. For ten years to come I shall have to economise rigidly with my own fortune in order to restore our finances."

Bachelin had ceased pacing up and down the drawing-room. He had become calm again, and he now listened with feeling respect to Madame de Beaulieu's reply. He knew that the lawsuit was irremediably lost. He had received a copy of the judgment, and no further litigation, no appeal, was possible. The Marquis's disdainful carelessness had enabled his adversaries to acquire a superior position in the suit, and henceforward the struggle could not possibly be carried on.

"Misfortunes seldom come singly," resumed the Marchioness, "so I suppose you have some other bad news to tell me, Bachelin. While we are about it, tell me everything," added Madame de Beaulieu; "I don't think any blow could affect me more grievously than this one."

"I wish I could share your confidence, Madame la Marquise, for what I have still to tell you would then not seem so painful. But I am acquainted with the delicacy of your feelings, and I fear that the pecuniary loss which the failure of the English lawsuit entails will seem to you the less grievous of the two misfortunes."

The Marchioness turned very pale and became intensely agitated. She divined what her confidential adviser was about to tell her, and, unable to restrain herself, she eagerly exclaimed, "You have news of the Duc de Bligny?"

"I was charged by you, madame, to inquire into your nephew's conduct," rejoined the notary, with a touch of disdain in his tone which was highly significant coming from a man who, as a rule, fervently worshipped the aristocracy. "I followed your instructions to the letter. For the last six weeks Monsieur le Duc de Bligny has been in Paris——"

"For six weeks!" repeated the Marchioness with stupefaction, "and we were not aware of it!"

"M. de Bligny advisedly refrained from informing you."

"And he hasn't come here! He isn't here to-day—knowing the misfortune that has overtaken us! For he is aware of it, no doubt?"

"He knew of it one of the first, Madame la Marquise."

Madame de Beaulieu made a gesture of painful surprise, and then, in a tone of profound affliction, she exclaimed, "Ah! you were right, Bachelin, this grieves me more cruelly than the money loss. The Duke abandons us. He has not come, nor will he come; I had a presentiment of it. All that he wanted from us was a fortune. The fortune has vanished and the suitor hurries off. Ah! money is the password of these venal, avaricious times. Beauty, virtue and intelligence count for nothing. People no longer say, 'Room for the worthiest,' but 'Room for the wealthiest.' Now we are almost poor, and so we are abandoned."

Bachelin had listened quietly to the violent outburst of this grieved and angered mother. In spite of himself the notary could not conceal a feeling akin to satisfaction. He had become very red again in the face, and vigorously rubbed his hands together behind his back.

"Madame la Marquise," said he, "I think that you slander

the times we live in. No doubt positive ideas are dominant, and the cupidity which is natural to the human species has made great progress. But we must not pass the same sentence on all of our contemporaries. There are still some disinterested men who consider beauty, virtue, and intelligence as gifts which make the woman possessing them desirable above all others. I won't say that I know many men of the kind. But at least I know one, and for the point at issue a single example suffices."

"What do you mean?" asked the astonished Marchioness.

"Simply this," replied the notary, "that a gallant friend of mine has not been able to see Mademoiselle de Beaulieu without falling passionately in love with her. Knowing that she was engaged to the Duke, he would not have dared to declare himself. But if he learns she is free, he will speak, providing you condescend to authorise him to do so."

The Marchioness looked fixedly at Bachelin. "You are referring to Monsieur Philippe Derblay, are you not?" she asked.

"Yes, Madame la Marquise, precisely so," the notary boldly replied.

"I am not ignorant of the feelings with which my daughter has inspired the ironmaster," exclaimed the Marchioness. "He does not hide them; he does not hide them enough."

"Ah! that is because he loves Mademoiselle Claire, and sincerely too," the notary rejoined with warmth. "But you do not know Monsieur Derblay sufficiently, Madame la Marquise, to be able to judge him at his real value."

"I am aware that he is highly esteemed throughout the district. But you, my dear Bachelin, you are on intimate terms with his family?"

"I have known Monsieur Philippe and his sister, Mademoiselle Suzanne, ever since they were born. Their father was kind enough to call me his friend, and this will explain, Madame la Marquise, my boldness in acquainting you with Monsieur Derblay's sentiments. I hope you will forgive me for having taken this liberty. In my eyes my client only has one flaw—his name, which is written in one word without an apostrophe. However, if a search were made, who knows? The family is a very old one, and under the Revolution honest folks clustered close together, so maybe the letters of Monsieur Derblay's name did the same."

"Let him keep his name as it is," said the Marchioness sadly. "He bears it like an honourable man, and that suffices in the times we live in. Look at the Duc de Bligny, who abandons Claire because she is ruined; then turn to Monsieur Derblay, who solicits the hand of a dowerless girl, and tell me which of the two—high born and low born—is the real nobleman!"

"If Monsieur Derblay heard you he would feel very happy, madame."

"Pray do not repeat to him anything of what I have just told you," interrupted the Marchioness gravely. "Mademoiselle de Beaulieu accepts generosity from no one, and with the character she possesses it is probable she will die a spinster. Please God that she will prove strong and resigned when this double blow falls upon her."

The notary remained for a moment confused and speechless, and then, in a voice which trembled with emotion, he exclaimed, "Whatever happens, Madame la Marquise, pray remember that Monsieur Derblay would be the happiest man in the world were he even allowed to hope. He will wait, I am sure of it, for his heart also is unsusceptible of change. I can discern that these events will lead to great affliction for all of us—for I trust you will allow an old retainer like myself to be numbered among those who will share your tribulation. Now, if you will kindly permit me to offer a suggestion, I should advise you not to say anything to Mademoiselle de Beaulieu, at least for the present. Maybe the Duc de Bligny will return to more honourable feelings, and besides it will always be time enough for Mademoiselle Claire to suffer."

"You are right; but at all events I must inform my son of the blow that strikes him." And walking to the steps, the Marchioness beckoned to Octave, who was sitting on the terrace, patiently awaiting the end of the conference.

"Well," said he gaily, "is the sitting raised, or have you sent for me to deliberate with you?"

"I wish to acquaint you with some grave tidings which deeply grieve me," replied the Marchioness softly.

The Marquis immediately assumed a serious expression, and, turning to his mother, asked, "What is the matter?"

"Maître Bachelin has received a final communication from our legal representative in England."

"Respecting the lawsuit?"

"Yes."

Octave approached his mother, and, affectionately taking her by the hand, asked, "Well, it is lost, eh?"

Madame de Beaulieu, who was stupefied to find the Marquis so calm, looked at Bachelin as if seeking for an explanation, but the notary remained impassive, and so she turned to her son again. "You know it then?" she asked, breathing more freely, as if the Marquis's calm resignation had eased her heart.

"No, not precisely," replied the young man; "but I had my doubts. I did not wish to worry you; I respected your illusions, but in my own mind I was perfectly convinced that this action could not prove successful. I have therefore long been prepared to hear that it was lost. My only concern was for my sister, whose dowry was at stake. However, matters may be easily arranged. You must leave her the part of your fortune which you were reserving for me. As for myself, do not be anxious, mother; I shall always be able to weather the storm."

The Marchioness flushed with pride on hearing these generous words, and, turning towards the notary, she exclaimed, "What can I complain of when I am blessed with such a son?" Then opening her arms to the Marquis, who was smiling softly, she added, "You are a brave fellow, come and let me kiss you."

"Oh! I deserve no praise," rejoined the Marquis with emotion. "I love my sister, and I will do everything in my power to make her happy. But, come, as we are talking of these sad things, don't you think, mother, that our cousin De Bligny's silence has some connection with the loss of this lawsuit?"

"You are mistaken, child," replied the Marchioness eagerly, as she raised her hand to silence her son. "For the Duke——"

"Oh, fear nothing, mother," interrupted Octave with disdainful haughtiness; "if Gaston hesitated to keep his engagement now that Mademoiselle de Beaulieu no longer comes to him with a million in either hand, we are not, I fancy, the sort of folk to seize him by the collar and compel him to keep his promises. In fact, in my opinion, if the Duc de Bligny fails to marry my sister, it will be so much the worse for him and so much the better for her."

"Well said, my son," cried the Marchioness.

"Yes, well said, Monsieur le Marquis," echoed Bachelin. "And if Mademoiselle de Beaulieu is no longer wealthy enough to tempt a dowry-hunter, she will always be sufficiently perfect to captivate an honourable man."

The notary would perhaps have proceeded further, but the Marchioness silenced him with a glance. Delighted with the favourable issue of this crisis, which he had feared would be such a terrible one, Bachelin thereupon took respectful leave of his noble clients, and hurried off in the direction of Pont-Avesnes as fast as his old legs could carry him.

III.

As Bachelin had stated, it was really M. Derblay whom the Marquis de Beaulieu had met, clad like a poacher, in the woods of Pont-Avesnes. Letting Octave call after him as loud as he liked, he had hurried on through the wood, going straight before him, careless of the lashing branches and the tearing brambles. He laughed nervously, mingling muttered words with exclamations. Chance had brought him nearer to the woman whom he adored from afar, in a dream, as it were, like a young queen just espied, and his heart was full of joy.

He descended the slope which leads to the valley, scudding over the ground with his long legs, and unconscious of the rapidity of his movements although the perspiration oozed from his forehead. He was seemingly bent on keeping pace with his thoughts, which flew on the wings of the wind. When the young Marquis de Beaulieu learnt whom he had had to deal with, as would ultimately happen no doubt, he would certainly feel grateful for the courtesy shown him by the man he had called a troublesome neighbour; and then, who knows, they would be brought more closely together. He, Philippe, might then approach Claire, the adorable maiden whose soft smile lived in his memory. He would be able to speak to her. But at this thought a cloud passed before his eyes, for it seemed to him that the words would die away in his throat, and that he would remain dumb-stricken before her, crushed as it were by his emotion. However, he might take refuge in some dark corner of the drawing-room, and thence admire her at his ease. Lost in contemplation he would feel supremely happy.

Happy? How was that? What would be the issue of his amorous tenderness? He would suffer all the more acutely on beholding the woman he so passionately yearned for, married to another man. For the Duc de Bligny would certainly return. Could a man, beloved by such a woman, be mad enough to disdain her? And even if she did not marry the Duke, some other suitor would come forward—a brilliant nobleman, who would only have to show himself and give his name to be welcomed with open arms—whilst he, the low-born ironmaster, would be disdainfully rejected.

At this thought a feeling of deep sadness overcame him, and his strength waned. He no longer ran towards Pont-Avesnes, bounding like a deer through the cover. He trudged slowly on, mechanically tearing the leaves from the branches and crumpling them in his hand. What a misfortune it was that he durst not even aspire to win this ideal creature! At this thought he paused abruptly beside an oak-tree, and leaning against its trunk without thinking of sitting down, he remained in meditation there, his features pale and grave, and his eyes moistened by mental agony.

He recalled to mind all the exploits of his life, and asked himself if in virtue of the task he had accomplished he were not really deserving of happiness. After very brilliant studies he had left the Polytechnic School with first honours, and had chosen the State mining service. He had just obtained his appointment as an engineer when the Franco-German war broke out. He was then two-and-twenty. Without hesitating he had enlisted as a volunteer in one of the regiments of the army of the Rhine. He had been present at the sanguinary defeat of Wörth, and had returned to the camp of Châlons with the remnants of the first corps d'armée. Then he had taken part in the disastrous march on Sedan, and found himself, on the night of the battle, a prisoner of war guarded by Prussian uhlans. But he was not of a nature to relinquish liberty without an effort, and profiting by the darkness he crawled through the German lines during the night. Then, as soon as he reached Belgium, he made for Lille, where he was incorporated in one of the new regiments then being formed.

The war continued, and he saw the invasion stretch like gangrene over the country. Under the orders of General Faidherbe, who recognised his merits, he took part in the campaign of the North. At St. Quentin he received a bullet wound, and for six weeks he remained between life and death at the hospital, only awaking from his long trance to shudder on learning that Paris was in the hands of the Commune. His convalescence spared him the sad obligation of firing upon his misguided fellow-countrymen, and he started for the paternal home, still suffering from his wound, but wearing on his breast the ribbon of the Legion of Honour, which his General had brought him in person whilst he lay stretched on his bed of suffering at the hospital.

He had experienced many sorrows in an exceedingly short space of time, but a greater grief than all awaited him at home. He found the house in mourning. His mother had just died, leaving his little sister Suzanne, then only seven years old, to the care of others. M. Derblay, senior, forced to absent himself to attend to important business matters, had left his daughter under the guardianship of some devoted servants. Philippe's arrival was attended by a fresh explosion of grief, a fresh flow of tears. Little Suzanne attached herself to her brother with the convulsive tenderness peculiar to bereaved, abandoned children. Poor weak, wee little girl, she clung to him as if appealing for support and help. Philippe, who had a simple, tender heart, adored this child, who so greatly needed affection and found so little; placed as she was between her father, absorbed by business, and the servants, who, faithful as they might be, were not apt to treat her with that delicate tenderness which is even more necessary than material care for children and women.

However it was necessary he should leave home and go into harness again. His departure caused Suzanne bitter grief. The despair she felt when her brother bade her good-bye was akin to that which had crushed her when her mother died. But Fate had decided that their separation should not be a long one. Six months later M. Derblay died in his turn, overcome by excessive work, and henceforth Philippe and Suzanne were all alone in life.

Fresh duties then fell to the young man's lot. The winding-up of his father's affairs proved very complicated and fruitful in painful surprises. Although M. Derblay, senior, had been a remarkably intelligent man, he had possessed one great fault. He undertook more than he could properly accomplish. He expended his activity in various affairs without being able to carry them on all together and with equal success. The profits of one enterprise were absorbed by the losses of another, and he was incessantly assailed by a swelling flood of difficulties, which he momentarily mastered by dint of skill and energy, but which, sooner or later, would inevitably have ended by submerging him. However, as it happened, he had died before the catastrophe, leaving his affairs in a most confused state.

As an engineer Philippe had a splendid career already chalked out before him. He might have abandoned his father's enterprises, have wound them up as well as possible, and have then resumed his own course. But in that case the whole of the paternal inheritance would have been needed to save the name, and Suzanne would have remained dowerless. Under these circumstances the young man did not hesitate. He renounced his career and sent in his resignation; and then taking up the heavy burden which had proved too weighty for his father, he became a manufacturer.

The task before him was a mighty one. There was some of everything in the paternal inheritance—some glassworks at Courtalin, a foundry in the Nivernais, some slate quarries in the Var, and the forges and furnaces of Pont-Avesnes. Philippe sprang boldly into the abyss, and tried to save the scattered remains of his father's property. He worked intrepidly, and during six years he devoted not merely the daytime, but also many hours of the night, to the task of redemption which he had so bravely undertaken. All the ready money he could command was employed in setting the various concerns going again; and then as they recovered by degrees, at first activity and then prosperity (thanks to his exertions), he disposed of them, retaining only the ironworks, the value of which he fully recognised.

Thus in seven years he had liquidated the paternal inheritance, and now he only possessed the foundry in the Nivernais, which he utilised conjointly with the works at Pont-Avesnes, feeding the former establishment with the metal turned out at the latter one. He was altogether beyond the reach of danger; the property he had retained was really his own, and he felt capable of greatly extending his enterprises. Popular as he was throughout the district, he might come forward at the elections to be returned as a deputy. Who knew? Such a position was calculated to flatter a woman's vanity. And, besides, a great industrial establishment is itself a power in this money-loving century.

Little by little as these reflections crossed his mind, hope revived in Philippe Derblay's heart. He had set off again, and had already reached the edge of the wood. On his right hand stretched the meadows spreading over the valley, whilst on his left rose the rocks forming the base of the hill. It was here that the entrances to the mine were pierced. A little railroad ran up a gentle incline towards the galleries, and served to convey the mineral to the works.

Suddenly aroused from his meditation, Philippe resolved to go and see how the labour was progressing, and turning aside he directed his steps towards the mine. The overseer whose duty it was to control the output occupied a hut standing on a little hillock. Philippe made straight for this shanty, but as he drew nearer he fancied he could hear some people shouting. There was, indeed, an unusual stir at the entrance to the galleries, and on perceiving it the ironmaster so quickened his pace that in a few minutes he was on the spot. He at once realised the cause of this unwonted tumult.

The prolonged infiltration of water had caused a subsidence of part of the railway embankment. Several trucks were overturned, and below the bank a mass of sand and a number of beams and sleepers had buried the conductor of a train which was passing when the accident occurred. A few workmen and a number of women, who had speedily arrived from the village, made up an animated group, in the midst of which a woman who seemed half crazy was weeping and gesticulating.

Philippe eagerly elbowed his way into the circle. "What has happened?" he anxiously asked.

"Ah! Monsieur Derblay," exclaimed the weeping woman, who had broken forth into still more boisterous lamentation at sight of the ironmaster, "it's my poor lad, my little Jacques, who was overturned with his truck, and has been buried under all that sand for the last three-quarters of an hour."

"And what has been done to rescue him?" asked Philippe eagerly, as he turned towards the miners.

"We have removed as much of the sand as possible, sir," replied a foreman, pointing to a large excavation. "But we don't dare go any farther for fear the beams and sleepers might fall in and crush the little chap."

"He still spoke to us only ten minutes ago," cried the mother in despair, "but now we can't hear him. He's no doubt been stifled. Oh! my poor little lad! Are you going to leave him buried there?" And overcome by her emotion, the poor woman burst into sobs and sank on to the grassy slope of the embankment.

Throwing his gun to the bystanders, M. Derblay had flung himself on the ground, where he remained listening with his head just inside the excavation, underneath the crossed sleepers. All was silent in the poor lad's sandy tomb.

"Jacques!" cried the ironmaster, whose voice had a mournful muffled sound under the sand and the beams, "Jacques! Can you hear me?"

At first only a moan came in reply, but a moment later these words reached him, faintly and disconnectedly, "Ah! master! It's you! Ah! My God! If you're there—then I'm saved."

This simple confidence touched Philippe deeply, and he determined to make every effort, and attempt even the impossible so as to make the poor lad's hope reality.

"Can you still move?" he asked.

"No," murmured the lad, with failing breath, as if he were almost stifled. "Besides, I think I have a leg broken."

These words, which were heard in the midst of a deathlike silence, elicited a sorrowful murmur from the bystanders.

"Don't be frightened, my lad, we are going to get you out," resumed Philippe, and then rising to his feet, he added to the workmen, "Come, you others, just get some stanchions and raise this beam." At the same time he pointed to a long beam deeply buried under the *débris*, and the projecting portion of which formed a kind of lever.

"That won't do, master," rejoined the foreman, shaking his head sadly. "Everything would then fall in. There's only one plan possible. Three or four strong men ought to crawl into the hole we've dug and try and pull the lad out, as he can't move. At the same time one might try and shore these sleepers up. But all the same, it's awfully risky, and the men who go in might possibly stop there."

"Nevertheless it must be done," said the ironmaster resolutely, as he looked at his workmen; and as they all remained motionless and silent his face flushed.

"If one of you were lying under that sand, what would he think of his comrades who left him there?" he asked. "Come, as none of you dare, I'll go myself." And bending down Philippe glided into the excavation.

A cry of admiration and gratitude arose among the bystanders; and as if an example had sufficed to restore every one's courage, three men crawled in after the ironmaster, whilst the remainder, combining their strength, stooped beneath the projecting beams and raised them up by dint of incredible efforts. Silence had again ensued. One could only hear the sobs of the woebegone, moaning mother, and the husky breathing of the workmen, staggering under the weight they supported. A few minutes—long as centuries, and during which the life of five men remained in suspense—elapsed, and then all on a sudden a joyful outcry arose. Begrimed with soil, with hands gashed and shoulders lacerated, the four men emerged from the excavation, and Philippe, who came last, carried in his arms the swooning lad.

A frightful crash resounded. The workmen had ceased supporting the beams, which now gave way, filling up the space left vacant by the rescue of the lad. The latter's mother, who now seemed half crazy with delight, lavished her joy and gratitude on her son and the ironmaster, whilst the crowd, impressed and silent, respectfully surrounded them.

"Come, carry that lad home," said M. Derblay gaily, "and let some one go for the doctor." Then adjusting his dress and taking his gun again, the ironmaster strode off towards Pont-Avesnes.

News of the rescue had speedily followed the announcement of the accident, and as Philippe came in sight of the château gate he espied his sister, escorted by Bachelin, coming towards him. On perceiving her brother, Suzanne quickened her pace. She approached, attired in a light dress and carrying a large pink parasol, which serviceably sheltered her charming head on this fine sunshiny day. Mademoiselle Derblay was seventeen years of age, and her fresh, gay face, wore a delightful expression of trustfulness and candour. Her brown eyes smiled even more than her lips. No doubt her beauty was not of a regular character, but her tender, naïve gracefulness rendered her irresistibly charming. In her impatience she began to run towards her brother, tilting her parasol, which outspread like a full-blown sail. She had opened her arms and was about to spring on to Philippe's neck, when he gently repulsed her, crying, "Don't touch me! I'm covered with mud, and I should spoil your dress."

"What does that matter?" exclaimed Suzanne with joyful eagerness. "Oh! I must kiss you! You have saved the child! Oh, Philippe! you are always ready when there is something good and beautiful to be done!" So saying she took her brother's head in her hands and kissed him tenderly.

Bachelin, whom Suzanne had outstripped, now came up greatly out of breath. "Well, my dear friend," said the notary, "here's another good action to be set down to your credit account."

"Pray don't mention it," interrupted Philippe, with a smile. "It really isn't worth while. The worst of the business is that I fear the child is badly hurt. You would do well to go and see him with your medicine-chest, Suzanne, and if there is any expense to be incurred, pray defray it."

"I will go at once, brother," said the young girl. "Shall I take Brigitte with me?"

"Do so. As for ourselves, my dear notary, let us go indoors," added Philippe, turning towards Bachelin; "I look like a vagabond, and must change my clothes."

As Suzanne went off in the direction of the domestic offices, Philippe and the notary crossed the large square courtyard, which was encompassed by old lime-trees, whilst in the centre, from a large rectangular sheet of water, edged with parterres of flowers, a jet spurted into mid air, falling again in fine spray scattered by the wind, and tinged by the sunrays with iridescent sheen. This basin contained all that remained of the water which had belted the château when the Avesnes was diverted from its course and turned into the moats by the old lords of the place. However, the channel which admitted of this was dammed up in the reign of Louis XIII.

and the moats were drained. The slime at the bottom
of them was mixed with mould brought from a distance
at great expense, and from this admirably fertile soil sprang
the fruit-trees which are even nowadays the pride of Pont-
Avesnes. There are here pear-trees and peach-trees nearly
two hundred years old and yielding unique fruit; for these
broad moats, with their stone facings serving as espaliers, are
like reservoirs in which the sun deposits its vivifying rays. It
is as warm here as in a hothouse, and the bitter winds cannot penetrate to dry and wither the trees.

The château is built on an elevation, but although it lacks
none of the advantages of site, it is sombre and gloomy, and
its tall slate roofs stand out grimly against the sky. As
Philippe had limited himself to occupying one wing of the
vast frigid pile, the rest remained closed, and if it were not
for careful Brigitte, Suzanne's foster-sister, who despite her
youth and thanks to her happy precocity, ably discharges
the duties of housekeeper, the château would be altogether
neglected. But the active girl, infusing her zeal into the
servants under her orders, has the whole place cleaned regularly every fortnight, and sees that the admirable Louis-
Quatorze furniture in the reception rooms is properly cared
for. When Brigitte opens the shutters of the grand drawing
room and the light streams into the vast apartment, the effect
is like that of a curtain rising in a theatre and disclosing some
marvellously luxurious scene. On the walls hang beautiful
Gobelins tapestry, portraying the history of Alexander the
Great. The large arm-chairs scintillate with their coverings
of Genoa velvet and their gilded framework of stately design.
The flowers of the parterres, the water-jet, and a corner of
blue sky are reflected for a moment n ithe great Venetian
mirrors with bevelled edges. Then active Brigitte passes by

carrying a light feather-brush and a broom. Finally, as soon as the cleaning is over, the shutters are closed again, and the artistic riches of the château relapse once more into darkness.

On the ground-floor of the wing which is inhabited Philippe has reserved for himself a large study, surrounded with bookshelves, the upper ones of which are only reached by means of steps. In the centre of the room stands a large writing-table covered with papers, which might seem in disorder to any one but the master; and here, moreover, is a very fine bronze inkstand representing a pair of struggling Cupids, the victor jocosely pressing a bunch of grapes to the mouth of his vanquished antagonist. On the mantelshelf figures an admirable ebony clock with brass ornaments, executed by Boule in his earlier manner. From the study one may reach the dining-room, where the staid-looking furniture is of carved pear wood; the sideboard being adorned with several pieces of richly wrought massive silver plate, which, by the way, is never used. On the other hand, the little drawing-room is furnished in modern middle-class style, with hangings of blue poplin and chairs and couches upholstered in the same material. The clock on the mantelshelf and the fire-dogs of the grate are all three of the *rocaille* style. On a little marquetry table there lies some unfinished embroidery seemingly awaiting Suzanne's return, while on the walls hang two portraits, those of Philippe's father and mother, painted more conscientiously than successfully by a scarcely proficient pupil of Flandrin.

On the first-floor are two large bedrooms, occupied by Philippe and Suzanne, with dressing-rooms attached. That of Philippe has a dark sober aspect, with its hangings of Havannah-tinted stamped velvet and its black furniture, the only ornaments being a panoply of modern arms, in the centre of which figures a linesman's metal liquor-flask, pierced with three bullet-holes—a souvenir of the engagement of Pont-Noyelles. Suzanne's room, on the contrary, is as fresh and virginal as its occupant. The hangings are a combination of some blue material and white muslin caught up with pink favours, while the white-lacquered furniture is picked out with blue lines. Here and there, moreover, are scattered all the little trifles which ornament so prettily a maiden's room. From her window Suzanne can follow the long avenues of the park, vaguely limited by distant foliage, and her balcony would be a fit spot for reverie, could reverie for one moment bedim the gaiety of a youth to which care is unknown.

It was to his study that Philippe took Bachelin when his sister had tripped away. He had a presentiment that the notary had just come from Beaulieu, and like all lovers he was eager to learn such important or futile particulars as his old friend invariably acquainted him with after each interview with the noble inmates of the château. However, on this occasion Bachelin did not seem inclined to speak. Ensconced in an arm-chair, he looked carelessly at the ironmaster, who stood bolt upright before him, like a note of interrogation. At last Philippe could restrain himself no longer, and he asked with affected calmness, "Well, have you spoken to Madame de Beaulieu of the arrangement I propose respecting the encroachment on her land?"

"Certainly I have."

"Well, does she find it sufficiently acceptable?"

"Quite so."

Philippe looked askance at Bachelin, annoyed by his laconic manner; but, deciding he would bring the conversation nearer to the subject he had at heart, he resumed, "Did you also offer the right of shooting over my preserves?"

"What was the use of doing so?" quietly rejoined the notary, at the same time giving the ironmaster an ironical look.

"You ask me what was the use?" cried the latter in astonishment.

"Well," replied Bachelin, "there was no necessity for my making the offer, since you made it yourself to the Marquis this morning, and in the most romantic fashion, too."

A slight flush came to Philippe's face, and he lowered his head with embarrassment. "Ah! So Monsieur de Beaulieu spoke to you of our meeting?" he asked. "But he did not know whom he had to deal with."

"I told him. Perhaps I ought to have added that if you filled his game bag so plentifully, it was because you were in love with his sister?"

"My friend!"

"Ah, ah! Do you retract?" asked Bachelin gaily. "Do you happen not to love Mademoiselle de Beaulieu any longer?"

"Would to Heaven I didn't, for it is great madness," replied Philippe. "How can I—a toiler who has long left society on one side—have thought of this young girl, who is at once so beautiful and so proud, and yet for this last reason perhaps all the more tempting? I saw her looking pale and thoughtful, somewhat anxious, no doubt, on account of the prolonged absence of the man she is betrothed to; and in spite of myself, without thinking of restraint, I gradually came to love her. I forgot the distance that separated us; I did not think of our difference of origin. I did not hear the voice of reason, the advice of experience; I only listened to my love which carolled irresistibly in my heart. Ah, my old friend, I am ashamed of myself, and yet I cannot overcome this mad passion which fills me with unknown joy, and transports me with exquisite sensations—which gives me everything, in fact, excepting hope! For there my blindness ceases, and I don't hope, I give you my word for it."

"You don't hope, it's agreed," rejoined Bachelin in a bantering tone. "But, at all events, you love, that's patent. So I conclude I acted rightly in speaking as I did to the Marchioness?"

"In speaking?" stammered Philippe, with emotion.. "What do you mean by 'speaking'? What did you speak of?"

"Why, I spoke about what you think, about what you have just expressed to me in such telling, passionate terms."

The ironmaster took a step backward, his eyes receded under his brows, and their expression darkened. He angrily bit his lips, but at last, striving to speak in a calm voice he asked, "But did I request you to inform Madame de Beaulieu of such matters?"

"No, that's true, you did not ask me to do so," rejoined Bachelin quietly. "But, to tell the truth, I found a favourable opportunity, and I didn't hesitate. Do you see, there's nothing like a well-defined situation. You would have continued beating about the bush for weeks and perhaps months; you would have plunged all the more deeply into this love adventure, and perhaps with serious consequences. It was much better to make a clean breast of it once and for all, even at the risk of being haughtily repelled. These are the reasons that led me to act as I did. Don't you think they have some weight?"

Philippe remained silent. He had scarcely heard Bachelin, for his mind was whirling, and he had lost all notion of existence. It seemed as if he were being carried rapidly through space. The wind whistled in his ears, and he was unable to fix his eyes on anything through the mist that obscured his gaze. In his aching head it seemed as if a mysterious voice persistently repeated what was perhaps a vague revelation of destiny, "Claire! if she were really to become yours!"

The notary at last aroused him from his torpor. "Well, why are you gazing fixedly at me like that?" asked Bachelin. "You look like a visionary."

Philippe passed his hand over his forehead, as if he were desirous of effacing a painful impression, and then, smiling at his friend, he replied, "Excuse me, I was troubled at thinking that you had taken such a serious step without my knowledge. I did not think it was in your nature, otherwise I should have asked you to say nothing. Since the day when I was weak enough to confess to you that I loved Mademoiselle de Beaulieu I have not ceased regretting that I had spoken so indiscreetly. But it would seem that when a man is in love his heart becomes too small for all the tenderness it should contain, and in spite of one's self more than is proper escapes one. Avowals come to one's lips and cannot be restrained. But scarcely had I spoken to you than my illusion was dispelled, and the pitiless reality appeared to me. Mademoiselle de Beaulieu has never done me the honour to notice that I existed. She is wealthy, she is betrothed to her cousin, and she will become a duchess. I must be a perfect madman to love her. I deserve punishment undoubtedly, and I am ready to submit to it. Come, tell me everything; you need not spare me."

"Well, to begin with, I will tell you that Mademoiselle de Beaulieu is no longer wealthy, that she will probably never be a duchess, and that an honourable man like yourself never had a better chance than now of being accepted as her husband."

On hearing this Philippe became so pale that it seemed as

if he were about to faint. He raised a cry of joy, and then, giving way to emotion, sank heavily into an arm-chair. "Oh, take care! Beware of giving me hope! It would be too hard if I were compelled to renounce it afterwards."

"But yet I mean to give you hope," rejoined Bachelin, "although in doing so I betray, for your sake, all the secrets of the Beaulieu family. However, it is so much in your own interest to remain discreet that I am sure you will never repeat what I have just told you."

Philippe caught hold of the notary's hands, and gazed at him with burning eyes full of inquisitiveness.

"Mademoiselle de Beaulieu is ruined by the loss of the English lawsuit," resumed Bachelin, "and she is not aware of it. For the last six weeks the Duc de Bligny has been in Paris without occupying himself about her, and she has no more knowledge of this than of the other matter. However, whenever Mademoiselle Claire learns that she is abandoned, a frightful tempest will burst forth in her heart, and there will be plenty of fragments to be rescued by those who are near her."

"Ruined and abandoned!" cried Philippe. "That accomplished and adorable girl! But what need has she of any fortune? The only treasure a man should expect from her is herself."

"Yes, certainly; and in speaking of you to the Marchioness I insisted on your absolute disinterestedness."

"You were right," cried Philippe warmly. "Tell Madame de Beaulieu what I think; tell it to *her* also, I beg of you." He paused abruptly, as if saddened by some discouraging thought. "But no," he resumed, "say nothing. She is proud and haughty. The idea of owing anything to the man who will be her husband would raise a barrier between us and induce her to reject me. However, warn the Marchioness, acquaint her with my scruples, try and win her approbation. Above all, let it be formally understood that I am a suitor for her daughter's hand. Oh! I would receive Mademoiselle de Beaulieu's hand on my knees. But I wish she should still believe herself rich, so as to accept or refuse me freely. Even if I had to settle on her everything I possess, I should still be her debtor."

"Come, come," said Bachelin, interrupting Philippe with an affectionate sign of the hand. "You are dashing off post haste. What fine things youth and passion are! But you must proceed more sedately. At the present moment the only thing for you is to visit the château. In default of other satisfaction, you will at least have that of contemplating the object of your desires, as people said in the last century. Be calm and grave, bear yourself discreetly in accordance with your situation, and take your sister with you. She will serve you as a screen; the others will occupy themselves with her, and in the meanwhile you will be at ease."

"And when ought I to go to Beaulieu?" asked Philippe, with evident trepidation.

"Come, now, are you already afraid, before even starting off? Well, I should go to-morrow. A good night's rest will set you on your legs again. You will be in the enjoyment of all your faculties and appear to the best advantage."

As the notary spoke he slowly rose, placed his portfolio under his arm, and took a few steps towards the door. Pausing suddenly, however, in the centre of the room, and giving the ironmaster a bantering look, he asked, "Well, do you still regret that I spoke to Madame de Beaulieu without having your authorisation to do so? In your emotion you haven't asked me what she answered."

"It's true," cried Philippe, whose joy by a sudden change now gave way to anxiety. "What did she say?"

"She said what I expected she would say in such a case, that is, she declared she had nothing to say, that she would never force Mademoiselle Claire to marry—in one word, she answered me with all the usual commonplaces. But, believe me, the strength of the position you wish to conquer is not on the mother's side but on the daughter's; so be brave. And now I'm going off to dinner." Thereupon Bachelin shook hands affectionately with the ironmaster, and withdrew.

Left alone, Philippe fell into deep meditation. He calmly considered the situation, and was obliged to confess to himself that it was not unfavourable to his hopes. Dishonourably betrayed by her cousin, Mademoiselle de Beaulieu would necessarily sojourn for some months longer in the Jura, so that time might in some measure efface the humiliation inflicted on her. Thus he would have opportunities of seeing her, of paying her discreet attentions, and maybe he might succeed in pleasing her. Suzanne would surely be a useful auxiliary, and in lieu of sending her back to the convent at Besançon as soon as the holidays were over, he would keep her at home. She would become Claire's companion, and win her friendship with her gentle naïve gracefulness. By degrees she might instil some thought of her brother into Mademoiselle de Beaulieu's heart.

As these ideas flashed through Philippe's mind, the dream seemed to become reality. He fancied he could see the two young girls slowly pacing under the overspreading trees of Pont-Avesnes. They walked side by side and arm in arm, like a pair of sisters, one of them tall and proud, the other slight and gentle. He watched them, and it seemed as if he could inhale the discreet perfume emanating from their persons. The delicious scent intoxicated him, and he was about to touch them, when suddenly a pair of fresh lips were pressed to his forehead and aroused him from his dream. Then Suzanne's dear voice whispered in his ear, "What are you thinking of, Philippe?"

As the ironmaster remained seated, vaguely smiling at her, and without replying, she speedily resumed, "You won't tell me? Then I suppose *I* must speak. Well, I've no doubt but you are thinking of a very beautiful young lady with golden hair."

Philippe sprang to his feet, and catching hold of his sister's hand, "Suzanne!" he cried.

But on espying the young girl's malicious glance, he lost confidence, and was unable to continue. He remained standing in a state of stupefaction, asking himself how it happened that this child had guessed his thoughts so accurately.

"How disturbed you are," resumed Suzanne tenderly. "Did you think your secret was so well concealed that no one could divine it? But for a month or more you have not been the same, and I didn't need much penetration to perceive that your heart no longer belonged to me alone. Oh! I'm not jealous, I love you too much for that. And if I feel anxious when I see you so pensive and absorbed, it is not that I fear you might divert some of your affection from me to bestow it on another, but because I fear you have some grief. I owe you so much, Philippe. It was you who protected me, loved me, and brought me up when I was alone without father or mother. And it seems to me that I am not merely your sister, but your daughter, the child of your care and toil. Go; love and be loved in return! You will only see me rejoice; for I know of no happiness complete enough on earth to reward such a perfect being as you are."

The tears started from the ironmaster's eyes and trickled down his cheeks. His sister's gentle words had affected his excited nerves. He felt crushed and stood motionless, leaning against the mantelshelf, and looking at Suzanne, who smiled at him.

"But now you are crying," she said. "But come; is it so very sad to be in love?"

"Don't ever speak of that folly again," interrupted Philippe in a husky voice.

"Folly! Why, pray? What woman who knew you could help trying to please you?" And standing in front of him with a bold expression and resolute gestures, she continued, "Come, if necessary, I will go and say to her you love, 'Mademoiselle, you act very wrongly in not loving my brother, for he is superior to all other men on earth. I can declare it, for I have known him long and I know him well.' And I'll be so eloquent that she'll come to you of her own accord, and hold out her hand with a beautiful curtsey, and say, 'Monsieur, you have such an extraordinary little sister that I have not been able to close my eyes to your merit any longer. Will you do me the favour to become my husband?' Then you'll bow to her gracefully, and reply with a thoughtful air, '*Mon Dieu!* Mademoiselle, as it is to oblige you, I will.' Then I'll bless you both with an air of solemn protection, and you'll be very happy. Ah! you see you are laughing. I knew I should end by consoling you."

Thereupon, taking the arm of her brother, whose feelings could not stand such vivacious communicative gaiety, Suzanne led him outside, exclaiming, "Let us take a walk round the garden while we're waiting for the wedding!"

IV.

Six weeks previously, when the Duc de Bligny alighted from the train which had brought him from St. Petersburg to Paris, he drove at once to his club. Having no apartment prepared for his reception, and his aunt's mansion being closed, Gaston thought the most practical course was to install himself in one of the rooms which a good club always keeps ready for the accommodation of its members. He meant to remain merely a week or so in Paris; in fact to start for Beaulieu as soon as he had transacted his business at the Ministry of Foreign Affairs and made a few purchases.

Nearly a year had elapsed since his last visit to France, and he had been leading in Russian society that artificial *vie Parisienne* which is considered supreme *bon ton* abroad, although it resembles the true high life of Paris merely as much as a Rhine pebble resembles a Wisapoor diamond.

And yet the refined corruption of the Slavs had seized hold of him, and he had found a great charm in leading a life which blended Asiatic languor with European activity. The Russian ladies had captivated him by the undulating grace and enigmatical charm of their beauty. He had been seized with a desire to learn the secret of these smiling sphinxes, whose eyes were full of fascination while their claws were full of threats. A handsome fellow, well bred, and bearing a famous name, he had been greatly sought after, and by degrees the image of Claire, faithfully engraved as it was on his heart, faded away as if it were but one of those charming crayon drawings of Latour, the colours of which grow pale with age.

Far away from Claire, he at first considered himself in exile, and determined to lead a sober, retired life. But how is it possible for a man to cloister himself when he is the youngest attaché of a French embassy and is gracefully courted in all directions? After a week's stern retirement, Gaston was unable to dispense with attending at one of the ambassador's receptions, and so he assumed his fête attire and made his entry into St. Petersburg society.

On the very first evening the young Duke became the favourite of the Russian aristocracy. His grandfather, after emigrating with the Comte d'Artois, had lived in the intimacy of the Nesselrodes, the Pahlens, and the Gortschakoffs. Bligny was welcomed in the most flattering manner by the great personages of the court, and was even presented to the Czar, who treated the young attaché with a favour that was much remarked. This diplomatist of five-and-twenty acquired in a single evening a highly important position, and his superiors, far from grudging their subordinate his success, only thought of profiting by the influence which he had so swiftly acquired.

But although Gaston was an elegant cavalier, and highly gifted in social accomplishments, he proved a very indifferent politician. He plunged into pleasure and neglected intrigue, and it was promptly shown that if St. Petersburg society had gained a brilliant recruit, France had not acquired a useful servant. Buzzing and fluttering from flower to flower, the Duc de Bligny was not the toiling bee absorbed in producing honey, but rather the brilliant wasp intent on rapine, with his golden corselet scintillating in the sunshine. In a few weeks he revealed himself as an intrepid *viveur*. His admirably tempered nerves defied the most crushing fatigue. At supper he stood his ground against the most renowned tipplers, and everybody knows how prodigiously the Russians drink. At the Nobleman's Club he played a game of baccarat which remained legendary, for it lasted three days and nights, during which the Duke and his adversaries only rose from table to recruit their strength with the necessary nourishment. Gaston vanquished his rivals not by his persistent luck, however, but by the drowsiness which ultimately stretched them out on the carpet. Then he became the lover of fascinating Lucie Tellier, the "star" of the French company at the Michael Theatre, and retained his hold on her despite all the attempts at corruption of the most lavishly prodigal boyards. One fine day, however, tired of her probably because she remained faithful to him, he was pleased to restore her to her Muscovite admirers.

Madame de Beaulieu had guessed rightly. The Duke was the lion of the Russian winter season. There were no good fêtes without him. He might have aspired to the hand of the richest heiress of St. Petersburg, but he disdained every overture that was made to him, and for this very reason was all the more ardently sought after.

However, Bligny had the blood of a *blasé* in his veins, so that after six months or so the life he led caused him prodigious weariness, and his only resource against spleen was the gaming-table. The very first time he had taken cards in his hand he had felt he was a gambler to the backbone. Thus he gambled and with insolent good luck. It seemed as if he were a predestined conqueror. Each morning, laden with the spoils of his adversaries, he returned home, feeling an iron circle round his head and with a taste of dust on his lips. He went to bed as the day broke, the dark overcast day, resembling twilight, of Russian winter-time. Worn out, he slept until the afternoon. Towards four o'clock he rose, and his day began just as the gas-lamps were being lighted through the city. He had arranged his existence in a contrary fashion to other peoples'. He lived as it were inversely, for during two years he hardly ever saw the sun. He was no longer a butterfly, but a moth. His features, which were graceful and delicately chiselled when he left home, had now a stern hard outline. Handsome they still were, no doubt, but the charm and freshness of youth had disappeared, and he wore as it were a *viveur's* mask upon his face. His dark curly hair was moreover becoming scanty about the temples, and his blue eyes were sunken far under his brows. The mad life he led left a more distinct mark upon him every day.

His aunt would have had some difficulty in recognising him. He was no longer the timid young stripling with a gentle voice who passed his evenings so peacefully between the Marchioness and Claire in the quiet drawing-room of the old family mansion. Mademoiselle de Beaulieu, who was resolute and decided, and of a somewhat masculine nature, had then laughingly called him "Miss Gaston." But now he had lost all that graceful pliancy which had made him look like a young girl. He was a man and a dangerous one. He had discovered treasures of innate scepticism in his mind. He really believed in nothing, and set his good pleasure above aught else. The paternal blood, which the peaceful enjoyments of retired life had momentarily calmed within him, had begun to boil again; and the ardent passionate race of the Bligny's, who from the reign of Henri III. downwards had given the court of France its most dissolute *mignons*, its boldest *raffinés*, its most gallant *menins*, and most debauched *roués*,* found in his person a worthy representative of the ancestral traditions.

Slight as his figure was, he nevertheless possessed a giant's vigour. He was like one of those lords of former times who painted their faces and perfumed their hands; who, rather than stoop, bade their pages pick up their cup and ball; who had themselves carried about in litters to avoid the fatigues of horsemanship, and yet who, on days of battle, charged like madmen in the *mêlée*, with a hundredweight of iron on their bodies, and accomplished heroic feats. Gaston would certainly not have walked a mile with any useful object, but he was a man to go out shooting or hunting for an entire day, to fence foil in hand for hours without cessation, so as to weary even those who considered themselves beyond fatigue.

It was at the gaming-table that he really appeared in all his strength. It seemed as if his will sufficed to impel luck to his side. He won with unheard-of persistency. The worst "hands" became good when dealt to him. The "bank," of which short work was made when he attacked it, became unconquerable when he held it. During two years indeed luck treated him like a spoilt child, and he was nicknamed "Lucky Gaston." Another person would perhaps have been regarded with distrust, but his honesty was too patent for him to incur suspicion.

The remnants of his patrimony, with the resources he derived from the gaming-table, enabled him to live in style. He had some marvellous horses, a superb abode, and all the luxurious comfort indispensable to a man living in the highest

---

* The reader will bear in mind that the *mignons, menins, raffinés*, and *roués* were more or less the fops and "mashers" of other times.—*Trans.*

society. When he arrived at the Nobleman's Club the game assumed a new aspect. Everyone at once realised that the engagement would be serious, and that large sums would quickly cover the *tapis vert*. He did not merely confine himself to baccarat and lansquenet, but willingly played a game of piquet as well, his stakes being usually a louis the point, with a hundred others tacked on at the end for luck. It was to him that old Narischkine, more than forty times a millionaire, addressed his memorable *mot*. Gaston had just won three thousand louis from him, and he rose from the table saying, "I prefer to go home, for if I stayed I should end by losing money."

After frequenting the performance at the Opera House or the French Theatre, or on leaving the house where he had spent the evening, Gaston habitually sprang into his sledge and had himself driven along the Perspective. Warmly enveloped in his furs, he liked to feel the cold night wind pass over his face. His nerves were thus strengthened for the game, and he felt quite fresh when he reached the club at two o'clock in the morning. He found his adversaries already excited, and his cool calculating audacity triumphed over the boldest of them. He remained impassive seated at the gaming-table, under the burning light; neither gain nor loss affected his coolness. The oldest gamblers did not remember having ever seen such perfect bearing before. He was grave and almost disdainful when puerile superstitions revealed themselves around him. He only counted on himself, and shrugged his shoulders when fetishes were spoken of or displayed.

Although he was scarcely of a passionate nature, and too deeply egotistical to love, he nevertheless had several *bonnes fortunes*. The fact is, he behaved generously, and by no means drove the beauties who smiled on him to despair. He

F

detested tears, and was anxious not to grieve any one for fear of the lamentations and reproaches that would follow. Only on one occasion did he really fancy that he was seriously enamoured, but subsequent events showed that he had flattered himself. One of the greatest ladies of the Russian aristocracy, the Countess Woreseff, famous for her emeralds and her golden hair, fell in love with him. Closely watched by her husband, who was exceedingly jealous of her, the beautiful Countess was unable to write to Gaston or to see him otherwise than in society. At the first moment Gaston, who seemed quite smitten, almost forgot the gaming-tables. He sedulously followed the Countess about to social gatherings, waltzing with her under her husband's jealous glance, but unable to devise an expedient for a private meeting.

At last, with the view of deceiving the husband, Gaston pretended to start for Moscow. He disappeared for a couple of days, and secretly returned home. The Count, who felt reassured, thereupon relaxed his wakefulness, and the Countess was able to meet her lover on three occasions. She left her carriage before the front entrance of Saint Alexis, entered the church, and leaving it by a side door, tripped lightly away to the rendezvous. The third time, however, an alarm was raised by her footman, who having stealthily followed her, hastened to warn the Count. The latter arrived in a fury at Bligny's residence, but he was obliged to parley with the Duke's valet, a Parsian as wily as Mascarille; and in the meanwhile the Countess, who was half crazy, implored Gaston to find her some means of escape. It was in this emergency that the young man's nervous vigour fully revealed itself. His bathroom, on the ground-floor, looked on to the courtard of an adjoining house, but the window was protected with iron bars. However, by a powerful effort of his distended muscles, Gaston instantly tore one of them down, and Madame Woreseff was able to pass through and escape. A few seconds later, when the Count was introduced into the presence of Bligny, who had assumed a peaceful, smiling look, he discovered nothing to justify his suspicions, and was obliged to withdraw and apologise.

The Count devoured his rage in silence, and contrived to show a calm face to his wife. But a skilful inquiry strengthened his conviction, and he determined to compel the Duke to fight him. He went to the club, and took the "bank" at the baccarat table. The cards being exhausted, Gaston had just cut a fresh pack, when the Count rudely declined to go on with the game. The Duke coldly asked him for an explanation, but he refused to give any, and a provocation followed.

Woreseff's conduct was unanimously blamed, but the result he sought for was attained. The duel took place on the morrow, in a little wood of birch-trees. It was a fine frosty morning. The conditions were, pistols, twenty paces, fire at will. Gaston, who by no means cared to lose his life, showed no generosity whatever to his mistress's husband. As soon as the seconds gave the signal he fired, lodging a bullet in his adversary's stomach. The Count sank on the snow, which was tinted with his blood, but rising on one knee with ferocious energy, he calmly aimed at Bligny. However, the weakness caused by the loss of blood made his hand tremble, and the ball only slightly wounded the Duke's shoulder.

The Count survived his terrible wound. As for Gaston, six weeks afterwards he had resumed his usual life. Singular to state, however, Count Woreseff's bullet seemed to have killed the young Duke's extraordinary luck. Was it the loss of blood that had deranged the happy equilibrium of his faculties; or, favoured so far, had Gaston ended by wearying Fortune? At all events, from that day forward he ceased to be on good terms with her. Indeed, he lost incessantly. His superb assurance departed from him, and he came to know the anxieties of the gambler who scents a bad card. He no longer flung his money on the table with a conqueror's self-confidence, nor looked down upon his adversaries from the height of his imperturbable serenity. He frequently turned pale now. His fingers nervously beat a tremulous march on the edge of the table. His eyes darkened and retreated under his brows, and his white teeth were for ever gnawing his lips. He had moments of weakness and depression. His perfect bearing of other times was gone, and he would leave the gaming-table at daybreak with his hair disarranged, his necktie awry, and his shirtfront creased and soiled by contact with the green table-covers.

He thus descended one by one the steps of the capitol up which he had climbed so triumphantly. Much of the money he had won at cards was dissipated, moreover, with frightful rapidity, and at last the Duke became embarrassed. He had to negociate loans—a sure sign of coming ruin. This necessity of applying to others for help made him realise his fallen position, and greatly affected him. Formerly he had enjoyed delicious sensations as the sovereign of this world of *viveurs*. Luck had raised him above all his companions. He was then treated as a master, and was proud of his supremacy. But in an instant his pedestal gave way. On the day he no longer won he ceased to exist for these gamblers. No hush now attended his arrival at the club. He merely gleaned a few shakes of the hand here and there, but no one turned aside from his game. He remained isolated in the midst of groups of people who treated him with indifference, for they had ceased to fear him.

Never, however, had his passion for gambling been so intense as in this difficult emergency. He attacked with blind frenzy, instead of calmly calculating his play. In a single night he would lose or win enormous sums. He was no longer the skilled horseman who guides his steed at will, but rather the reckless rider, carried away at a furious gallop by a horse he does not seek to control—the rider who has more chances of breaking his neck than of ever reaching the goal. And in point of fact he did not reach the goal. Besides, casual returns of luck were useless; he did not know how to profit by them. He plunged on like a madman, and speedily lost whatever he won.

A disaster seemed inevitable when his ambassador saved him, by entrusting him with a mission for the Government in Paris. Gaston's duel with Count Woreseff had caused a very bad impression, and the ambassador thought it advisable that his attaché should absent himself for some little time. Accordingly he gave him three months' leave. Bligny had not asked for this mission, for in doing so he would have looked like a combatant anxious to forsake the fray, but upon its being offered him he joyfully accepted it. He felt that he was "used up" at St. Petersburg, and he was anxious to disappear, think over the situation, and decide on a plan of future conduct.

Of all his previous winnings, which had once formed a seemingly inexhaustible treasure, there now only remained to him some fifty thousand francs in hard cash, and with poverty his ideas suddenly underwent a change. In the disorderly fast life he had been leading he had lost all remembrance of Claire; but now he began to think of his betrothed again. In a delightful mirage, as it were, he seemed to see the calm, quiet drawing-room of the Beaulieu mansion. Claire was working by the soft lamplight, and as she leant over her embroidery her beautiful fair hair sparkled with the effulgence of gold. She was patiently waiting for him, sighing, perhaps; and at the thought he began to love her again, and swore he would for ever renounce the feverish life to which he was indebted for so many bitter joys and so many cruel cares. He reflected that if he had dissipated the remnants of a fortune which his father had bequeathed to him, Mademoiselle de Beaulieu was wealthy, and that with the hundred thousand francs a year which her dowry represented, a young household might yet figure presentably. Life was far from being as expensive in Paris as at St. Petersburg, and, besides, the time of folly was over. They would remain for six months in the year on their estates in the country, and devote the larger part of their income to living in proper style in the capital during the winter.

The Duke imbued himself with these ideas, and felt as if he had become good and tender-hearted again. He found himself another man, and derived delicious enjoyment from this return to the first dreams of his youth. All the way back to France he built up charming projects for the future, and, when the train at last drew up under the glass roof of the Northern railway station in Paris, he sprang eagerly on to the platform, joyfully setting foot once more in the city which his heart and his mind had forgotten so long and so grievously.

It was evening, and he took a childish pleasure in following from the windows of his cab the long vista of the Rue Lafayette, dotted with innumerable gas-lamps. The motion and turmoil of the great city powerfully impressed him. The passers-by seemed gifted with peculiar vivacity and gaiety. The streets were full of noise. Where the Faubourg Montmartre crossed the Rue Lafayette he encountered a block of vehicles. The drivers roughly jeered and snarled at one another, and pedestrians, eager to pass, glided under the very heads of the horses. At last the cab started off again, skirted the wall of brown freestone which encloses the gardens of the Rothschild mansion, turned up the Rue du Helder, and then, all on a sudden, the Duke found himself on the Boulevard.

The beating of his heart quickened. A number of equipages, bound for the Opera, were filing by. Women in elegant opera cloaks, with lace scarfs over their heads, sat back in the roomy landaus. The intermittent flames of the Jabloschkoff electric-lamps, whilst shedding a pale light on the façade of the theatre, pierced with dark apertures, lent a gleam to the helmets of the municipal guards on horseback, who, shrouded in their cloaks, remained as motionless as statues in the centre of the Place. Here, where so many streets and the Boulevard meet, the traffic and the turmoil were enormous. The shop-fronts blazed out in the darkness, the foot-pavements were black with promenaders. 'Twas the magic picture of Paris by night displayed in all its powerful splendour.

The cab turned into the Rue de la Paix, and a few minutes later Gaston alighted at the door of his club, feeling somewhat giddy; he still seemed to hear the irritating rumble of the train, and his eyes were dazed by the light. Tired out, he went up-stairs to the room prepared for him, and slept without waking till the following morning.

The Duke had not been absent from Paris sufficiently long to lose his boulevardian habits, and he felt quite at home when he set foot on the asphalte once more. His flashy Russian varnish immediately melted away, and he felt himself a Parisian again from head to foot. For a couple of days, however, he yielded to the fascination of the city. He strolled up the Champs Elysée and promenaded in the Bois; he lounged at the Hôtel Drouot, sauntered from the Madeleine to the Boulevard Montmartre, delighted to shake hands with the friends he met and raise his hat to his acquaintances. He patronised the little theatres, leaning back with a delightful sensation of beatitude on the narrow, badly-stuffed stalls. He looked even on idiotic pieces as exquisite, and the content which filled him was ever overflowing in admiration. The fact is, he had, so to speak, regained his liberty since leaving Russia. He was like a ticket-of-leave man who has placed himself beyond surveillance, like a convict escaped from the penitentiary. He was free now, and he breathed again.

His business at the Foreign Office was concluded in three days, and he decided he would leave Paris at the end of the week. He knew that Claire and the Marchioness were at Beaulieu, and he wished to surprise them. He pictured their astonishment, and seemed to hear their joyful exclamations. For nothing in the world would he have renounced the pleasure of coming upon them unawares.

He strolled one day up the Rue de la Paix to purchase of Bassot, the family jeweller, an admirable betrothal ring—a large sapphire surrounded by brilliants, and set with rare perfection. He saw himself offering the white velvet case to Claire; and she opened it, smiling softly, and handed him the golden circlet, so that he might himself slip it over her tapering finger, tipped with a rosy nail. Then it would be really decided that he should be her husband; the ring would be the first link in the chain that was to unite them.

As the Duke returned from the theatre on the eve of his departure, he found the club far more animated than usual, and on inquiring he learnt that all the movement, the display, and the illumination were caused by a theatrical performance which was to be given in the Salle des Fêtes. A distinguished audience had assembled to witness *L'Education de la Princesse*, a two-act operetta, due to the collaboration of two talented amateurs—the Duc de Féras for the words, and M. Jules Trélan for the music. The display of vocal and histrionic talent promised to be remarkable. Baron, of the Variétés, lent his innate distinction to the *rôle* of the Grand Chamberlain; Daubray, of the Palais Royal Theatre, figured as that questionable personage the Chevalier Alphonse de Rouflaquette; Saint-Germain, of the Gymnase, had consented, for that occasion only, to reveal himself as a great vocalist in the part of Pepinster; young Baron Trésorier, a member of the club who possessed a charming *tenorino* voice, had been entrusted with the *rôle* of Triolet; Madame Judic appeared as the Princess Hortensia; and Suzanne Lagier as the Queen-mother.

A formidable success was expected. The footmen on duty hardly knew which way to turn, for every one arrived at the same moment in order to secure good places. From the vast vestibule, adorned with Louis Quatorze tapestry, there came a murmur of voices and a rustling of dresses smoothed by dainty hands, with puffs of warm air saturated with the scent of powder *à la maréchale*.

Instead of going up-stairs to bed, the Duke handed his overcoat to an attendant, and flattening his crush-hat entered the Salle des Fêtes. An apparently futile circumstance often modifies a man's destiny, but Bligny, in going to witness the performance of *L'Education de la Princesse*, certainly had no idea of the great change he was about to effect in his future.

The Salle des Fêtes was brilliant with illumination. There was already a large audience seated in comfortable rows of chairs. Satin, velvet, gauze, and silk, and the whole scale of vivid colours, with beautiful fair shoulders resplendent in their alabaster whiteness, were all here. The flutter of fans lent a winglike motion to the assemblage. A subdued buzz of conversation arose from time to time when some well-known personage entered the hall, at the end of which was the silent stage, concealed from view by its red curtain.

The Duke walked towards a group of gentlemen in evening dress, among whom he recognised several friends. Maître Escande, a young notary, heir of a millionaire family, and who had but recently been invested with his legal functions, was superbly attitudinising in the centre of the throng. He was dressed with irreproachable elegance, and was speaking with an important air, but as he caught sight of Bligny his tongue seemed to cleave to his palate, and he remained with open mouth gazing half stupefied at the Duke, who approached with a smiling face. A moment's silence followed, only broken by the exclamation, "Oh! what a pity!" raised in a compassionate tone by a tall bald-headed man, wearing a dress-coat the cut of which plainly indicated that its owner was some retired merchant. This individual had a very red face, and very large ears surmounted by tufts of yellowish hair. His neck was imprisoned in a tall white cravat, and his shirt-front was adorned with diamond studs, while on his feet he wore a pair of polished leather shoes, cut low in front so as to disclose a strip of his white cotton socks.

Bligny had reached the group, and after shaking hands with his friends he remained waiting, puzzling his mind as to the cause of this extremely eloquent silence. He was about to ask what the matter was, and why his presence made every one else seem so uncomfortable, when the old man with the diamond studs, leaning towards one of Gaston's friends, asked in an under tone, but loud enough to be overheard, so that a refusal would be out of the question, "Pray introduce me to the Duke!"

The individual he had spoken to turned towards Gaston with an air of mingled annoyance and surprise, as much as to say, "What strange fancy has come over this old bore"? However, as there was no help for it, he resignedly exclaimed, "My dear Duke, Monsieur Moulinet."

"Manufacturer," quickly added the man with the diamond studs, "formerly judge of the Tribunal of Commerce." And then, taking hold of Gaston's hand, he resumed, with a deferential air, "I have the honour of knowing your family, Monsieur le Duc. Mademoiselle Moulinet, my daughter, was educated at the same convent as Mademoiselle de Beaulieu, your cousin. Yes, monsieur, at the 'Sacred Heart,' the first educational establishment in Paris. But then I was never niggardly with Athénaïs. I have always thought that the best things were not good enough for her. Ah! I beg you to believe that I deeply regret the sad news——"

For a moment or so Maître Escande, the young notary, had been wriggling in the most singular fashion, at the risk of crumpling his shirt-front or disarranging the artistic bow of his cravat. His arms moved like semaphores, he stamped impatiently, and coughed "hem, hem" almost without cessation. But Moulinet was either too well launched to stop, or else he was determined not to heed the notary's gesticulations, as what subsequently happened would seem to show. At all events, he still continued pouring forth his compliments of condolence.

"Excuse me," said the Duke, knitting his brow, "but I don't quite understand. You are speaking, monsieur, of some sad news which seems to touch my family, and especially

Mademoiselle de Beaulieu. I have no notion what you mean. Pray be more explicit."

Maître Escande seemed greatly worried, and as Moulinet remained silent with downcast eyes, the young notary gathered up his courage, and approaching Bligny said, in a solemn tone, "*Mon Dieu,* my dear Duke, I am sorry you should learn what Monsieur Moulinet has been alluding to this evening, and in a place like this, so unfitted for the communication of such news. But as you would certainly be apprised of it to-morrow, there is perhaps no reason why you should not be enlightened on the spot. Well, when you came in, I was telling these gentlemen that when I was in London a couple of days ago I learnt that the lawsuit commenced by the late Marquis de Beaulieu, and continued by his heirs, had just been lost by them beyond power of appeal."

This unexpected revelation made the Duke turn pale. The loss of this lawsuit, in the success of which Madame de Beaulieu had placed such hopes, meant that Claire was ruined. However, Gaston made an effort, and mastering his emotion haughtily rejoined, "I must say I am astonished at the readiness with which you communicated matters interesting the Beaulieu family to these gentlemen. I did not think that the affairs of my relatives were of a nature to serve as gossip and tittle-tattle for unconcerned idlers. I should feel obliged if you would show yourself rather more circumspect in the future."

On hearing this the young notary became extremely pale, and a number of little wrinkles, caused by the agitated state of his nerves, overspread his puffy face. He shook his head and breathed hard, and then in a wounded tone began, "But, my dear Duke, pray don't think——"

"I think what is proper," interrupted Bligny curtly, and

after taking the notary's measure with a glance he slowly walked away, followed by his friends in silence.

Moulinet and Escande had remained together, and for a moment they looked at each other without speaking. But at last, with a smile which strangely resembled a grimace, the manufacturer exclaimed, "Quick-blooded men, these Blignys! You were speedily silenced, eh! my dear maître? And I had my own share in it too. But no matter, fine blood and no mistake. He's ruined, isn't he?"

"Ruined! I should think so," said the notary with disdain. "And yet he plays the high and mighty lord, lays down the law, and gives lessons——"

"Quite so. Do you see, my dear fellow, in spite of revolutions, we shall never be these folks' equals. Why, even this ruined Duke will be an advantageous husband for a wealthy girl."

Three solemn raps, resounding at intervals on the stage, interrupted their conversation. Escande and Moulinet sat down. The Duke had found a vacant place some little distance off. The orchestra struck up the overture, and the harmonious melody of a brilliant waltz expanded with delightful rhythm. Although Bligny seemed attentive, he was in reality seriously reflecting. Claire's ruin was a thunderbolt calculated to wreck his future. He was betrothed to Mademoiselle de Beaulieu, and she was now poor. To Gaston's praise, it must be admitted that he did not once think of repudiating his engagements. The idea that he might marry some other woman never occurred to him. He considered himself absolutely bound. The white velvet case, stamped with the coupled escutcheons of Bligny and Beaulieu, and containing the betrothal ring, was in his pocket near his heart; but he was far more surely bound by his word than by the golden circlet.

And yet Claire's ruin meant impoverished circumstances for life. He would have to shut himself up in some country château, and vegetate like a bearish gentleman farmer, never inviting a friend for fear of the expense a visit would entail. For handsome, fascinating, courted Gaston this implied burial in the heydey of life. He bitterly regretted having dissipated the enormous sums he had won at play. However tainted the source that money had been derived from, it was money still; and life without money in this positive century, when men are only estimated at their pecuniary value, was not life at all. Then he felt touched on thinking of the grief Claire and her mother would feel when they learned the fatal news. They were still ignorant of it, no doubt, since that fool Escande had just brought it fresh from England. Gaston would have liked to expedite his journey, so as to be sooner by the side of these poor women, and soften the blow and console them.

Meanwhile the curtain had risen, revealing a gay and smiling scene. A band of reapers of either sex appeared in a sunshiny landscape, and to a rattling *bourrée** tune they sang at the top of their voices—

> "Sing, pretty maids,
> Reap, handsome swains,
> Your sickles raise
> To the gay refrains!"

Feeble as the words were, they seemed to inspire the Duke with a fresh strain of thought. He pictured himself with Claire at Beaulieu under the blue sky. The reapers were singing among the corn, and sultry heat rose from the ground. A sensation of delightful languor stole over him. In the company of her he loved he felt supremely happy, and gave no thought to poverty. It seemed such profound calm, such

* The *bourrée* is the popular dance of Auvergne.—*Trans.*

sweet peacefulness after the storms of his short life as a *viveur!* He enjoyed it thoroughly, and in the modest circumstances to which Claire's ruin condemned him he divined captivating delight such as he had never before known.

On the stage the performance was progressing, and the Chevalier Alphonse de Rouflaquette was singing his grand duo with the Princess. Judic's mellow, caressing voice was murmuring with passionate ardour—

"Oh! come! I renounce all my grandeur for thee,
Let's fly from my court, and my palace forsake!"—

Whereupon Daubray, curling his "knockers," responded with a killing glance—

"Nay, grandeur and love rightly mated may be;
So keep all your wealth and your power for me,
Ay, keep them for Alphonse's sake!"

The favourite *artiste* crowned his phrase with a vocal flourish which elicited thunders of applause. Indeed the *Education de la Princesse* announced itself as a great success, and the lessee of the Variétés, who looked very much absorbed, was thinking of trying this little "machine"* at his own place during the ensuing winter.

In the meanwhile Moulinet leant back in his chair and nodded his head like a bear listening to a flute player. He had no inclination to follow the adventures of the Princess Hortensia. He was far more interested in another princess— his daughter, the raven-haired Athénaïs. He saw her again as she was at the convent, a little girl wearing ill-made shoes

---

* In French theatrical parlance an opera, an operetta, a *vaudeville*, a tragedy, a drama, or a comedy is invariably styled a "machine." Mr. Grenville Murray has humourously noted this in his "High Life in France."—*Trans.*

and a dress too short for her, with red hands, a plain, shapeless face, and an angular, gawky figure, as yet undeveloped. She came to the parlour in the midst of her elegantly attired companions, who looked down on her disdainfully. He was not a rich man in those days, old Moulinet; he had not then founded his great chocolate works at Villepinte, nor invented those prospectuses on blue paper, couched in a travelling dentist's style, which had since made his products known even in the smallest villages of France. He was, in fact, simply a wholesale dealer in "colonial produce," and the noble mothers of Athénaïs's companions did not conceal their astonishment that this grocer's daughter should have been admitted as a boarder to the convent. He had heard all about the little class-room intrigues. He knew how arrogantly the other girls had treated his daughter, and he recollected that it was proud Mademoiselle de Beaulieu who had led the coterie of the nobles, as it was called.

How many times, indeed, he had heard Athénaïs speak angrily of her enemy—swearing with tears in her eyes that she would be revenged. And vengeance had come, without need of being prepared. Athénaïs Moulinet was now one of the richest heiresses in Paris, while proud Claire de Beaulieu was dowerless. The grocer's daughter, habituated to luxury, dressed by Worth, and with her hair becomingly arranged, had lost all her whilom gawkiness, become transformed as it were; and illumined by an aureole of millions, she was considered to be one of the best-looking girls of the upper middle-class. The Marchioness's daughter, clad in a simple woollen dress, would have to live in the provinces, disappear into obscurity, and perhaps—who knew?—she might even miss the marriage so long prepared for her.

The Duc de Bligny, such a brilliant nobleman, bearing

such a beautiful name! Often, when the young Duke came with his aunt, the Marchioness, to visit Claire at the convent, Athénaïs had turned pale with rage on seeing them side by side. She divined that they were intended for each other. Claire would become a duchess, whilst she, Athénaïs, would marry some notary, an Escande, or a tradesman like her father, and bear her husband sons and daughters destined to be humiliated and looked down upon.

At this thought a proud smile came over Moulinet's face. He leant back farther still, and thrusting his hand into one of his pockets, jingled some silver coins. "And why should that be?" he muttered. "Don't my means allow me to buy her any husband she pleases?" So saying, he turned round with a grave expression on his face, and, gazing at the elegant assemblage, seemed to be seeking for the son-in-law who would best please him. Standing on the pedestal of his millions nothing appeared impossible to him. Who would be audacious enough to refuse Athénaïs, holding a blank cheque in her hand? A count or a marquis? What sum would buy him? He had only to name his figure. Moulinet could give his daughter a million of francs, or ten millions if he pleased. To auction, the husband! The father was rich enough to buy his daughter a prince!

As he followed this train of thought his glance became bold and almost threatening; it strayed vaguely over all these unknown faces, and at last fell on Bligny. The young man looked gloomy, and Moulinet said to himself, "He is thinking of his cousin." The chocolate manufacturer felt greatly irritated at this idea, but why? What were these confused fancies stealing over him? He could not explain them himself, and yet the semblance of a project was already dawning in his mind.

At this moment there was a great stir in the hall. The curtain had just fallen on the finish of the first act, and in the midst of the applause and the calls for various performers, the Duke had risen, accompanied by his friends, and was walking with an indifferent air towards the door. For a moment Moulinet remained watching him, half undecided, and then suddenly leaving his seat he started off in the same direction as Bligny.

The fête had by no means interrupted the gambling on the second floor. The rooms reserved for play were well-nigh as quiet as usual; the refrains of the operetta being wafted merely as a vague murmur to the ears of the gamblers. Nothing had been able to turn them from their customary pastime. They knew that something very amusing was being performed down-stairs, but what did they care for it? Their pleasure was here, on this horse-shoe table, under the burning gas which heated their brains. On the floor below, elegant and beautiful women, sweet scented and arranged in bewitching toilettes, were grouped together like bouquets of flowers. The gamblers gave them no thought, however. They found the Queen of Spades and the Queen of Hearts a hundred times more attractive; and, insensible to the charms of the fête, deaf to the voices of the singers and the joyous strains of the orchestra, they remained up-stairs in a heavy, enervating atmosphere, flinging their money on the *tapis vert*.

As the Duke listlessly strolled about without aim or purpose, he unwittingly reached the card-rooms. Was it Fate that brought him once more, after all his fine resolutions, to the edge of the gaming table? At all events, as the banker exclaimed: "Gentlemen, make your game," Gaston drew a thousand franc note from his pocket and carelessly flung it on the table. He won. "Dear me!" he exclaimed with no little surprise, for Fortune now seldom favoured him, and curious to ascertain if his luck would last, he installed himself in a vacant chair. At that same moment Moulinet entered the card-room. It was the first time he had ever set foot there. He held all games of chance in horror on principle; and if ever he touched a card it was only in view of conquering luck by skill. He thus willingly played at besique. As for whist it was above his comprehension. However, he now approached the baccarat table, and on perceiving that Gaston had left his hundred louis on the *tapis*, he gravely laid a ten franc piece beside them. Plainly enough Moulinet was anxious to have an opportunity of watching the Duke, and, desirous of avoiding apparent indiscretion, he secured this opportunity by risking a trifle on his own account. The chocolate manufacturer believed in useful concessions on matters of principle.

The game continued, but luck had changed. It seemed as if the virtuous manufacturer's ten francs had broken the charm. Bligny, pale with rage, and again mastered by his passion, furiously produced his lost bank notes, whilst Moulinet, who disdained winning, placidly continued staking a ten franc piece. At daybreak, when the game ceased for want of players, the Duke had lost some forty thousand francs. Moulinet, sufficiently edified as to the fate of Mademoiselle de Beaulieu's betrothed, had long since been peacefully snoring in his superb mansion on the Boulevard Malesherbes.

At the hour when Gaston ought to have taken the train for Beaulieu he went up-stairs into his bedroom, feeling feverishly enervated. Leaning on the rail in front of the open window, he watched the matutinal street sweepers already at work in the Rue de la Paix. The clear sky was tinted with the roseate flush of Aurora, and the fresh air speedily revived him. "I was very foolish last night," he muttered to himself, "but I'll start this evening. To the deuce with baccarat!" He thereupon changed his clothes, went down-stairs, hailed a cab, and gave orders to be driven to the Bois de Boulogne. In the evening, however, he failed to start for Beaulieu. He repaired to the gaming table again.

Meanwhile, Claire, strong in her confidence and unchanging in her love, was waiting for the return of her betrothed.

V.

On the evening of the day when Bachelin came to Beaulieu with the sad news that the lawsuit had been lost, and that Gaston was sojourning in Paris, the Marchioness, still grievously affected by these hard blows, sat meditating in her cosy arm-chair in the grand drawing-room facing the terrace. She was deeply absorbed, and the expression of her countenance indicated that her thoughts were painful ones. However, she was roused from her sorrowful reverie by her son abruptly entering the room. She started on perceiving him, and gave him an anxious look as if she had expected some fresh misfortune, but noting the calm expression of his eyes and the quiet smile on his lips, she heaved a sigh of relief and asked: "What is the matter?"

"Our cousins, the Préfonts, are arriving, mother," the young man answered. "The carriage has just passed through the gates and is coming up the avenue."

In the stillness of the evening, the noise of wheels grating on the gravel was distinctly audible, and the Marchioness at once rose. Always chilly, she covered her head with a lace scarf, and wrapped her shawl around her. Then, crossing the broad paved vestibule, hung with old figured tapestry, and adorned with cabinets in carved pear-wood, she advanced to the steps, in front of which the carriage had just drawn up, after artistically whisking round the sweep. A laughing face, crowned by a toque trimmed with the plumage of the lophophorus, peeped out of the window. A gloved hand was waved excitedly, and a full fresh voice exclaimed: "Good day, good day, all of you!"

The young Marquis had already reached the vehicle. A hurricane of silk swept out; a dainty bronze-leather boot, surmounted by a grey silk stocking, showing a well-shaped ankle to advantage, was poised for one moment on the carriage step; and then the Baronne de Préfont in person darted into the Marchioness's arms, embracing her and jerkily exclaiming: "Ah! my dear aunt! How pleased I am! Ah! my good aunt! How long it is—— And you, my dear friends?"

Thereupon she lovingly threw herself into the arms of Mademoiselle de Beaulieu, intermingling vivacious exclamations with affectionate caresses: "My dear Claire! It seems a century since I saw you!" Next she unhesitatingly passed to Octave, allowing him to kiss her on both cheeks; after which she shook hands with him in the English style—laughing all the while, making her dress rustle with her sprightly movements, pausing every now and then in her cries of satisfaction so as to regain breath, and taking the whole château and its inmates by storm with her affectionate, overflowing joy. All on a sudden, however, she became serious, and eagerly asked: "Ah! good gracious me, what has become of my husband?" And looking anxiously around her she added: "Have I lost him already?"

"Here I am, dear," answered a soft voice; "I was patiently waiting for the end of your effusions to pay my respects in my turn." At the same moment a young man of thirty or thereabouts, dressed in a sober-looking travelling suit, with a courier-bag hanging at his side, stepped forward, and with quiet, smiling politeness approached the Marchioness and Claire.

"Well, well, pay your respects," petulantly exclaimed the Baroness. "There that'll do. Now pray go and see after my luggage. Be particularly careful about my large black bonnet-box. I hold you responsible for it on your head."

"Yes, dear," replied the Baron quietly, and, turning to Octave, who had approached to shake hands: "nineteen trunks and boxes, my dear fellow," he added with a smile of resignation. "Six hundredweight of extra luggage! I really believe my wife carries artillery about with her."

As the ladies now entered the drawing-room the Baroness leant towards Madame de Beaulieu, and, raising her eyes above, hurriedly whispered: "Ah! my dear aunt, what a deal we have to tell each other." Then pressing the Marchioness's hand with emotion: "You know that we love you, and that nothing that concerns you can be regarded with indifference by us——"

Madame de Beaulieu glanced at Claire, who had already pricked up her ears and become attentive, perceiving which the Baroness resumed: "Yes, I know. However, my husband will tell you everything." Then darting up to Claire she observed, as though seeking to efface the effect of her imprudent words, "You know we are going to Switzerland, dear? But we did not like to pass so near Beaulieu without coming to see you. We shall remain here for a few days and then start off by road. We shall reach Switzerland by the pass of Verrières. Ah! our poor army of the East! · The Baron was wounded at Joux in the last combat between our rearguard and that terrible Werder's men—— So, you understand, it's a pilgrimage for me. My husband behaved like a hero!—— Of the two hundred men his company counted—poor, suffering, frost-bitten fellows—there were only eighty left after the engagement. And they didn't decorate him!—— It's true we are Legitimists—— Ah! what an abominable government, my friends! And, hereabouts, do folks think that Gambetta will consent to become prime minister?"

Thus did the little Baroness rattle on, smiling and animated, as talkative as a parrot, at one moment even dramatic, but passing swiftly from one subject to the other, regardless of all transition, although she employed a surprising variety of language. She seemed, as it were, a living kaleidoscope, instantly changing in aspect and effect. The Marchioness and Claire became astonished and bewildered as they listened to her. In the quiet calm of their country life they had grown grave and thoughtful, and the animation of this noisy, airy Parisienne imparted a sensation of vertigo.

Without waiting for any answer to her question the Baroness crossed the drawing-room, and approaching a window whence the view extended far over the shadowy valley, from the depth of which rose the tall chimneys of the ironworks launching a fiery glow into the darkness, she clapped her hands with childish admiration and exclaimed: "How beautiful! It looks like an opera scene! Ah, nature, nature!—— How happy you are, to be able to live in the midst of the fields and woods! What a beautiful life, and how it preserves one! Look at me, aunt, and compare me with Claire. We are of the same age, and yet I look as if I were her mother!—— It's all the fault of the dinners and visiting, the balls and the theatres. We fade away in the whirl of Parisian life; and so much pleasure becomes perfect toil. You are smiling, aunt? Perhaps you think that we might manage differently, my husband and I, and spend four months a year at our place in Burgundy—— Perhaps so, but

I hardly see the way. The Baron, who is a learned man, needs to reside in the capital for the sake of its intellectual life. He has his Academy of Sciences and all his solemn societies there—— Ah! heavens. That Academy, how it affects my nerves!—— As for myself I've a thousand duties to attend to, which I can't possibly neglect—social connections to keep up, charitable societies to promote and manage—And then there's my little girl, whom I can't always leave with her governess. So when we have been for a couple of months at the seaside, a couple of months touring, and a couple of months at Nice—you see what remains—— Ah! it's an extenuating life I can assure you. But suppose we sat down!"

And darting like a hurricane between Madame de Beaulieu and Claire, the Baroness ensconced herself in the cosy arm-chair, which was the Marchioness's favourite. "There," she said. "Now talk to me about yourselves. What do you do here? How do you occupy your time? And Octave? And your neighbour, the ironmaster?—— You see I remember what you write to me about. Heavens! what would become of one if one hadn't a little memory?"

Seating herself comfortably in the roomy arm-chair the Baroness gently closed her eyes and prepared to listen attentively to her aunt and cousin. There was a moment's silence, and then almost without transition, as a bird after warbling its last note falls asleep at the edge of its nest, our Parisienne, who was no doubt really fatigued by her journey, let her head fall back gently on to the antimacassar of old guipure, and the faint sound of breathing that escaped from between her parted lips showed she was giving way to sleep. The Marchioness and Claire exchanged a good-natured smile, and, taking up their work, prepared to wait till this charming woman, who had remained in many respects so childish, woke up again.

The Baronne de Préfont, *née* Sophie d'Hennecourt—How ironical names sometimes are! "Sophie," applicable to wisdom, bestowed on such a madcap—was the only daughter of one of the late Marquis de Beaulieu's sisters. She had been educated at the same convent as Claire, where she had formed part of the aristocratic clan which so persecuted the girls belonging to the middle classes. Thus she had become well acquainted with M. Moulinet's daughter. Gifted with an angel's heart, but having no more brains than a bird, she spent her time striving to repair, by dint of kindliness, all the harm she wrought in ever-recurring moments of thoughtlessness. It happened that she had in no small degree contributed to increase the hatred which Athénaïs had vowed against Mademoiselle de Beaulieu. It was she, indeed, who as soon as Mademoiselle Moulinet reached the convent surnamed her "Little Cocoa;" and as a battle royal was on the point of being fought by these schoolgirls of thirteen, it was Claire, the strongest and most reasonable, who with a tinge of haughtiness stayed the combat. Such was Athénaïs's nature, however, that she felt more irritated against Claire for intervening, than against Sophie for attacking her. Besides, Mademoiselle de Beaulieu overawed her companions by her precocious firmness of character. She was, so to say, the incarnation of this aristocratic set which made life so hard for M. Moulinet's daughter; and by reason of her very superiority she became the object of all Athénaïs's spite. The truth is that Claire personally never did anything intentionally to wound Athénaïs, but their natures were naturally hostile. Everything in connection with this patrician damsel offended or hurt her sensitive schoolfellow of the middle classes, even the elegance of her figure and the whiteness of her hands, the crest on her note paper and the gloves she wore during play time.

Claire and her friends were in the habit of saying "thou" and "thee" to one another; and Athénaïs at once followed their example, whereupon some terrible discussions ensued in this miniature world. Sophie d'Hennecourt, especially, was quite exasperated, and persistently addressed the chocolate manufacturer's daughter as "you." Claire, however, laughed at what she considered a puerile distinction, and thou'd and thee'd Athénaïs as much as she did the other girls.* But Mademoiselle Moulinet thereupon resented Claire's familiarity as an insult. Although Claire pretended not to notice her hostility, it by no means escaped her. In spite of herself, perhaps, her disdain for Athénaïs was increased.

In the meantime, a bitter warfare was waged incessantly between Mademoiselle d'Hennecourt and "Little Cocoa." One day, as Sophie returned from seeing some relatives in the parlour, she entered the playground carrying a bag of chocolate sweetmeats, which she offered to all her companions. Athénaïs's turn came at last, and Sophie approached her with seeming graciousness and held out the bag so that she might help herself. "Will you have some?" she asked in a honeyed voice; and then, as Athénaïs half hesitated, she added

* All readers conversant with the French language will remember that this is a constant practice among relatives and friends in France—as much among those of the masculine sex as among girls and women. However, in translation into English, it is impossible to render "thou" and "thee" otherwise than as "you." Among us, Quakers alone use the former pronouns in ordinary conversation. It is true that English Protestants address the Divinity as "Thou;" whereas French Catholics, who, in this instance, invariably say "You," are grievously shocked, for, to their minds, the thee-and-thou-ing of the Creator is scandalously irreverent.—*Trans.*

with deliberate irony, "Oh, you needn't fear for the consequences. They don't come from your place, but from Marquis's." Mademoiselle Moulinet turned pale with rage, and snatching the bag from Sophie's hand, she flung it against a window, which broke with a crash, the pane of glass falling in fragments on the sandy court. A tussle ensued, in the course of which Athénaïs was almost pushed down, when one of her hands came in contact with a bit of glass and was rather badly cut. Excessive rage and the fear of seeing her blood flow had such an effect upon her system that she positively fainted away; whereupon Sophie, whose good heart at once gained the upper hand, caught her in her arms, and helped to take her to the school infirmary—at the same time weeping and blaming herself for having caused this misfortune.

Thenceforward the scene changed. Athénaïs openly placed herself at the head of the girls of the middle classes, and the playground was divided into two camps—that of the juvenile aristocrats, and that of the moneyed damsels without handles to their names. However, as these girls grew up their quarrels assumed a more underhand character, evincing better acquaintance with the usages of society. They no longer scratched each other with their finger nails, but relied on their tongues to wound and hurt one another. Although Claire, more haughty and disdainful than ever, remained seemingly aloof, taking no part in the warfare, she was none the less bitterly execrated. There was a covert struggle waging between herself and Athénaïs. It was evident that Mademoiselle Moulinet was Mademoiselle de Beaulieu's personal antagonist, and, to say the truth, they were fairly matched.

Father Moulinet was then engaged in amassing a colossal fortune. People pretended that he had discovered a means of making vanilla out of coal, and that in preparing his chocolate he used burnt almonds instead of cocoa. It was reported that this alimentary chemistry yielded him immense profit, and thus he was beginning to rank as a financial notability in the world of Paris. He had, moreover, just received his appointment as one of the judges of the Tribunal of Commerce, and whenever he was spoken of his friends nodded their heads gravely and remarked: "He's a wonderfully clever man." On his side, jovial Moulinet, one of whose characteristics was a surprising familiarity of language, willingly observed: "Ah! the old boy (meaning himself) has a long purse." He was, indeed, exceedingly vulgar, but by no means an evil-minded individual. He readily did any one a good turn when he thought he might himself reap some advantage from it. On the other hand, although extremely desirous of enlarging his circle of acquaintances, he warily gave all black sheep the go-by. He always looked above and never below him, and had thus succeeded in steadily climbing higher and higher up the social ladder.

One fine day he drove up to the Convent of the Sacred Heart in an admirable landau drawn by a pair of horses, and on reaching the parlour had his daughter sent for. The result was that Athénaïs left the convent. She was then sixteen years of age. On the following Sunday, in the Bois de Boulogne, her companions perceived her seated in her father's superb carriage, and she smiled on them and eagerly recognised them from afar, as if particularly anxious to bow to them from such a stylish turn-out. A few months later Sophie and Claire also returned home, and the convent warfare ceased for want of combatants.

But hatred was still rife in Mademoiselle Moulinet's heart, and she kept her eyes on her rivals. From her box on the second row, which her father had with difficulty secured for the season at the Grand Opera House, she angrily watched Mesdemoiselles d'Hennecourt and de Beaulieu, installed in one of the best boxes on the grand tier, where they received innumerable visits from elegant cavaliers between the acts. In the salon, at the rear, conversation was carried on, and Sophie and Claire listened smilingly to their visitors and regaled themselves with bonbons. But Moulinet's box—alas!—remained unvisited, and all was silent there. Over and over again Athénaïs remarked to herself: "Surely among all those visitors there must be some suitor for Claire's hand, some nobleman who will eventually marry her." The fact is Mademoiselle de Beaulieu's beauty had become most fascinating. Her skin was exquisitely white, and when she appeared in a low-cut pink robe, without a jewel, every one gazed at her admiringly.

Nevertheless Sophie was the first to marry. The Baron de Préfont asked for her hand, and the wedding was celebrated with great pomp at the church of St. Augustine. There was a splendid service, to which Mademoiselle Moulinet was not invited. Still some of her old companions at the convent pretended they had seen her—thickly veiled, and accompanied by a maid—watching the ceremony from one of the transepts. This was never proved, still it was true. Screened by the shade of a pillar, Athénaïs viewed the wedding and fairly devoured her enemies with her eyes. Claire was bridesmaid, and collected in company with the young Viscomte de Pontac;[*] but as soon as Mademoiselle Moulinet perceived her enemy ap-

---

[*] At all the fashionable Parisian weddings the bridesmaids collect for the poor, under escort. It is worthy of remark that there are never more than two bridesmaids or *demoiselles d'honneur*, and usually only one.—*Trans.*

proaching her observatory, she retreated into the throng and went off. This little manœuvre was not noticed by Mademoiselle de Beaulieu, who continued her collection with a gentle smile on her face—never for one moment imagining that if eyes could kill she would have already fallen dead in the centre of the church.

Sophie being married and the Duc de Bligny having started for St. Petersburg, Claire's life became a very retired one. Of late she had spent six months away from Paris, and all recollection of Athénaïs had faded from her mind. As she watched the Baronne de Préfont, sleeping composedly in the cosy arm-chair, she did not give a thought to the many quarrels which this charming madcap had initiated during their convent days.

Presently the drawing-room door was abruptly opened, and the Baroness started at the sound and woke up. On perceiving her husband and Octave enter the room, she sprang at once to her feet, and exclaimed with sudden lucidity of mind: "Why, you let me fall asleep." Then beginning to laugh: "Why, it's like in the fairy tales. This must be the castle of the Sleeping Beauty! Scarcely arrived, I must needs fall asleep. But who is the Prince Charming that has just woke me up? Is it you, Baron? No, it must be Octave. Aunt, pray excuse me! It is your air that did all the harm! It overcame me. We are not accustomed to such atmosphere in Paris."

"It's nothing!" replied the Marchioness. "You were taken unawares. It is merely the first effect; but you will get used to it."

Meanwhile the Baron had stepped forward with quiet gravity. "I have just carried out your instructions, dear," said he. "Your luggage has been brought in, and the whole château is encumbered with it."

"Very good," replied the Baroness, with the air of a queen satisfied with a subject's obedience.

"Shall I show you your rooms?" asked Claire, perceiving that the Baroness remained standing with an undecided air.

"Willingly, dear," replied Sophie; and taking up a red leather bag which she had laid on a chair when entering the room, she gave her husband a keen sharp glance. He immediately approached her to rid her of the bag, but she quickly wrested it from him. "No, not you," said she. "You are too absent-minded. And this needs to be treated carefully. Come, Octave, you shall have the privilege of carrying it." With these words she glanced again at her husband, and then from him to the Marchioness, in a most significant manner.

"I'm highly flattered by your confidence, dear," said Préfont with a smile. "Come, Octave, my dear fellow, the work is for you. I'll keep your mother company."

Delighted at having been understood, the Baroness favoured her husband with an approving gesture, and then, linking her arm through Claire's so as to make sure that Mademoiselle de Beaulieu would not linger behind and prevent the tête-à-tête she had planned between her husband and the Marchioness, she left the room humming a gay refrain.

The Baron, who looked grave and thoughtful, advanced a few steps in silence. The Marchioness, ensconced in her easy-chair, gazed vacantly in front of her. The room was dark, but the fire, which had been lighted in this chilly October evening, sparkled in the grate of the pink granite chimney-piece, and its leaping flames cast dancing gleams of light over the ceiling. The Marchioness was thinking to herself that perhaps the news the Baron had brought from Paris was better than what Bachelin had informed her of a few hours earlier, and yielding to this idea she began to hope again.

On the floor above the eager steps of the young folks going from room to room could be plainly heard. The old château seemed full of unusual life and motion, and a subtle strain of the Baroness's gay carol was wafted through the air.

At last the Marchioness roused herself from her meditation and raised her eyes. Perceiving the Baron standing before her, as if awaiting her orders, she gave him a melancholy smile. "Well, nephew," she said, "and so you have something to tell me. I can guess pretty nearly what it is, and in fact you can see how it grieves me."

"It is certainly a sad business, aunt," answered the young man gravely, "and by no means calculated to increase the esteem in which our society is held. Unfortunately, whenever one of us acts dishonourably the odium of his conduct falls on all his equals. Nowadays our only superiority over other classes lies in the faithfulness with which we keep our engagements. 'A nobleman's word' is a proverbial expression. But, when it is seen that we don't keep our promises any better than other folks, people will soon cease to believe in our respect for verbal engagements, and we shall have lost the last vestige of our good fame."

A tear sparkled in the Marchioness's eyes, and, raising her thin delicate hands towards the Baron she exclaimed: "Tell me all. Don't hide anything. Thanks to our worthy Bachelin's investigations, I already know that the Duc de Bligny has been in Paris for the last six weeks."

"Ah, really, Marchioness, you know all that?" exclaimed the Baron bitterly; "and are you also aware that he is about to marry——"

"To marry!" exclaimed Madame de Beaulieu, rising, half stupefied, from her arm-chair, her face pallid with emotion.

"Yes, my dear aunt. Excuse my frankness and promptitude in telling you of it, but in matters of this kind I always think it best to go to the point at once."

"To marry!" the Marchioness slowly repeated.

"The Duke has done all he could to prevent it from being noised about. But his future father-in-law, who, it appears, is as vulgar a man as could be found, has by no means proved discreet. It seems he is in exultation. Fancy, his daughter is to become a Duchess! I learned the story from Castéran, who is one of the Duke's intimate friends, and well acquainted with the manner in which the negotiations were set on foot. I am sorry to have to confess to you, aunt, that the story is a most lamentable one. It appears that the Duke had scarcely arrived from St. Petersburg, when he began to gamble at the club. He was badly treated by luck and soon came to the end of his tether, which was by no means long. Thereupon he had recourse to the club cash-box, and obtained funds to meet his engagements. After that he went on playing again—playing such high stakes that in a single week his liabilities rose to two hundred and fifty thousand francs. It seems he had completely lost his head. Bad luck maddened him, and he rushed blindly into the mêlée. In a couple of evenings he had won back all he had lost. Then he lost another hundred thousand francs again, and finally he remained with a 'culotte' of a couple of hundred thousand——"

The Marchioness raised her eyebrows with surprise and exclaimed interrogatively: "A 'culotte?'".

"Excuse me, aunt," said the Baron phlegmatically; "it is the usual term. In speaking of a heavy loss at cards people say a 'culotte'—a pair of breeches."

"A culotte costing two hundred thousand francs," said the Marchioness with a dreary smile. "That is certainly very prodigal."

"All the more so as Gaston hadn't the first halfpenny to pay what he owed. Besides, at our clubs all debts of this kind must be paid in four-and-twenty hours, or else the debtor is liable to be 'posted' and excluded. So the Duke's situation was a most critical one. Of course he might have applied to his relatives. Although all our fortune is in land, we could have raised part of the sum, the Baroness and myself; and Gaston might have obtained a delay for the rest. But he did not think of applying to us, or rather he would not do so, although Castéran had advised him to take that course. The fact is, the unfortunate fellow shut himself up in his room at the club and gave way to the most painful reflections. He realised that he had grievously tampered with his social position and compromised all his future prospects. However, at this difficult juncture, Providence intervened in the person of the future father-in-law, whom Gaston, so I am told, had only met on a single previous occasion. This individual went to the point at once, speaking to Bligny in this fashion: 'Monsieur le Duc, you owe a couple of hundred thousand francs which you must procure in the course of the day; but you will not be able to do so.' Thereupon the Duke sprang up as if to cut all further conversation short, but this singular person, who had only been introduced to him a few evenings before, immediately added: 'It happens I have brought you these two hundred thousand francs. I possess an immense fortune, and I would not have it said that a man like myself, giving a dowry of ten millions to his only daughter, allowed one of the noblest names in the country to be compromised for the lack of ten thousand louis.' Such language is an enormity, of course; but you will understand that I don't guarantee these words as being absolutely correct. Castéran has a ready tongue, and, may be, he tried to embellish the story. However, I have only repeated what he told me. Bligny appears to have been dazzled. It seemed to him as if this obliging old man were made of gold, and, indeed, as he had benevolently opened his safe, the Duke dipped his little finger into it. His hand followed, and then, as if he had been caught in some machinery, everything else was drawn in—title and all. And that's how it happens that the Duke is about to be married."

A moment's silence followed. Night had now fallen, and, in the darkness, the Baron could barely discern the Marchioness's head, still proudly raised. The only sound was the monotonous ticking of the old Louis Quatorze clock, as its pendulum swung from side to side with regular cadence. Suddenly the Baron perceived a white cloud as it were pass before his aunt's face, and a sob, imperfectly repressed, told him that she was weeping. He hastily approached her and kneeling on a tapestried stool at her feet, tenderly took hold of her hand—at a loss for words to console her in the grief which had proved stronger even than pride.

" 'Tis nothing," said the Marchioness gently. "I was unable to master my sorrow, I own it; this is such a blow, I could not restrain my tears. I loved Gaston so dearly. He was a second son for me! He is of the same blood as myself, and his misconduct grieves me doubly. I cannot understand such ingratitude on his part, for as a lad he had a generous, loyal heart. How can he have changed so promptly? Has society the power of undoing all the work of long years, in a few months? I brought him up so gently, so tenderly! And this is how he rewards me! Ah! the ungrateful, the ungrateful fellow."

The Baron, who was deeply touched, had unwittingly taken from the table one of the long ivory needles with which the Marchioness knitted woollen waistcoats for the poor, and, with an irritated gesture, he obstinately kept pricking it into a large ball of grey wool. However, the Marchioness had regained her self-possession and was now drying her tears. "The important matter," said she firmly, "is that we must be most circumspect in reference to Claire. You know her. She is proud, and violent at times. Just like her father, who had a golden heart, but an iron head. This blow will come upon her at a time when she is full of confidence. She was speaking to me of Gaston only this afternoon. She has never for once thought that he might be jilting her for some one else. She has imputed his silence and delay to the necessities of the situation. The shadow of a doubt has never rested on her mind. Frank and loyal herself, she expects only frankness and loyalty from others, and the disclosure of the truth may have a most serious effect on such a nature as hers."

"But, my dear aunt, don't you think that the situation might be greatly modified by an interview with Bligny? He has been led astray. But by making him realise all the enormity of the offence he is about to commit, perhaps it would be possible to win him back? If you consented, I would willingly place myself at your disposal to make the attempt."

"No," replied the Marchioness proudly. "We are not folks to humble ourselves and implore. Sad as our position may be, it is none the less dignified and well defined. I should not care to change it. However, before acquainting my daughter with the sad tidings, I shall wait till my nephew's new engagements have become irrevocable. For with a man so capricious as the Duc de Bligny"—and here the Marchioness smiled bitterly—"one can rely on nothing with certainty—may be, he will change his mind again——"

"As you please, aunt," rejoined the Baron. "I cannot

blame you for deciding on this course. To tell the truth I anticipated such an answer from you; still I considered it my duty to offer you my services in the event of conciliation being thought of. At all events, no matter what may happen now, yours will be the honourable *rôle*; and if you have occasion to shed a few tears in secret, at least you will have no need to make a wry face. And I wouldn't say as much for Bligny."

A sound of rapid footsteps was now heard on the stairs, combined with the merry chatter of fresh young voices. Octave and Claire, light-hearted and smiling, were returning with the Baroness, whose impulsive gaiety had speedily enlivened them. The drawing-room door opened and Madame de Préfont, ahead of her cousins, swept like an avalanche into the gloomy apartment. "What! good heavens! You are in the dark! How dreadfully dismal!" cried the Baroness. "You seem to be talking in a tomb! Why it's dark enough not to hear one another speak! Aunt, you have spoiled us—you have given the Baron and me the finest rooms in the château. And, do you know, we shall find ourselves so comfortable that we shall be tempted to stay here for good!"

"So much the better, my dear. But I fancy your journey must have given you an appetite. We will go to dinner."

At the same moment, as if these words had been expected, the folding doors communicating with the dining-room were thrown open, a blaze of light illumined the sideboards adorned with old china and massive silver plate, and in a sedate, solemn voice the butler articulated the established formula: "Madame la Marquise is served."

VI.

On the morrow of Monsieur and Madame de Préfont's arrival at Beaulieu, Philippe Derblay, accompanied by his sister, presented himself at the château; and his visit was particularly well timed so far as the versatile Baroness was concerned, for it promised some little diversion in the midst of this country life, which she was already beginning to find insipidly monotonous.

Seated under a large garden tent, striped red and grey, the inmates of Beaulieu were enjoying the sunshine of one of those fine October afternoons which are, like the last smiles of the year, soon destined to become so cold and dreary. Deceived by the warmth of the sun, numerous feathered vocalists were carolling among the trees of the park as in the summer time; while on the warm gravel of the terrace a couple of blackbirds with yellow beaks whistled and fought for some crumbs of bread which the Marquis had thrown out of the diningroom window. Wrapped in her shawls and rendered somewhat drowsy by the warm air, the Marchioness listened with wandering attention to the prattle of the Baroness and Claire, who conversed together leaning over the pink granite balustrade. The Baron, who was gravely reclining in a rocking-chair, puffed slowly at his cigar, the smoke of which rose in wavy spirals towards the blue sky. The Marquis, with his pocket-book on his knee, was furtively sketching the profiles of the two young women, which stood out gracefully against the clear horizon. Profound peacefulness pervaded this cosy corner, and by degrees an invincible, delicious sensation of lassitude stole over one, enervating the body and lulling the mind to sleep.

The footsteps of a servant sounding on the gravel aroused every one from this moral and physical stupor. The Marchioness opened her eyes. Claire and the Baroness turned round, abandoning their dreamy contemplation of the valley. The Marquis hastily slipped his note-book into his pocket. The Baron, who did not believe in useless motion, alone contented himself with a mere inclination of the head.

"Monsieur and Mademoiselle Derblay inquire if Madame la Marquise receives," said the footman.

A slight frown came over Claire's proud brow as she heard these words. The name of the man by whom she instinctively felt she was pursued displeased her, thus pronounced in her own home. She had, as it were, a presentiment that this stranger would somehow influence her life, and her whole being revolted at the thought. Suddenly, however, her heart filled with bitterness, although a confused idea that she was abandoned already existed in the depths of her soul. She asked herself how it happened that, after M. Derblay's demonstrations of love, timid though they were, he dared to present himself at the château. It is true that Bachelin had announced the visit, giving as its motive a desire for conciliation on business matters. But the latter might only be a pretext. Because she was momentarily forsaken by the Duke, was this ironmaster bold enough to think of approaching her and wooing her? These reflections passed in a second through her mind, and prompted her aversion for Philippe.

"Receive him, aunt, receive him!" cried the Baroness. "I

am so curious to see this ironmaster! He will amuse us, and we will make his sister chatter about what is going on in the village. Perhaps she wears the costume of the province! How nice it would be!"

"But I am myself desirous of receiving, dear," replied the Marchioness, smiling; and turning towards the servant, who stood waiting, she added: "Request Monsieur and Mademoiselle Derblay to be kind enough to step as far as here."

There was a moment's silence, and then the glass door of the drawing-room opened, and Philippe and Suzanne appeared on the steps. A sun ray illumined the ironmaster's bronzed resolute countenance. He appeared in all his quiet, sedate strength. Clad in a long buttoned-up frock-coat, he seemed taller than he really was. His sister, who wore a simple dress of dark blue woollen stuff, approached close beside him. Emotion lent an animated expression of mingled nervousness and resolution to her features, and her loving eyes were fixed on her brother as if to inspire him with courage.

The Marchioness had risen and taken a few steps forward to meet her visitors. Philippe bent low before her and stammered a few disjointed words, the confusion of which brought a smile to the noble lady's lips. But as if to free him from his embarrassment she turned to Suzanne, and, with charming grace, took hold of her hand. "Tell your brother, child," she said, "that he is welcome here."

Philippe raised his head, and in a tone of deep gratitude, exclaimed: "I don't know how to thank you, Madame la Marquise, for the kind reception you give my sister. She has grown up under my guidance, but without a mother's care. She sadly needs advice and lessons, and she could obtain none better than yours, if you were gracious enough to take some interest in her."

Madame de Beaulieu looked at Suzanne more attentively, and was touched by her candid, tender gracefulness. "Come and let me kiss you, my beauty," she said. And touching Suzanne's fair hair with her lips, "There is peace signed on this child's forehead," she added, turning to Philippe. "All your sins are forgiven you, neighbour. And now come and let me introduce you to my family."

With a wave of the hand she indicated Octave who was approaching. "The Marquis de Beaulieu, my son," said she.

"Oh! an introduction is quite useless, mother," exclaimed the Marquis frankly, as he held out his hand to Philippe. "We have already met—Monsieur Derblay and I. You have good legs, my dear neighbour, and the hares I contrive to miss so well could never scamper off so fast as you do, when you don't wish to be overtaken."

"You must excuse me, Monsieur le Marquis," replied Philippe with a smile," if I did not tell you who I was. You did not seem to have a very favourable opinion of me, and I feared I should meet with scarcely a pleasant reception if I abandoned my incognito."

"Well, I only knew you by the misunderstanding which had arisen concerning our respected limits, but matters are different now, and I trust we shall be good friends. But, pray, be kind enough to introduce me to Mademoiselle Derblay."

The charm of Suzanne's person was having its effect already, for Octave at once approached her, gallantly polite and eager to please. Madame de Beaulieu thereupon turned to Philippe again, and designating him to the Baroness and Claire, exclaimed: "Monsieur Derblay, the ironmaster of Pont-Avesnes." Then indicating the two cousins, she added: "The Baronne de Préfont, my niece, and Mademoiselle de Beaulieu, my daughter,"

A burning flush suffused Philippe's face, and without daring to set eyes on the girl he adored, he bowed so low that one might almost have fancied he was about to kneel down.

"Why he's a gentleman, dear!" whispered the Baroness to Claire. "And think that I pictured him with bare arms, with a leather apron over his knees and iron-dust in his hair! Heaven forgive me! Why, he's decorated! And the Baron isn't!—It is true we live under a strange government, but all the same, it is very extraordinary! So he doesn't spend his time hammering then? Just look at him—— It's incredible. He's really very good looking. His eyes are superb."

Claire had hitherto averted her gaze, but now she looked at Philippe almost sternly. Her heart was full of anger, and she was tempted to greet this daring stranger with wounding words and offensive glances. She looked on his stalwart form as evidence of vulgarity, and was displeased even with his dark clothes, which gave him such a dignified, serious air. At the same moment the Duke's image flitted vision-like before her eyes. She seemed to see Gaston, with his slender figure and graceful bearing, his oval face and brown hair, his blue eyes and his expressive mouth, shaded by long drooping moustaches. The contrast was complete between Philippe, there present, and Bligny, far away. The robust figure of the former was the incarnation, so to say, of the healthful physique of the middle classes, while the latter exhibited in his person the delicate and somewhat effeminate grace peculiar to the aristocracy.

Philippe remained spell-bound under Claire's gaze, and his feet seemed rooted to the ground. In his confusion he was tempted to try and escape from this hostile examination, and thought of approaching the Marquis—who was still talking with Suzanne—so as to be near some one who bore him no ill-will. However, his limbs failed him. Almost unwittingly he glanced at himself, and suddenly imagined that he was unwieldy, common looking, and destitute of aught approaching elegance. He bitterly compared himself to the two young men near him, who walked about with such easy, natural grace in their well-cut clothes; and his black frock-coat of provincial make seemed hideous. He fancied he looked grotesque, standing there with his tall hat in his hand; and he suffered horribly. He would, at that moment, have given ten years of his life to have been dressed like the Baron and Octave, and to have possessed their easy bearing, for he said to himself that Claire would never forget the aspect under which he had first appeared before her, and that an unfavourable recollection of his person would always abide in her mind. He distinctly realised the distance that still separated Mademoiselle de Beaulieu, although ruined, from the ironmaster of Pont-Avesnes, and with profound despair, he reproached himself for his mad presumption in raising his eyes higher than his ambition could ever hope to attain.

However, Octave's voice at last roused him from his torpor. "My dear Monsieur Derblay," said the Marquis, "we have some one here who can readily talk to you about industrial questions—my cousin, the Baron de Préfont, a *savant*."

"Say a man of study, my dear Octave," softly interrupted the Baron. "The field of science is too vast for me to have any other pretension than that of having explored a small corner of it."

Regaining his self-possession Philippe looked around him for Mademoiselle de Beaulieu. She had gracefully sauntered off, and was now slowly walking up and down the terrace with the Baroness. With the tip of her crimson parasol she unwittingly struck at the flowers of a creeper twining round the balustrade. Philippe heaved a sigh, and averting his gaze: "This is not the first time," said he, "that I have heard Monsieur de Préfont's name mentioned." Then, as the Baron made a gesture of polite protest, he added: "Are you not the author of a remarkable treatise on cementation, monsieur? I have myself studied the question, and I read the treatise you sent to the Academy of Sciences with very great interest indeed."

"Oh! oh! Baron," cried Octave gaily. "You didn't fancy you were so well known in our mountains? Come, you are on the road to fame, my dear fellow; your name has penetrated even into remote rural districts, and you must supplement your old device, '*Fortis gladio*,' with the addendum '*et pennâ*.' Don't think I'm poking fun at you. I would gladly imitate you if I only could."

But the Baron cared little what the Marquis might say! Delighted to find an auditor who could understand him, he had already launched forth into a learned dissertation on the manufacture of steel. Even the intervention of the Baroness would not have turned him from his subject. He had divested himself of his English stiffness and reassumed all his natural mobility. He clapped his hands together and imitated the noise of machinery to illustrate his demonstration. Gesticulating vivaciously, he even caught hold of M. Derblay's arm, as if to prevent the ironmaster from taking himself off. But Philippe had no desire to try and escape from M. de Préfont's impulsive familiarity. Quite the contrary, he urged him on, happy to find an unexpected ally in one of these people among whom he had felt so ill at ease; and thus the Baron, who was quite delighted, rattled on with infinite loquacity, already calling Philippe "my dear sir," which he certainly would not have done with any one else after a three months' connection.

But then their mutual interest in science had brought and linked them together immediately, as if they had been a couple of freemasons and had exchanged certain mysterious signs in shaking hands.

"And you dig your own ore? How interesting your works must be!" said the Baron. "I must go down to Pont-Avesnes to-morrow morning for you to show me your forges. You must employ a good many workpeople?"

"About two thousand."

"That's capital! And how many furnaces?"

"Ten, the fires of which are kept alight from one year to another. You shall see my steam hammer. It weighs twenty tons, and can be worked with such precision that you might lower it to touch an egg without breaking the shell."

"Why, with such an implement as that you might compete with Le Creusot itself?"

"Exactly so; what Le Creusot does on a large scale we do on a small one."

"It is quite a piece of good fortune for me, to have met you, my dear sir," exclaimed the Baron joyfully. "I intended starting with the Baroness for Switzerland at the end of the month, but good-bye to our tour! I shall stop here. Do you understand? We will make some experiments together. Have you a laboratory? Yes! You are a chemist? Perfect! You are one of the most agreeable men I have ever met." And taking Philippe by the arm again, M. de Préfont began walking up and down the terrace.

"Dear me! what is the matter with my husband?" asked the Baroness, as she approached with Claire.

"The matter, my dear cousin?" responded Octave gaily, "why he is riding his favourite hobby with Monsieur Derblay before him."

"Then they may have a long journey, and no mistake, if my husband isn't stopped."

"And why should he be stopped?" asked the Marquis. "Don't you approve of Préfont's associating with Monsieur Derblay? Your husband, my dear cousin, is a descendant of the crusaders, and ten centuries of warlike fame are united in his person. Monsieur Derblay, a manufacturer's son, represents but one century—but it is the century which has produced, or at least found the means of utilising, steam, gas, and electricity. I must confess to you that, for my own part, I particularly admire the sudden association of these two men, who although apparently dissimilar, mutually esteem each other and blend together the greatest desiderata for a nation's grandeur—past glory and present progress."

"Octave, my friend," said the Baroness, "it can be seen that you are an advocate. You speak very fluently indeed. But allow me to say that I find you rather democratic for your father's son."

"Well, cousin," rejoined the young man smiling, "you know that democracy invades us on all sides. So let us try and constitute an aristocracy even in our democratic community. For instance, draw the line at mediocrity, and set all who are meritorious above it. We might thus found the aristocracy of talent, which is the only one worthy of succeeding the aristocracy of birth. And besides, in acting like that we shall only be imitating our ancestors. Do you imagine that the founders of our families were of noble birth? It was their courage which raised them above other men. The first Préfont was simply called Gaucher (the left-handed), which no doubt did not prevent him from being skilful, for it is stated that he was a doughty soldier. Ennobled for his warlike deeds, and enriched by booty, he took the name of his estate on returning from Palestine; and it is thanks to Captain Gaucher, my dear cousin, that you are a Baroness. So why should we deny men who are co-equal perhaps with your ancestor the right of stepping out of the crowd? In old times folks used to say: 'Honour to the bravest;' but nowadays let us rather cry: 'Room for the most intelligent.'"

"Well thought and well said, Monsieur le Marquis; and I beg Madame la Baronne to excuse me if I side against her." exclaimed a deep voice, proceeding from behind a clump of foliage. And the next moment Bachelin, with a very red face, his hat in his hand, and a portfolio bulky with papers under his arm as usual, appeared at the corner of the terrace.

"Ah! Bachelin, your arrival is well timed," cried the Baroness gaily. "That's just the style of you legal gentlemen. You all belong to the Third Estate, and the Revolution was made for your benefit. But you have sprung up like a jack-in-the-box. Which way did you come?"

"I crossed the park as I had just arrived from La Varenne, and I left my gig at the little gate. But excuse me—" And turning towards Madame de Beaulieu, who was approaching with Suzanne—"Madame la Marquise, your humble servant. Mademoiselle Suzanne, my sincere homage. How extraordinarily warm it is to-day! I came in great haste—I wished to be here at the same time as Monsieur Derblay. But a very important deed to sign detained me. A deed which has caused me much regret, Madame la Marquise. It was for the sale of La Varenne."

"Ah! so the D'Estrelles have at last found a purchaser?" exclaimed the Marquis in a questioning tone.

"Yes, a purchaser," replied Bachelin; "a purchaser who has paid a fancy price, too, I can assure you. But he particularly wished for this estate, and he has given at least a third more than could have been realised even if the property had been divided into lots. He is a Paris manufacturer. He even told me that he had the honour of knowing Madame la Marquise's family. No doubt this is why he was desirous of purchasing some property in the neighbourhood of Beaulieu."

"And can one know this gentleman's name?" asked the Marchioness coldly.

"His name is Monsieur Moulinet," quietly replied the notary.

Bachelin had certainly no idea of the effect he was about to produce when he opened his mouth to articulate these words. Mademoiselle de Beaulieu rose hastily to her feet, whilst the Baroness started, clapped her hands together and exclaimed: "Athénaïs's father!"

"Yes, Monsieur Moulinet had a young lady with him whom he called by that name," remarked the notary. "The estate has been purchased for her, and will figure as part of her jointure on the day of her marriage. It means a clear income of thirty thousand francs a year, and, indeed, the rents might be raised when the present leases expire."

"Dear me, it is really too bad! There, they have become our neighbours!" resumed the Baroness. "And Monsieur Moulinet will now be playing the lord of the manor! Poor man! He will look as if he were his own gardener!"

"He is said to be very rich?" exclaimed Bachelin, interrogatively.

"Excessively rich," the Baroness answered. "Ridiculously so! Ah! you see, Octave, that's what your theories bring us to, my dear fellow. There you have it—the aristocracy of intelligence! Monsieur Moulinet is one of its finest specimens. The D'Estrelles, who gave ten generals, two admirals, a marshal, and several ministers of state to France, whose ancestors' portraits are at Versailles, and whose names appear on all the grand pages of our history, have to vacate their château to make room for a chocolate-maker who never rendered a centime's worth of service to his country, and whose name only figures on the prospectuses which he has distributed at street corners. That's your democracy, my dear fellow! Ah! Don't talk to me of a country where such abominable things can happen. It is a lost land!"

"Calm yourself, Baroness," said Octave. "I agree with you that it is a great pity the D'Estelles should have to part with their château, but, frankly, how can we prevent it? Ought we to dispossess Monsieur Moulinet of his money to enrich our friends with? It would be rather arbitrary. And unless we heated his feet into the bargain, I don't see how he could be treated worse."

"Leave me alone! You are insupportable," cried Madame de Préfont. "Come, I believe you say all that merely to annoy me, and that you don't really believe a word of it." Thereupon, taking the Marchioness's arm she went forward to meet the Baron who was returning with Philippe.

Claire had remained behind—motionless and pensive. The sudden apparition of M. Derblay and Athénaïs Moulinet not merely disturbed the retirement of her life, but caused her a strange emotion. Reared in that aristocratic society, round which impassable barriers have been raised with rigorous pride, she beheld with bitter stupefaction this unexpected trespass on her private life. It seemed to her as if the old château had become as commonplace as a street, since M. Derblay could enter it so easily and be at once received on a footing of equality. She determined to show that she in nowise approved of the alacrity with which mere strangers were welcomed, and seeing her relatives all so smiling and affable, she became still more frigid and solemn. However, she divined that there was some threatening mystery in what transpired around her. The Duke's prolonged silence worried her more than she dared confess; and the frequent embarrassment of her relatives, a few scraps of phrases she had overheard, sudden pauses and silence when she approached unexpectedly, an increase of affection on her mother's part, all combined to make her apprehensive. She suffered grievously. Equivocation was unbearable to her proud, frank nature. As a rule she went straight to the point and tackled the situation in front. But in this instance she dared not do so. Her love made her timid. She was afraid she might learn that the Duke was faithless to her, and, ashamed for him, fearing she might be obliged to acknowledge his unworthiness, she refrained from questioning, and maintained her painful silence.

Thus she showed herself impassive and haughty, receiving Philippe's timid homage, with a disdain she took no trouble to hide, and merely paying sufficient attention to him to show how much his presence displeased her. Suzanne had in vain tried gentle words in hopes of parting Claire's compressed lips, but her endeavour having failed she lost countenance, and sought for a refuge beside Bachelin, who watched over her paternally. She felt sad and discouraged, despite all the graceful attentions of the Marchioness, whom she had captivated with her simple grace. The poor child's illusions had been instantly dispelled, and she realised that her brother's happiness was seriously compromised. With her precocious common sense she was able to comprehend the distance which separated Philippe from haughty, imposing

Claire. She divined that some unforeseen event could alone bring these two dissimilar beings together. Still she did not despair; for with a child's tenacious faith, she naïvely relied on Providence to dispel all obstacles.

The Marchioness, remembering Bachelin's confidential praise of Philippe, delighted with the enthusiasm of the Baron, who had decidedly appropriated the ironmaster, and really surprised to find that her neighbour was such a cultivated man, had asked M. Derblay if he would remain to dinner at the château. Claire immediately gave her such a look of astonishment and displeasure, that she asked herself if she had not been rather hasty in giving this invitation. On consideration, however, she decided she had only acted politely, and interpreted Claire's irritation as a sudden attack of unsociability. But Philippe himself promptly furnished a means of appeasement. With exquisite politeness he expressed his regret at not being able to profit by the very great favour shown him, for pressing business required he should return to Pont-Avesnes before the evening set in.

In reality he was anxious to leave. He had experienced acute mental torture during the two hours he had spent on the terrace, listening to the Baron without understanding him, with his temples compressed by a vice as it were, and with tumultuous thoughts hammering into his brain. He could endure this agony no longer. He had looked forward to this interview so impatiently, he had dreamt that it would yield him such joy, and yet it had proved one of the most cruel moments of his life. Thus, discouraged and saddened, ready to relinquish his ambitious hopes, he took leave of the inmates of the château. Claire did not seem to attach any more importance to his departure than to his arrival. She remained disdainfully silent, merely acknowledging his respectful bow with a slight inclination of the head—just as much as she would have granted to a tradesman.

Philippe's departure would have singularly resembled a rout, had it not been for the timely help of the allies he had won in the fortress. The Baron's conduct was a fresh example of how profoundly passion can modify character. Abandoning the last vestige of his customary reserve he accompanied M. Derblay as far as the gate, and shook hands with him as vigorously and as cordially as if they had been intimate old comrades. On the other hand the Marquis followed Suzanne, and by his extreme affability towards her brother evinced the particular interest he took in herself. Bachelin brought up the rear, with his eternal portfolio under his arm. At the little park gate where his gig was waiting, the old grey horse was found philosophically munching some green leaves. The notary helped Philippe and Suzanne to climb into the vehicle, while the Baron considerately held the nag's bridle—of which there was no need—and the Marquis exchanged a last smile with the young girl. Bachelin then touched up the horse with his whip, the wheels creaked, and the Baron and the Marquis cried out in touching unison: "*Au revoir!* Till we meet again."

In a quivering voice, Philippe responded with a "Never," which was fortunately lost in the rattle of the vehicle. The notary, however, abruptly turned round.

"Never?" said he, "Never? Come, my friend, have you lost your head? Why should you never return to Beaulieu?"

Thus questioned Philippe ceased to restrain himself, and opening his heart, he allowed the bitter flood of his mortification to pour forth. What was the use of persevering in an enterprise which as everything indicated was destined to result in miserable failure? He could only encounter unmerited humiliation and bitter grief. 'Twould be better to renounce his hopes at once, and uproot the evil ere it had time to spread.

"But, my dear fellow," interrupted Bachelin in a sarcastic tone, "what in heaven's name did you hope for? The violence of your regrets leads me to suppose that your pretensions were very far fetched indeed. Did you imagine that Mademoiselle de Beaulieu would throw herself at your head as if she had been a grisette and you a student? In the society you have just entered, my dear fellow, sentiments are usually expressed in extremely delicate shades of language. There is no glowing enthusiasm, nor any decided antipathy. Everything is done with tact and measure. And, besides, you have achieved incredible success for a first visit. You made a good impression on both of the men, the Marquis is your friend, and the Baron is only too eager to take charge of your laboratory. Finally, the Marchioness, herself, so shares the general impression that she invites you to dinner the very first day, as if you were a friend of twenty years' standing; and yet you complain! Come, you are really most unjust! To say the truth, Mademoiselle Claire gave you a cold greeting. What of that? It would have been a pretty business indeed if she had thrown her arms round your neck. Come, you are altogether too hasty! Yesterday afternoon the height of your ambition was to see and approach her for a few minutes. You have just spent a couple of hours in her company, and yet you raise a cry of despair, and accuse heaven and earth! And you declare besides that you won't return to the house again. Upon my word you must be mad! To begin with, you can't dispense with returning to Beaulieu, unless you wish to pass for an ill-bred cub. Besides, will you have sufficient power over yourself to resist the temptation of offering up your devotion at the feet of the beautiful Claire? Ah! my dear fellow, how happy you are to be in love! You are young, so weep and suffer, it is the best part of life. In fact, life would be nothing without it, believe me—believe an old man, who in his capacity as a notary has heard a good many confidential revelations during the last forty years, and who, himself, only regrets one thing at the present hour——"

Bachelin's face wore an unusually animated expression, and his eyes fairly sparkled. No doubt some very remarkable confession was on the point of escaping him when his glance lighted on Suzanne, who, whilst attentively listening, was pulling to pieces, petal by petal, a lovely rose which the Marquis had culled on the terrace at Beaulieu. Somehow or other this sight induced the notary to leave his sentence unfinished, and whipping up his nag, who was going at a jog trot with his head between his fore legs, he resumed: "Come, take my advice, my dear fellow, return and see the Marchioness. Mademoiselle Claire will shortly have to pass through some very cruel trials, and coming events may greatly change her manner towards you. Ah! you no longer say: 'Never!' That's something. To-morrow you will be saying 'Always!' But here we are at Pont-Avesnes. I won't go in with you. I have some pressing work to give my clerks. Come, a good appetite, and rosy dreams!"

Then, having shaken hands with Philippe and gallantly pressed his lips to Suzanne's fingers, Bachelin drove swiftly down the principal street of the village and speedily disappeared round the corner of the market-place.

Philippe heaved a sigh and opened the side door of the courtyard; then, with downcast brow, and followed by his sister, who respected his mute sadness, he re-entered his home, which he had left so hopefully only a few hours before.

VII.

The Château de la Varenne is one of the finest feudal piles remaining in France. Raised by Enguerrand d'Estrelles—who distinguished himself at Bouvines by rescuing King Philip Augustus, when the latter was unhorsed by a Flemish pikeman—its pointed towers, with their ornamental leaden roofs, had the honour of sheltering the Emperor Charles V. on his way to the siege of Nancy. However, during a brush which took place between Turenne and the Imperial forces, prior to the illustrious Marshal's sanguinary and savage campaign in the Palatinate, he cannonaded La Varenne with most destructive effect, and the whilom stronghold remained in ruins during the reigns of Louis the Well-Beloved and Louis the Martyr. The Revolution swept by almost powerless to harm it, for scarcely any more harm could be done. The citizens of Besançon contented themselves with cutting down the trees for firewood and stealing the stones for building purposes. Worked like a quarry, the château thus furnished walls for more than a score of dwellings. A dealer in old metal, living in the district, moreover, appropriated between two and three hundred tons of lead coming from the roofs, and impudently sold them. Naturally enough he made his fortune.

The D'Estelles, who had emigrated with the Comte d'Artois, were unable to complain of these depredations. They were fighting before Mayence, cutting down Biron's hussars and

Pichegru's grenadiers, with an ardour similar to that which gained the battle of Fontenoy. Curiously enough, it was the organized pillaging of La Varenne, in which the whole province participated, that virtually saved the D'Estrelles from ruin. The town of Besançon was never able to sell the La Varenne lands as "national property." No one would have dared to purchase them, for fear of the ill-will of the townsfolk and peasantry, who were in the habit of pillaging the estate as if it had been a strip of conquered country.

However, under the Directory, the D'Estelles were able to return to France, thanks to Barras's protection. They found their property fairly sacked, but free, and installed themselves in a keeper's lodge, which they re-provided with doors and windows. By carefully managing the remnants of their patrimony during the Empire, they were able to scrape something like a new fortune together, and in the early days of the Restoration, they returned to Paris in a position to keep up their rank. Moreover, under the July Monarchy, the head of the family espoused the richly dowered daughter of Claude Chrétien, the banker, who had just been created a baron as a reward for his pecuniary services. M. d'Estrelles had a passion for old-time architecture, and at immense expense he caused the château of La Varenne to be restored as it was in its days of splendour. The lofty walls crowned with battlemented terraces, the superb towers with their quaintly sculptured gargoyles, rose once more above the trees of the park. The work lasted ten years, and cost a stupendous sum. The magnificent pile was most tastefully re-furnished. In anticipation of the furore of nowadays M. d'Estrelles purchased all the finely carved credences, all the mirrors in splendid frames, all the most perfect ecclesiastical woodwork of an ornamental character—chefs-d'œuvre of the image cutters of the Middle

Ages—and all the superb Flanders tapestry that he could lay his hands on. La Varenne thus became a perfect museum, full of those artistic riches which were then so despised, but are now so eagerly sought after. This splendid residence proved a perfect paradise for the impassioned collector who had adorned it with so many marvels.

It was perfectly restored and embellished in all respects when M. d'Estrelles died, leaving it to his son, a lieutenant in the Guides. Four years later, however, this young madcap had mortgaged the estate of La Varenne for two-thirds of its value, and the priceless art collections were about to be removed to Paris to be sold by auction, when M. Moulinet appeared on the scene as a purchaser for the whole estate and its appurtenances. In view of his daughter's marriage with the Duke, he had at first thought of repurchasing the domain of Bligny in Touraine. But his future son-in-law's ancestral home, after changing hands several times, had fallen into the possession of a wealthy manufacturer of pottery, who treated Moulinet's offers, tempting as they were, with absolute disdain. As Bligny could not be bought, Athénaïs's father fell back on La Varenne, and, everything considered, he was delighted with his acquisition. The vicinity of Beaulieu especially pleased him. He would find himself *en famille*, as it were, and pleasant neighbourly intercourse would speedily follow.

It is true that, although Moulinet was a faithful executor of the dark designs which had guided his daughter in her selection of a husband, he had no idea of the real extent of Athénaïs's perfidy. The Duke's relatives might, of course, at first turn a cold shoulder to his attempts at familiarity; for it had certainly been said at one time that Gaston should marry his cousin. With superb egotism, however, ambitious

M. Moulinet looked down on this betrothal as a childish freak. Gaston and Claire had been "little husband" and "little wife" at an age when the heart has not yet developed a true power of feeling, when the mind wanders here and there without aim or plan. The chocolate-maker did not admit that this engagement, contracted at the outset of life, could have resulted in a deep attachment, even on the part of one of the betrothed. He himself had been bound by childish promises to the juvenile daughter of a carpenter, in the Rue de la Ferronnerie, at the time when he was a petty clerk employed by a wholesale druggist in the Rue des Lombards. This carpenter's daughter, whom he had quite forgotten, had ultimately married a butcher, doing business on the Place des Innocents, and one day he had caught sight of her—fat and ruddy, with white linen sleeve-protectors on her arms, and an Astrakan tippet over her shoulders—as she weighed some mutton chops in the bright brass scales. In the meanwhile he, Moulinet, had become a millionaire and resided in a superb mansion on the Boulevard Malesherbes. What connection could there be between a judge of the Tribunal of Commerce and this buxom butcheress, radiant with health? Life had nipped their foolish ideas, and by separating them, had set them both in their right place. Was it not the same with Mademoiselle de Beaulieu and the Duke? United, they would have been mutually condemned to impoverished circumstances. Parted, they might both retrieve their fortunes. The Duke being provided for, Claire would certainly succeed in marrying advantageously; and besides he, Moulinet, would offer all the help in his power. After all, perhaps, the feeling uppermost in the chocolate-maker's mind was that of his own good pleasure. Bligny suited him as a son-in-law, and a man who had taken fortune by storm was not to be prevented from doing as he pleased. He had decided that his daughter should be a duchess; it must be so, and so it would be.

The grandiose aspect of the Château de la Varenne had, moreover, prodigiously flattered Moulinet's vanity. The battlemented towers, the drawbridges, the solemn belfry which gravely chimed the hours, pleased this parvenu immensely. Puffed up by pride this enriched trader considered himself fittingly at home in the lofty guard-room, on the walls of which were painted the escutcheons of all the illustrious families related by alliance to the ancient house of Estrelles. He even had the impudence to install himself in the room that the Emperor Charles V. had occupied—an apartment which had been restored with scrupulous exactitude—and it was with unparalleled satisfaction that he snored in the chamber where the victor of Pavia had slept. On hearing the old servants of the château call his apartment the Emperor's room, he forgot the recent restoration and the purchase of new furniture. He imagined that the floor and the walls were precisely the same as when the Kaiser sojourned for a few hours at La Varenne, and hence he chose this room for his own use. He stretched his plebeian limbs in the colonnaded bed, pompously raised on a platform and hung with curtains of Venetian point, and he ofttimes proudly remarked: "Charles V. used to wind up my clock." Indeed he sincerely imagined that the great Emperor spent his whole lifetime in regulating clocks, whereas it is well known that this fancy only seized hold of him at Saint-Just, when his powerful mind sought relief from weariness.

For Athénaïs, who cared less than her father about satisfying vanity, the château was but a threatening fortress, whence she might pounce down upon her enemy. In her eyes the great charm of La Varenne was that its proud and splendid towers rose within a distance of two leagues from Beaulieu. From this estate she would command the situation, and here she might wait at ease and choose her own time to deal a deadly blow at the girl she hated with all the strength of her soul. As soon as she was installed at the château after the signing of the deed drawn up by Bachelin, she skilfully made inquiries, and learnt that the Baroness de Préfont was at Beaulieu with Claire. An adversary the more did not intimidate her, however; on the contrary, she rejoiced at the thought of humiliating proud Mademoiselle de Beaulieu in the presence of Madame de Préfont.

Moulinet and Athénaïs had been residing for three days at the château, and after repeatedly exploring his park, kitchen-garden, stables, and household offices in detail, the new lord of La Varenne was beginning to feel at a great loss what to do with himself on his estate, when a special messenger came from the town with a telegram announcing the arrival of the Duke, who had not been expected so soon. This intelligence displeased Athénaïs exceedingly. She feared that the Duke might try to prevent the execution of her plans. Indeed Gaston would surely wish to spare the feelings of his relatives, and seriously oppose anything that she might attempt in view of humiliating Claire. Athénaïs, accordingly, decided to act before Bligny could interfere. The telegram stated that he would arrive at La Varenne at three o'clock the same afternoon. Thus there was not a moment to be lost.

Moulinet, still carelessly crumpling the telegram in his hand, was walking up and down the superb parterre which extended in front of the château, when his daughter, arrayed in a bewitching toilette, came towards him, veiling her fixed determination under a semblance of cheerful liveliness.

"Well, papa, we must go to the Château de Beaulieu this afternoon," she said with a smile.

"And why this afternoon?" asked Moulinet in surprise. "The Duke is coming, so wouldn't it be better to wait for him? Under his auspices we shall be much better received. Let him introduce us to his relatives himself."

"No, that would never do," replied Athénaïs with a calm expression. "There is no need of any cat's-paw between Claire de Beaulieu and me; and, in fact, she might rightly express surprise at my not informing her of my marriage myself. Besides, between you and me, Monsieur de Bligny would be rather awkwardly situated, and I think he would feel grateful if we smoothed the way and saved him the annoyance attaching to the first interview. When once the situation is well defined there will be no reverting to old plans, and everything will be for the best. I don't suppose you fear being badly received?"

"Badly received!" cried Moulinet, drawing himself up to his full height and resolutely plunging his hands into his trousers pockets. "A man in my position, an ex-judge of the Tribunal of Commerce, is never badly received! If we did not live under such a worthless government, if there were a Court at the Tuileries or elsewhere, I should go there as I go into my own house. Badly received, indeed! By folks who haven't sixty thousand francs a year left, perhaps! That would be singular and no mistake! Wait a moment! I'll give orders to have the grand barouche got ready, and the footmen shall wear their gala liveries."

"No, no, papa," interrupted Athénaïs. "The usual liveries, please, and a victoria. Don't let us display our fortune. The richer we are the more modest we ought to show ourselves. People would laugh at our display, but they will praise our simplicity."

"Do you think so?" asked Moulinet regretfully. "But it seemed to me that the livery breeches and silk stockings would have created a favourable impression. However, I leave the matter in your hands. You are a girl of taste, and are acquainted with the customs of high society. Get ready, and I will go to the stables and give the necessary orders."

A quarter of an hour later Athénaïs and her father, seated in a pair-horse victoria, were driving through a cloud of dust along the road to Beaulieu.

Forgetful of the resolution he had formed in a moment of discouragement, Philippe had returned to the Château de Beaulieu. To tell the truth, the Baron had not allowed him to seclude himself. On the morrow of Philippe's visit to the Marchioness M. de Préfont, who imitated the sixteenth Louis in his passion for mechanical art, had reached the ironworks at an early hour, and, taking off his coat and rolling up his shirt-sleeves, had soon put himself in such a state that Philippe was obliged to lend him a change of clothes and keep him to lunch. After that he could scarcely help seeing him back to Beaulieu. Philippe had furnished himself with such excellent reasons to excuse what he called his weakness, that he experienced no discomfort on reaching the terrace, where he had spent two hours of mortal agony only the day before. It is true that Claire had shown herself as frigid and as indifferent as at the first interview, but her haughty, disdainful attitude, in lieu of disconcerting the ironmaster, on this occasion only irritated him; and the more Mademoiselle de Beaulieu pretended to ignore his presence, the more determined he became to compel her to notice him.

The Marchioness was one of those fortunate women on whom nature has bestowed an admirably balanced disposition. As she appeared one day, so she appeared on the morrow. She had been pleased with Philippe at once, and the opinion she had formed of him would never change. Thus she greeted him with her usual affability and put him completely at his ease.

The little Baroness, who was curious to study the character of a man whom she had pictured in her imagination as a kind of Cyclops, displayed for M. Derblay's benefit all the graces of her frivolously vivacious mind. She found Philippe amiable, though he made no effort to please, and interesting in his conversation, although he was in nowise pretentious. Accordingly, she declared him to be as solid morally as physically, and began to esteem him greatly. As for the Marquis, he had met a most delightful companion in Suzanne. They engaged together in terrible games of billiards and Dutch top, in which even the more serious-minded inmates of the château did not disdain to take part at times.

On the day that Moulinet and Athénaïs set out for Beaulieu it chanced that a warmly disputed game of croquet had been commenced between the Baroness and Octave on the one side and Suzanne and the Baron on the other. The battle-field was a lawn lying between the great iron entrance-gate and the domestic offices. The Marchioness and Claire, who took no interest in the pastime, sat together in the drawing-room, and as the windows were open they could hear the thuds of the mallets and the exclamations of the players whenever a skilful or an unlucky stroke turned the chances of victory. Philippe and Bachelin, who had been appointed umpires, followed the balls and gravely measured the distances with a foot-rule whenever any dispute arose. Having attentively and conscientiously followed the game, they were about to award the victory to the Baron and Suzanne, when the attention of players and umpires alike was attracted by a vehicle which drew up abruptly in front of the iron gate. At the same time a footman pulled at the bell, which responded with a sonorous peal. Doubt was no longer possible, some visitors were awaiting admission.

In a second, like a flight of frightened birds, the players decamped, hastened up the steps and reached the drawing-room just as a servant with a card on a silver salver was approaching the Marchioness. Madame de Beaulieu adjusted her glasses, glanced at the card, and raising her head with an air of great astonishment, exclaimed: "Monsieur and Mademoiselle Moulinet!"

Silence ensued, so solemn that it seemed as if everybody present had divined that some serious event was on the point of happening. The Baroness was the first to recover her self-possession, and clapping her hands together, she muttered, "This is really *too* much!"

"What can these people want?" asked Madame de Beaulieu quietly.

As no one else seemed desirous of speaking, Bachelin ventured to intervene: "Dear me, Madame la Marquise," said he, "as Monsieur and Mademoiselle Moulinet are new-comers in the district, they have probably thought it only polite to call on their neighbours. You know that it is the custom to do so. They have accordingly commenced with the château, which was only just and natural, for the Beaulieu family is one of the oldest and most important in the province. Besides, did not Monsieur Moulinet assert that his daughter had long been acquainted with Mademoiselle Claire? I think that these reasons are more than sufficient to explain his visit."

"I suppose, aunt," exclaimed the Baroness impetuously, "that you are not going to submit to the familiarity of the Moulinets? There can't be anything in common between you and them. The father is an extremely common individual, not to say vulgar; and as for the daughter, she is certainly the most dangerous little pest in the world. It is just like these parvenus to imagine they are going to procure themselves an introduction into society in the same way as they have purchased a château, thanks to their millions! But don't lend a hand to it, aunt; be brave, and resist this attempt at burglary!"

"I fancy, my dear," said the Baron coldly, "that your aunt knows very well how she ought to act, and that she has no need of your advice."

The Marchioness, however, was nodding her head with perplexity. Plainly enough she was greatly annoyed, and this was not surprising, for with her indolent nature she held all complications and difficulties in horror. At length she turned towards her daughter, who had remained motionless and silent, as if taking no interest in the controversy. "Claire," asked Madame de Beaulieu, "what do you think I ought to do?"

"*Mon Dieu*, mother," replied the young girl calmly, "it seems to me rather difficult to close our door to Monsieur and Mademoiselle Moulinet. We should have to find some pretence for doing so, and what one could we employ? We could hardly say that we are not at home, for they must have seen these ladies and gentlemen playing at croquet on the lawn. We were at the window ourselves. To say simply that you don't receive, would be an impolite way of acknowledging what is after all a visit of courtesy. Would it be worthy of us? I don't think so. My idea is that you ought to receive them; but once this visit over, I should not go any farther. Isn't that your opinion too?"

"Yes, child, you are right; we will do as you say. Octave, tell the servant to answer that we receive."

A moment later Monsieur and Mademoiselle Moulinet entered the drawing-room of the Château de Beaulieu. Every woman has in a varying degree the stuff of an actress in her nature; and thus, despite Athénaïs's great emotion and the rapid beating of her heart, she curtailed the embarrassment of the first moment by an extremely audacious movement. With extended hands, a smile on her lips and joyously sparkling eyes, she advanced towards Mademoiselle de Beaulieu, threw her arms round her neck as if she were some dearly treasured friend, and boldly exclaimed: "Ah! my beautiful Claire, how happy I am to see you!"

This effusion caused Mademoiselle de Beaulieu such surprise that, despite her usual presence of mind, she was unable to articulate a word of reply. Meanwhile Athénaïs, profiting by her advantage, turned towards the Marchioness, and curtseying with perfect deference and modesty, resumed: "It is a very great joy for me, Madame la Marquise, to find myself near Mademoiselle de Beaulieu again. Since I have known her—and I have known her long," she added, smiling most affectionately at Claire, "I have always endeavoured to imitate her in every respect. I do not think it would be possible to find a more perfect model."

"To imitate me merely?" said Claire quietly. "You are really modest."

"And this is certainly the first time you happen to be so," muttered the Baroness, stepping forward.

As Athénaïs perceived Madame de Préfont, her delight seemed to overleap all bounds; but she did not venture to throw herself into the arms of petulant, vivacious Sophie. She had too often left them badly punished, to risk in public the consequences of such a close embrace. Who knew but what this madcap might publicly inflict on her one of those humiliations which overturn the best combined plans, and snap asunder all the threads of the web most cunningly contrived? Thus Athénaïs prudently contented herself with a vigorous shake of the hand which made her bracelets jingle, at the same time mitigating this relative coldness by the warmth of her affectionate language. She was doubly happy, she declared; she had not hoped to meet dear d'Hennecourt also!

Not having been invited to Sophie's wedding, she pretended to be quite ignorant of it, and thus addressed Madame de Préfont by her maiden name. To put a stop to this skilful equivocation Sophie had to introduce the Baron to Athénaïs, who found some honeyed words to congratulate M. de Préfont on having chosen such a charming wife. Manœuvring on this battle-field, so full of obstacles and ambuscades, with the skill and composure of a great tactician, Mademoiselle Moulinet paralyzed her adversaries by her audacity, stupefied her father by her presence of mind, and gave every one a very high opinion of her intelligence. Sophie and Claire were obliged to admit that she was a far more redoubtable foe than they had imagined.

In two years this young person had wonderfully improved. She had become very pretty in the face. Rather short, perhaps, and with a certain tendency to stoutness, which lent her an air of deceitful but pleasing nonchalance, she had an abundant crop of jet black hair and most expressive blue eyes. It is true that her hands—encased in long gloves of Swedish kid, which disappeared under the ruches of her sleeve, tight fitting at the elbow—were of plebeian dimensions, just like her feet, which were apparent under her short skirt; and, on being attentively examined, she seemed rather vulgar. But at the first glance she was certainly prepossessing.

Moulinet had for some minutes remained in mute ecstasy, thinking to himself that his daughter was certainly a superior little being, born specially to be a duchess. His excessive admiration suddenly made him feel sentimental. He thought of his poor defunct wife, who would have been so delighted and so astonished, could she have only seen her daughter. This conjugal emotion brought a tear to the chocolate-maker's eyes, and he drew forth a huge pocket-handkerchief and blew his nose with a terrible noise. A reproving glance from Athénaïs recalled him to the necessities of the situation, and reminded him that noses should be blown with moderation in aristocratic society. Thereupon, leaning towards the Marchioness, with his arms curved and his hat pressed against his heart, "Mademoiselle de Beaulieu and Madame," he said —at the same time indicating the Baroness—"were my daughter's schoolfellows at the 'Sacred Heart.' I have always congratulated myself, and I do so more than ever to-day, on having sent Athénaïs to that establishment, which is undoubtedly the best of its kind in Paris. The young persons who are sent there receive a first-class education, and at the same time make most desirable acquaintances."

A smile escaped the Marchioness, and looking at Moulinet: "So I perceive," she said, with a touch of irony, unnoticed by the chocolate-maker, though it made Athénaïs turn pale with impotent rage.

"As for myself, Madame la Marquise," continued Moulinet, delighted with this encouragement, "I am greatly touched by the favour you have done me in allowing me to present you my homage. I owed it you for more reasons than one, first as a new-comer in the district, where I have recently purchased some property."

The Marchioness exchanged a glance with Bachelin, who made a gesture implying, "What did I tell you?" whereupon Madame de Beaulieu responded with a nod, as much as to say, "You were right."

"Some very important property," resumed Moulinet, who had been momentarily disconcerted by this exchange of signs, "La Varenne—belonging to the D'Estelles. I was not personally anxious for it, but my daughter, who has great knowledge of established usages, made me understand that land is the necessary complement of a great fortune like mine. Besides, let me confess it to you, Madame la Marquise, I am liberal in my opinions, but I only understand intercourse with the aristocracy." Thereupon, filliping the collar of his white waistcoat with eighteenth-century grace, he smiled encouragingly all round.

The lookers-on were stupefied, and Athénaïs was so crushed by her father's monstrous vulgarity, that, heaving a sigh, she sank helplessly on to an arm-chair.

The Marchioness on this occasion displayed all the tact incumbent on her as mistress of the house, mingled with the veiled impertinence of a real great lady. She did not wish that Moulinet should realise how severely he was judged, and yet she was unable to renounce the pleasure of indulging in a few delicate epigrams. Thus she enacted an exquisite little comedy for those who were able to understand the situation. "Believe me, monsieur," she said to Moulinet, "I am greatly touched by the sentiments you express with such candid simplicity. They are worthy of a man who has risen by his *intelligence* to such a position as yours."

Moulinet, who was delighted with this reply, in which he

failed to detect an under-current of irony, considered the Marchioness to be really a most worthy woman, and decided to treat her with especial regard. He fancied himself on the high-road to intimacy and thought he had only to clap his hands together and cry "It's settled." "That's how I am!" he exclaimed expansively. "And if my character suits your fancy, Madame la Marquise, why I think we shall get on swimmingly together."

The Baroness, who was so exasperated that she could barely remain calm, now rose and drew Philippe towards the recess of a window, where she eased herself in some measure by exclaiming: "That man's a perfect monster!"

As for Moulinet, who perceived he had created an impression, though he had no notion that it was an unfavourable one, he rattled on in the same bland, self-sufficient style: "The estate of La Varenne," said he, "is of very considerable extent. You know the castle, no doubt? You know that it is historical? I occupy the room where Charles the Fifth slept, according to what has been told me. Yes, Madame la Marquise, I sleep in an emperor's bed." Then, with a gesture of affected modesty, the ex-judge of the Tribunal of Commerce added: "Upon my soul I'm none the prouder for it."

This time, Athénaïs could no longer restrain herself. She perceived that her father had in a few minutes compromised her chances. So, abruptly rising, with a changed expression of face and a wicked look in her eyes, she dryly exclaimed: "Papa, ask Madame la Marquise to show you her beautiful terrace. It seems a lovely view can be had from it."

With these words, and so as to curtail her father's effusions, she resolutely walked towards the glass door facing the steps. The Marchioness rose, showing Moulinet the way, and every one else followed. Claire came the last, looking as thoughtful as if she divined some approaching catastrophe. Just as she passed out of the drawing-room and was about to put her foot on the first step, she found herself face to face with Athénaïs, who, having skilfully contrived to leave the others, was returning towards her. Claire involuntarily stepped back. The eyes of the two girls met. Those of Mademoiselle de Beaulieu wore a look of questioning astonishment, while those of Athénaïs had a serious and almost threatening expression.

"Suppose we step indoors?" said Mademoiselle Moulinet, taking a step towards the drawing-room.

"Willingly," replied Mademoiselle de Beaulieu, with a sudden pain at her heart. "You wish to speak to me?"

Certain now that the crisis she had divined was imminent, Claire at once recovered all her self-possession and energy. She drew her beautiful figure up to its full height, and sure alike of her heart and mind she awaited with superb confidence the attack of her implacable enemy.

"You don't know how pleased I am to find myself alone with you," said Athénaïs, without answering Mademoiselle de Beaulieu's question. "Since we lost sight of each other two years ago, I have reflected a great deal and seen a great deal. I have acquired some little experience, and my feelings have greatly changed. For instance, at the convent, we were not precisely good friends."

"But——" began Claire, with a frown and a gesture of haughty protest.

"Oh! don't say the contrary!" resumed Athénaïs quickly. "I did not like you. I was jealous of you; I can own it now. I have risen sufficiently since then to have the right of being frank without appearing humble. But if I didn't like you, I instinctively admired you, and my dream was to become your equal."

"My equal!" exclaimed Claire with a bitter smile. "Why, I am of such little account! You eclipse me, I assure you. Judge yourself more fairly—beauty, elegance, luxury—you have everything that can be obtained——"

"Everything, yes," said Athénaïs coldly; "everything excepting a name!"

"But, dear me," rejoined Claire with seeming simplicity; "a name can be easily bought nowadays. There are titles at all prices, petty ones, average ones, and high ones. If you really care for a handle to your name, you can secure yourself the best in the market. Your means will allow you to do so."

"True," replied Athénaïs, trying to steady her voice, which was beginning to tremble with anger. "And, in fact, just now there is a question of my marrying——"

"Indeed! But that's delightful. Allow me to congratulate you sincerely."

"But I wish for something more than congratulations, from you."

"Indeed! And what, pray?" asked Claire in astonishment.

"A little advice."

"Advice—about what?"

"About my marriage."

"You are really too flattering! How can I advise you on your family affairs? I should be greatly embarrassed to do so, for we know each other so little. Could you not dispense with my opinion?"

"No, it isn't possible," answered Athénaïs gravely.

"Well, I no longer understand you," rejoined Claire, who felt troubled despite herself.

"Listen to me attentively," resumed Mademoiselle Moulinet.

"It is really worth your while. The marriage proposed to me is a very grand one, a great deal above what I might expect in my position, and it eclipses all my hopes. It is a question of my wearing a coronet——"

"A prince's coronet?" asked Claire, trying to smile.

"No, only a ducal one," replied Athénaïs, giving her rival a keen look. "If this marriage came off I should be a duchess."

On hearing this, Mademoiselle de Beaulieu shuddered. It seemed to her as if a veil that had hung before her mind had been suddenly torn aside. She instantly divined what her relatives had been hiding from her so carefully and so long. She did not doubt for a moment but that Gaston was the suitor Mademoiselle Moulinet had spoken of. His delay, his silence were all explained, and a feeling of bitter anguish came over her. A flow of blood caused her heart to expand, her beautiful face turned deadly pale, and a sigh of despair died away on her lips.

Athénaïs perceived this sudden change with fiendish delight. She exulted at the sight of Claire's anguish, and noted with rapture the precipitate beating of her temples. It was a delicious pleasure to be able to repay with one blow all the humiliation she had undergone during the last quarter of an hour. But, on seeing Claire motionless and icy cold, she feared she might faint, and thus escape her ere the hateful revelation was completed. "You don't ask me my suitor's name?" she said, still scrutinizing her rival, who stood half-staggering beside her with her eyes gazing into space.

"N—o," stammered Mademoiselle de Beaulieu, unconscious of what she answered, so absorbed was she in her sad reflections.

"But I must tell you who he is," replied Athénaïs. "It is

my duty to do so." And then, taking her time as if she wished to choose the best place for her thrust, she slowly added, "He is the Duc de Bligny."

Claire expected the blow, for all her illusions were already dispelled, and she felt certain of the Duke's faithlessness. Still the name of Bligny, which was to have been hers, coming as it did from Athénaïs, made her quiver with anguish. She remained motionless, not daring to try and speak, for she feared her voice would fail her. With trembling hands and parched lips she drained the bitter cup of mortification to the very dregs.

"Monsieur de Bligny is your relative," resumed Athénaïs, who was exasperated by her rival's mournful impassibility. "He was your companion in childhood; and I have even heard it said that there was some question of marrying you together. Under these circumstances—you will understand it now—I thought it only right on my part to come to you loyally, and consult you."

Mademoiselle de Beaulieu fancied she could discern a ray of hope in Athénaïs's seemingly generous words. Perhaps matters were not so far advanced as she had imagined. Accordingly she regained her courage, and determined to fight on till the last extremity. "Consult me?" she said, "and respecting what?"

"Why respecting the Duke's position in reference to yourself," answered Mademoiselle Moulinet with apparent simplicity. "You will understand, if it were really true that you were engaged to each other, you might accuse me of carrying off your betrothed. The Duke has asked for my hand; but I'm by no means in love with him. In fact I scarcely know him. He or another, what do *I* care?—Come, be frank with me. Do you love him? Would you feel hurt or even simply displeased if I married him?—You have only to say the word and I will engage to break off the match."

Perhaps, if Claire had courageously confessed her love, Athénaïs would have allowed herself the supreme satisfaction of playing the generous, and would have renounced her ambition, in view of crushing Mademoiselle de Beaulieu all the better. For an instant the fate of these two girls trembled in the balance. But Claire only remembered one sentence of all that Mademoiselle Moulinet had said: "The Duke has asked for my hand." As she recalled it a burning blush rose to her forehead, and, determined to die rather than own her love for Gaston, she exerted all her will to master her voice and eyes and assume an air of quiet self-possession.

"Thank you," she said, with a cold smile. "But you may rest assured that I am not a girl to be forsaken and slighted. Don't think that the Duke would marry any one else if we were really engaged. No! But in childhood it is the custom among cousins—your relatives betroth and marry you between two smiles. It is a childish pastime and nothing more. But reason comes with age, and the requirements of life soon upset all these little plans. The Duke has asked for your hand, you say? Marry him by all means. It would really have been a pity if you had not been united, for you are worthy of each other."

Athénaïs turned pale as she heard this branding taunt. With one thrust Claire had revenged herself for all the agony she had endured. They looked at each other with deadly smiles, carrying on the struggle with every outward form of courtesy. It was like a battle waged with golden pins, which penetrated into the flesh as sharply and as dangerously as daggers. It was like a combat with fans, fingered smilingly although their perfidious fluttering was as insulting as blows. A woman's warfare in truth—each attack combined with refined science, and the victory so ardently disputed, that both combatants would be cruelly wounded ere it was won.

"So there is really nothing to annoy you in this marriage?" resumed Mademoiselle Moulinet, injecting subtle venom into the wounds she had inflicted. "How happy your answer makes me! Think, what a dream it is! Your relative, really your equal now, and a duchess as well!"

"Just what you deserve!" said Claire ironically.

"Let me kiss you!" cried Athénaïs, darting at her rival and catching her by the neck as if she wished to bite her. Mademoiselle de Beaulieu offered no resistance, and Athénaïs was able to print on her enemy's cheek the most hypocritical kiss that ever emanated from woman's lips. Then looking gravely at Mademoiselle de Beaulieu, she exclaimed: "You must know that you have a sincere, devoted friend in me."

Claire had sufficient strength to answer: "You have just given me convincing proof of that." And then feeling that her limbs were failing her, she sank on to the sofa.

It fortunately happened that when the Baroness noted the prolonged absence of the rivals, she became nervous, and, suspecting some act of perfidy on Athénaïs's part, she returned as soon as possible to the house. At this moment, indeed, she entered the drawing-room, and when at the first glance she perceived Claire so pale and crushed, and Athénaïs erect and radiant, she divined in a great measure what had taken place.

"Why, what have you two been doing, shut up in here for the last half-hour?" she asked; and then leaning towards her cousin she anxiously added: "What is the matter?"

Mademoiselle de Beaulieu made no audible reply, but with

a gesture of despair she pointed to her rival, who was composedly putting on her gloves again, like a duellist who has just killed his adversary. This supplicating appeal for assistance quite upset the Baroness. Anger flew to her brain, her tiny ears became fiery red, and darting towards Mademoiselle Moulinet with a threatening gesture, she showed her the door exclaiming: "You will just please go——"

But ere she had time to finish her phrase, Athénaïs, with wonderful presence of mind, intervened so ingeniously that one might have supposed she did not understand these words as an insulting order to quit the premises. "Yes, I am going —to join my father on the terrace," she said; and then turning to Claire: "Till by-and-by."

Thereupon composedly and leisurely, so as to show that she was victorious and abandoned the battle-field which belonged to her of her own free-will, she advanced to the glass door and left the room.

VIII.

MADEMOISELLE MOULINET had hardly disappeared, when Claire, bounding to her feet, sprang towards the Baroness, her eyes all aflame with the rage she no longer had need to restrain. "You knew it—you knew that he was going to marry!" she cried. "Why did you not tell me of it?" And as Madame de Préfont remained silent in her astonishment, "Betrayed! Forsaken!" resumed Mademoiselle de Beaulieu, wringing her hands in a paroxysm of mad despair, "and for whom? For that creature? And you allowed me to learn it from her lips! She was left free to deal me such a blow! But you were her accomplices then! Isn't there one among you that loves me? And he—he—*for money!* The scoundrel!"

Dismayed by the sight of this furious grief, the Baroness tried to calm her cousin. "Oh! Claire," she cried, "for Heaven's sake be calm. You frighten me!"

But Mademoiselle de Beaulieu had lost all power over herself. Her violent nature, so long kept under control, had dashed every restraint aside. The efforts she had made during that horrible interview now seemed to her so many cowardly acts of weakness. She asked herself with stupefaction, how she had been able to forbear hurling all the insults that now rose to her lips, at the head of the girl who had so impudently exulted in her anguish. She regretted she had not struck her and dealt her grievous wounds. Her cries were full of exasperation at the thought that her lover had been stolen from her; her fury disregarded all social conventionalities; she had no care for what others might think, but strode to and fro, stamping on the floor, feverish with excitement, and deaf to the appeals of reason. The blood of the old barons who meted out justice, high and low, was boiling in Mademoiselle de Beaulieu's veins, and she dreamt of inflicting infamous cruel tortures upon her hated rival.

At last, however, the consciousness that she was powerless returned to her, and crushed her again. She realised that all her hopes were destroyed, that no prospect of revenge existed. Her overstrained nerves suddenly relaxed, and with her bosom heaving with sobs of anguish and tears fast streaming down her face, she fell into the Baroness's arms. "Ah! How miserable I am!" she stammered, "how miserable!"

Madame de Préfont, who was deeply grieved, pressed her cousin to her bosom, and supported her heavy head upon her shoulder. Then, in the gentle language which mothers use to quiet the sorrow and allay the sufferings of children, she endeavoured to stanch the wounds in Claire's lacerated heart. The poor girl wept despairingly; but at least her tears did her good service, for they washed away the venom which Athénaïs had injected into her wounds and mitigated their excruciating pain. As Mademoiselle de Beaulieu recovered consciousness, she blushed at the thought that she had given way to such excessive rage. Now, her only object was to master her feelings, galling though they were, and by a supreme effort of pride she succeeded in doing so.

When the Marchioness reached the drawing-room—terrified

by an announcement which Moulinet had just confided to her, she found her daughter, if not resigned—resignation was so far impossible—at all events courageous and dignified. Breathless with mingled haste and emotion, Madame de Beaulieu gazed in affright at Claire, who was still livid and trembling. Then, after seeking for some words which failed her in her agitation, she threw herself into her daughter's arms, sobbing piteously, "Ah! my poor, poor child!"

"You know it, mother?" asked Claire, the tears starting from her eyes afresh.

"The father has told me everything this very moment; and when I think," cried the Marchioness, raising her arms to heaven in her indignation, "when I think it was you who advised me to receive them, so as not to seem impolite!"

"Ah! I am well rewarded for it," said Claire bitterly. "I was very imprudent. I ought to have shunned that—person carefully. I knew so well what sentiments she entertained towards me. Perhaps we girls may have teased her at the convent, but how cruelly she revenges herself. She has never forgiven nor forgotten. She has waited for the propitious hour, and struck the happiest of her old schoolfellows in the heart. Ah! she has broken my life. The Duke's faithlessness will always weigh upon me, and even if I were mad enough to think of marrying, after such humiliation, what man would ever consent to take me for his wife?"

"What man, indeed!" cried the Marchioness vivaciously. "Why all those who have eyes to see you, and ears to hear you! If any one is disgraced, my child, in this sad circumstance it is the Duke, not you. And if you care to marry you will have plenty of suitors to select from in our society and elsewhere. A girl like Mademoiselle de Beaulieu does not go a-begging for a husband. Why, less than six months ago I had to decline the proposals of several honourable families, and the suitors who then asked for your hand were so disappointed on being refused that I am sure they would gladly come forward again if they thought there was any chance of success."

But Claire made a gesture of discouragement. "After the Duc de Bligny, mother, I can only marry a man who is superior to him in every respect, or else a man whom I might seem to love. My only possible justification in the eyes of society can be the grandeur or the impulsiveness of my choice. But you know very well, mother, that all this is impossible; after such a deception a girl like myself can only be wedded to religion. I can only look forward to a convent now."

"Come, child," said the Marchioness gently. "You are wandering. A convent indeed! Well, and don't you think of us? No, you are too young to have a right to despair. With your moral qualities and beauty the future surely has some compensation in reserve for you. In fact, I may perhaps tell you that there is some one very near here who would accept your hand on bended knees."

Mademoiselle de Beaulieu raised her proud eyebrows slowly, and turned towards her mother. "Monsieur Derblay?" she said quietly.

"Yes, Monsieur Derblay," replied the Marchioness. "But I only mention his name as an example. Who could approach you without loving you? Shall we return to Paris? Would you like to go to Switzerland with Monsieur and Madame de Préfont? Speak, I am ready to consent to anything that could satisfy or console you. What would you like to do?"

"Ah! do I even know?" cried Claire in a transport. "I wish I could disappear at once—fly from everybody, escape from myself. I hold everything in hatred and contempt. Alas! why can't I die?"

"Death, my dear child, is the only evil beyond all remedy. If all the women whom their lovers or husbands abandoned died, the world would be depopulated. Men are very, very rarely faithful, and when they don't deceive you beforehand, they do so afterwards."

At that same moment, as if in speaking of man's inconstancy the Marchioness had invoked the ungrateful fellow who had just caused so many sighs and tears, the noise of a furious gallop resounded, and through the open gateway the Duc de Bligny dashed into the courtyard on a horse that was white with foam.

He sprang at once to the ground, and throwing his reins to a stupefied servant, darted up the front steps. He walked straight towards the drawing-room, and would have entered it if the Baron and Bachelin, hastening to meet him, had not stopped him in the hall. Pale, with a contracted brow, the Duke tried to prevent them from barring the way. "Are Monsieur and Mademoiselle Moulinet still here?" he asked in a quivering voice; and as the Baron replied affirmatively, "My aunt?" he added, "I must see the Marchioness at once. Perhaps it is not too late."

"Undeceive yourself, Duke," gravely replied Monsieur de Préfont, who now understood the cause of Gaston's precipitation. "It is too late, for Monsieur and Mademoiselle Moulinet have already spoken."

The Duke heaved a bitter sigh, and sinking on to one of the carved benches of the hall he gazed sorrowfully at the Baron and Bachelin, and said, "What can I do now to remedy the harm that has been done?"

"Alas! the harm is irreparable, Monsieur le Duc," replied

Bachelin in a tone of respectful reproach. "The best thing you can do now is to leave without trying to see Madame de Beaulieu."

"Oh! I can't consent to that," hastily responded Gaston, rising to his feet again. "The Marchioness will blame me and hold me responsible for what has occurred here this afternoon; but I must explain my conduct to her. I must show her that I took no part in this infamous step. I will do what she pleases. But I wish to see her, speak to her, and weep with her. You can see that what has happened drives me to despair."

The Duke's features wore such an expression of genuine affliction that although the Baron and Bachelin were strongly prepossessed against him, they could not help feeling touched.

"Very well," said Bachelin. "Monsieur de Préfont will be kind enough to keep you company, Monsieur le Duc, while I go and ask Madame de Beaulieu if she will accede to your request." Thereupon, leaving the two cousins together, Bachelin passed round on to the terrace, and discreetly knocked at the glass door of the drawing-room.

In the meantime, as if totally unconscious of the perturbation reigning inside the château, Philippe, Moulinet, Suzanne, Athénaïs, and the Marquis still continued conversing on the terrace. The sun was slowly sinking behind the horizon, tinging the greenish blue sky with purple streaks. With evening a delightful calm descended into the valley, already full of shade. The bell of the church of Pont-Avesnes resounded clearly and solemnly in the distance, announcing the Mass of the Departed for the morrow.* Such profound peace per-

* November 2nd is the Day of the Dead (*Les Trépassés*) in the Roman calendar. Services for the souls in purgatory are then celebrated at all the churches.—*Trans.*

vaded the beautiful landscape that Athénaïs experienced its influence. She felt less aggressive, and having triumphed over her rival so completely, she thought of treating her more leniently in the future.

On entering the drawing-room Bachelin found its three inmates a prey to inexpressible emotion. When, by one of the windows looking on to the courtyard, Claire perceived the Duke gallop through the gateway, she sprang to her feet stupefied and distracted. She tried to speak, but was unable, and stretching out her hands towards her faithless lover she gave way to hysterical laughter and stuttering. It seemed as if she were going mad, and the Marchioness and the Baroness were terrified. They hastened to the poor girl, who was quivering convulsively, and whose lips were already white. They feared she was about to faint, and wished to ring for assistance; but, with an imperious gesture, Claire prevented them from doing so. Making a stupendous effort she managed to articulate these words through her clenched teeth, "No, nothing, no one. Leave me, I shall be right soon."

She sat down. A cold perspiration started from her forehead, which the Baroness carefully wiped. The Marchioness divested herself of her shawl and her woollen fichu, and wrapped them round her daughter, who was shivering. Supported by cushions, but with her head bowed down, Claire sat there as motionless as if she were dozing; but her bright eyes, which stared fixedly, obstinately at the carpet, showed that she was not asleep. She was plunged in profound meditation, and there was a deep crease between her eyebrows, testifying to the great mental effort she was making. After a few minutes the colour returned to her cheeks again, a sigh relieved her breast, and she abruptly cast the *wrappers with which her mother had covered her on one side.

On hearing Bachelin open the glass door she turned her head, and desirous of hiding her sufferings, contrived to smile at the notary. The latter wore an air of consternation, and approached Madame de Beaulieu on tiptoe, as if he had been in a sick-room. Bowing even lower than was his wont, as if indeed he felt ashamed of his mission, he began, "Pray forgive me, Madame la Marquise, but what has happened is so extraordinary——"

"I know it," interrupted the Marchioness hastily. "The Duke is there. Well?"

"Well, madame," resumed the notary, quite out of countenance, "in spite of all we have said to him he insists on seeing you."

"That is strange audacity!" cried the Marchioness, springing to her feet with unusual vivacity and walking towards the door.

"Where are you going, mother?" asked Claire.

"I'm going to have him turned out of the house, as he deserves to be," replied Madame de Beaulieu, who was red with indignation.

For a second Claire remained silent, reflecting, as if she hesitated to take some serious resolution; then, shaking her head, she rejoined, "No, mother. You must not turn the Duc de Bligny out of the house. It would be better to receive him."

"Receive him?" repeated the Marchioness, stupefied, and asking herself if her daughter had really lost her mind.

"Yes, receive him, and receive him politely, too. I would not for anything in the world have him think that I have suffered from his faithlessness. To be mourned by such a girl as me, *he*—he would be too proud of it. Anything rather than his insulting pity. No, receive him. We can surely open the door to him, since we did not close it to his intended wife."

"But what do you mean to do?" asked Madame de Beaulieu nervously.

"I mean to revenge myself!" replied Claire with a frightful expression of anger. Then turning towards Bachelin, "Be kind enough," she added, "to ask the Duke to go round on to the terrace and wait there for a moment. Don't bring him in here till I make a sign to you from the window; but, in the meanwhile, pray send Monsieur Derblay to me."

The Baroness and the Marchioness exchanged glances of astonishment. They were unable to divine why Claire acted in this manner. But Bachelin was more perspicuous, and guessing that his plans were on the point of succeeding, he hastened away with the alacrity of a young man. A moment later Philippe entered the drawing-room.

"Mother and you, Sophie, dear," said Claire, "pray step a little on one side, so that I may speak privately with Monsieur Derblay."

Madame de Beaulieu and the Baroness at once retired into the recess of a window, and, greatly perplexed, waited for the finish of the interview. Philippe, who was in a state of intense emotion, for he realised that his fate was trembling in the balance—and, moreover, he had been warned by Bachelin that matters were fast reaching a crisis—stood motionless, with bowed head, in front of the girl he adored.

"Monsieur," said Claire, addressing him personally for the first time, "our old friend and excellent adviser, Maître Bachelin, has told my mother that you did me the honour to aspire to my hand."

Philippe did not speak, but bowed in token of assent.

"I believe you to be an honourable man," continued Mademoiselle de Beaulieu firmly, "and I presume that in forming such projects you were, like my relatives, aware that the Duc de Bligny had—long ago, perhaps—discarded his engagements ——"

"Yes, mademoiselle, I was aware of it," replied Philippe, speaking with difficulty. "And pray believe that if it depended on me, even at this moment, to assure your happiness by bringing the Duke back to you, I would not hesitate, even at the price of my life."

"I thank you," said Claire; "but all ties between the Duc de Bligny and myself are now for ever severed, and the most certain proof I can give you of it is that if you still retain the same views I am ready to offer you my hand."

Mademoiselle de Beaulieu's voice grew faint as she spoke, and Philippe divined rather than heard the last words. At the same moment there flashed through his mind a recollection of the day when his sister, seeing him so sad and discouraged, laughingly declared, "You'll see; she will come herself and ask you to do her the favour of becoming her husband."

Thus Suzanne's prediction was realised. Enlightened by her affection, this child had foreseen her brother's happiness. He was not dreaming; it was all really true. Claire herself offered him her hand. Deep joy pervaded Philippe's heart, and taking hold of that charming hand, which he had so often despaired of ever feeling in his own, he printed on the tips of the icy fingers a timid but most delicious kiss.

"I have a favour to ask of you, monsieur," resumed Claire. "I should like you to do all you can to let it be supposed that our engagement dates from several days ago. I have no need to explain to you the reason of this request. It is prompted by my pride. Alas! you can have no illusions as to the state of my heart; but I assure you you will find in me a faithful and loyal wife. Pray leave me now, but do not go too far, for I may have need of your presence." And letting Philippe depart, she made a sign to Bachelin, so that he might now bring the Duke into the drawing-room.

The notary had occupied Bligny very skilfully during the few minutes that the interview between Mademoiselle de Beaulieu and M. Derblay had lasted, and when Philippe left the drawing-room with a radiant face, he had only just opened the door communicating with the terrace. Moulinet and Athénaïs were astounded on perceiving Gaston. When Napoleon, waiting for Grouchy, saw Blucher's advance guard emerge from the woods of Frischermont, he was not more overcome than the chocolate-maker's daughter on this occasion. Nothing was more calculated to compromise the success of her combinations than the Duke's presence at Beaulieu. A feeling of acute anxiety came over her. She had considered the victory as won; but was there a disastrous humiliating defeat in store for her after all? What would happen when Gaston and Claire found themselves face to face? Had matters really come to such a pass that all reconciliation was impossible? Or would the two lovers, exchanging a single glance, feel that they still belonged to each other, and in a supreme embrace exchange the most solemn and binding of oaths?

On his side, Moulinet was excessively surprised, but his surmises by no means went so far as his daughter's. He did not understand why the Duke had not waited for him at La Varenne, but he had no suspicion of Gaston's real object in coming to Beaulieu. Accordingly he approached his future son-in-law with an amicable smile, held out his hand, and remained thunderstruck by the glance which Bligny gave him as he passed by without even bowing to Athénaïs. However, he had still sufficient self-possession to follow the Duke into the drawing-room.

The Marchioness and the Baroness had immediately improvised a *mise-en-scène*, so that when Bligny entered, he perceived the Marchioness ensconced, as usual, in her easy-chair, the Baroness standing near the chimney-piece with her arms crossed, so that Gaston might not offer to shake hands with her as was his wont, and Mademoiselle de Beaulieu seated between her mother and Sophie, with her back to the window, so that the traces of her suffering should be less apparent. It was Claire's beautiful hair that first attracted the Duke's attention. He quivered despite himself, and, seized with acute emotion, he was on the point of hastening to the girl whom he still tenderly loved, and throwing himself at her feet, careless of the consequences of this passionate demonstration; but the calm, severe look in the Marchioness's eyes restrained him; and, bowing low before the noble woman who had been his second mother, "Madame la Marquise," he said, in a husky voice, "my dear aunt, you see my emotion —my regret—my grief! On arriving at La Varenne at—this gentleman's house (the Duke was apparently ashamed to pronounce the name of Moulinet) I learned what an unpardonable step——"

"But, Monsieur le Duc," interrupted the ex-judge of the Tribunal of Commerce, who evidently felt hurt.

Turning towards his future father-in-law with superlative haughtiness, the Duke resumed, "A most improper step, monsieur, and I wish to have it known that I was in no degree your accomplice. I may have greatly erred, I may have acted lightly and ungratefully, but as for having authorised such outrageous conduct towards my relatives, no, on my honour, no!"

"A simple visit of politeness," muttered Moulinet, who was impressed by the Duke's energy. "I really don't understand——"

"You don't understand," interrupted Gaston with crushing contempt; "that is your only excuse!"

Moulinet, however, was too much infatuated with his own importance to allow himself to be treated any longer in this style, even by a man whom he considered to be of superior origin. So, assuming a dignified air, and bowing gravely, he began, "If I have acted in any respect wrongly, my son-in-law, pray tell me how. I am ready to offer all reparation in my power."

But Gaston's irritation was increased tenfold on hearing Moulinet call him "my son-in-law," and, discarding all restraint, he silenced the ex-judge for good, by exclaiming, "Enough, monsieur!" in a voice which was as cutting as a slash from a riding-whip. Then, for the first time since he had entered the room, daring to look at Claire, who sat motionless and imperturbable, he resumed, "Aunt, I owe you an explanation; pray allow me to give it you. Claire, I cannot leave the room till you have forgiven me."

On hearing these words, which were addressed to her personally, and as if she had been waiting for them, Mademoiselle de Beaulieu rose proudly to her feet, and looked at her lover with amazing serenity. "But you owe us no explanation, Duke," said she, "and you need no forgiveness. I have been told that you intend to marry this gentleman's daughter"—and in pronouncing these last words she assumed a supremely contemptuous tone. "You had the right to do so, it seems to me. Were you not as free as myself?"

When the Duke heard this unexpected language, he asked himself if he were dreaming. He looked at Claire, the Baroness, and his aunt, and noticed no apparent emotion, sadness, or anger. He had fancied he would have to wipe tears away, and he found himself confronted by smiles. Was it possible! Had Mademoiselle de Beaulieu so thoroughly ceased to care for him during that year of absence which he had so fatally employed?

"Your betrothed came to tell me of the happy news," resumed Claire. "It was only right, and I do not wish to remain in arrear with you."

Thereupon, approaching the open doorway looking on to the terrace, she made a sign to Philippe. Athénaïs, who was dying of curiosity, boldly followed the ironmaster, and a moment later all the inmates of the château were assembled in the drawing-room.

"I must introduce you to each other, gentlemen," said Mademoiselle de Beaulieu, with amazing composure; and pointing to Gaston, with a wave of her hand, she exclaimed, "Monsieur le Duc de Bligny, my cousin." Then, turning towards her faithless lover, and defying him, as it were, with her proud gaze, "Duke," she added, "Monsieur Derblay, my future husband!"

If a thunderbolt had fallen on the château, it would not have had a greater moral effect than these last words. The Duke staggered. Athénaïs felt giddy, and turned ashy pale.

The Baron and the Baroness exchanged looks of surprise. Bachelin and Suzanne alone evinced no astonishment, the former because he had toiled to bring this result about, and the latter because she so loved her brother that she had never doubted but that Mademoiselle de Beaulieu would end by appreciating his sterling merits.

The Duke at least showed that he had not practised diplomacy unprofitably. He speedily recovered, and, assuming an irreproachable attitude, smiled graciously at M. Derblay. "Receive my congratulations, monsieur," he said, in a tolerably steady voice. "You marry a woman whom very few of us would have been worthy of."

Although Athénaïs smarted under the counterblow which Mademoiselle de Beaulieu had thus dealt her, she realised that she must at all events show a bold front. So, stepping forward in her turn, and looking at Claire attentively, she exclaimed, "All my congratulations, dear!" And then, in an undertone, she added, with a perfidious smile, "A love match, no doubt!"

Mademoiselle de Beaulieu tottered, and abruptly realised all the horror of her position. The man she worshipped was there before her; but, alas! he would soon depart with her rival. Claire's unexpected revelation had dispelled the Duke's anger, and he stood beside Athénaïs, holding her finger-tips as he talked to her, and laughing with the careless gaiety of a happy man. And she, Claire, prompted by her ungovernable pride, had just decided her life, and forfeited her liberty. She had promised her hand to a man she could not love, for her heart was still full of the dear and painful remembrance of another! She glanced at the Duke in mortal anguish. She was about to cross the room, draw him away from Athénaïs's exaggerated coquetry, and tell him the whole truth; but he looked so calm, so indifferent, so light-hearted, that her pride and anger returned, and saved her from this weakness. She despairingly determined that she would not appear to have been forsaken. She resolutely sacrificed her whole future to the victory of her self-esteem, and, including Bligny and Mademoiselle Moulinet in the same triumphant glance, she muttered, "My marriage shall take place before theirs!"

IX.

The preparations for the wedding were carried on with incredible speed. Every one at Beaulieu and Pont-Avesnes seemed anxious to further Claire's scheme. Philippe started abruptly for Berry to obtain certain family papers he needed, and at the same time the Marquis set out for Paris. The postal and telegraphic services were constantly employed to urge on dilatory milliners, modistes, and other purveyors of feminine raiment, and a most agitated, unsettled life followed the calm in which the Marchioness had been living for a year.

The worthy lady, who was somewhat dazed by the rapidity of events, sanctioned her daughter's sudden determination without finding strength enough even to discuss its bearings. Relying on Bachelin, who had given her such a favourable account of M. Derblay, and touched, moreover, by the disinterested delicacy of the ironmaster's conduct, she saw the marriage decided on with astonishment rather than anxiety. She regretted that Claire had not waited a little while in view of finding a husband in their own circle; but she asked herself if a rich man of noble birth would have consented to take Mademoiselle de Beaulieu, dowerless, in this positive, practical century. The reply seemed so doubtful to her that she at last began to consider it rather fortunate M. Derblay had appeared on the scene just at the critical moment.

Claire did all that she was capable of to dispel her mother's distrust and to set her mind at ease; for in her presence she showed a smiling face, and displayed every outward sign of happiness. The Baroness alone was acquainted with her sufferings and regrets. She witnessed her cousin's fits of weakness, and calmed her attacks of anger. In the seclusion of her room Claire would spend days without saying a word, physically and morally crushed, unable even to move. Stretched on a sofa, with a contracted brow and an aching head, and a dark look in her eyes, she would dwell incessantly on the cruel episodes of the rupture, unable to accustom herself to this sudden collapse of all her hopes. She asked herself how she could have deserved such misfortune, and found no reason for self-reproach. The catastrophe was entirely due to her rival's hatred and her lover's cowardice. Considering herself to be the victim of pitiless foes—a martyr selected by implacable Fate—Claire at last began to indulge in thoughts of revenge. She looked upon life as a battle in which each combatant must be steeled with contempt to avoid being wounded, and armed with audacity if anxious to conquer. She uprooted from her mind all the scruples which had placed her, bound and defenceless, at the mercy of her adversaries. She vowed that nothing should prevent her from attaining her object in the future. Her heart became bitter and her mind disturbed. She grew unrelenting and spiteful, till nought remained of the noble, disinterested, tender-hearted Claire. She was now harsh and selfish, and egotistical, setting her own good pleasure above everything else. It seemed as if the flames of grief and pain had withered her heart. Even her style of beauty changed; it was as if she had been transformed into marble, for she was as cold and as stately as a statue.

Reflecting on the approaching change in her life, she determined on a plan of conduct from which she resolved she would never swerve. She felt thorough indifference for M. Derblay. She was in no degree grateful to him for his blind devotion. Left ignorant of the ironmaster's generous intentions, she attributed his ready deference to all her wishes exclusively to his ambition to become her husband. Was it not natural he should consent to everything in view of marrying such a wealthy girl and entering such a noble family? She even had some contempt for the readiness with which M. Derblay had enacted his part in the humiliating comedy played before the Duke, and in fact Philippe's admirable generosity seemed to Claire only so much abasement. She said to herself that he would prove a yielding, pliant husband, easily managed; and this was exactly what she wished for. If M. Derblay showed himself docile, she would interest herself in his favour, take his future in hand, and by means of all the influence within her reach enable him to rise to a very high position. The importance of her husband's station would in some degree compensate for his lack of noble birth. After all, they lived in a century of parvenus.

The little Baroness became anxious on noting with what terrible calmness her cousin prepared for a union which was surely not one of inclination, and she resolved to try and discover what was really passing in Mademoiselle de Beaulieu's mind. She began to question her, varying her inquiries, and darting from one subject to another, but at the same time retaining her usual frivolous, careless manner as a veil wherewith to conceal her purpose. It was in vain that Claire tried to affect indifference. Despite her efforts bitter feelings rose to her lips, and she allowed the Baroness to perceive how grievously her wound was bleeding. At last, having confided in Madame de Préfont, she experienced immense relief. The

Baroness learned how acutely the proud young girl was tortured. She was able to admire her courage and divine her resolutions. With the experience derived from three years of married life, she realised all the gravity of Mademoiselle de Beaulieu's conduct. By showing her things as they really were, she tried to turn her from her purpose, but Claire's resolutions, based on her ungovernable pride, were not to be shaken.

It was a kind of *lex talionis* that Claire had devised for her own especial use. Others had made her suffer, now others should suffer through her. So much the worse for them if they were innocent. Was she guilty? As injustice was the law of humanity, she would cast equity and duty on one side and sacrifice everything to her own good pleasure. She began to look upon human beings as implements, and determined to make them march, men and women alike, like pawns on a chessboard, so as to win the game she had in mind. Her only object now was to avenge herself on Athénaïs and to humiliate the Duke. In view of this sorry satisfaction she was prepared for every sacrifice. And the first victim she selected was none other than passionate, generous-hearted Philippe, whose only dream was to restore to her the happiness and peace of mind she had lost.

Madame de Préfont severely blamed Claire's despotic intentions. The cold manner in which Mademoiselle de Beaulieu mingled what was just and what was unjust together, solely guided by her egotism, seemed so senseless to the Baroness that she ascribed it to a passing mental aberration, destined to subside with time. Still she endeavoured to show her friend that it was not so easy as she imagined to tyrannize over human beings possessed of such gifts as thought and action. Certainly M. Derblay could only be greatly flattered by the prospect of entering the Beaulieu family, and no doubt he was ready for any sacrifice that might conduce to his marriage with Claire. In exchange for the service he had rendered her by enabling her to crush her enemies at a moment when they thought her vanquished and humiliated, she had promised him her hand. That was all well and good. But what was the life she held in reserve for him, and how would Philippe behave when, on coming to his wife with open arms and words of affection on his lips, he found her cold and solemn? Mademoiselle de Beaulieu considered that the ironmaster was solely guided by ambition in wishing to marry her. But might it not happen that he was in love with her? Nowadays, no doubt, the pecuniary side of the question was not lost sight of in matrimony. A man did not neglect to inquire into the amount of his wife's dower; and yet all the same, there were still husbands who loved their wives, and might not M. Derblay be one of these phenomena?

Claire had only looked at one side of the question, and the Baroness told her so, and insisted on the point. In married life the wife was seldom the master, and the husband's character was usually inclined to domination. Now M. Derblay seemed to know very well what he wished for, and suppose he revolted and upset all the plans which Claire had prepared? Supposing their two wills clashed together, what would be the result? This was no passing alliance, of a few hours' duration, such as is signed behind a fan, in view of carrying on some ordinary drawing-room intrigue or resisting some social machination. No, it would last for a lifetime. And the auxiliary could not be dismissed with the mere permission to kiss one's finger-tips as a reward for the service he had rendered. He was a husband, and his wife was bound to him by ties that could not be severed. This should be reflected upon before matters were carried any further. Once married, no "crying off" would be possible. Marriage was not a one-act comedy that can be disposed of in a few minutes. It might become a drama if Claire were not careful; and so, perhaps, it would be better for her to pause whilst there was still time.

These reasons failed to touch Mademoiselle de Beaulieu. Rather than modify her plans, she was prepared for any risk. She wished it to seem as if she had jilted the Duke, and she had resolved to be married before he was. The wedding-day was fixed, moreover, and nothing would have induced her to postpone it. Still she realised that she had been imprudent in allowing the Baroness to read her mind so fully; and she considered it necessary to try and reassure her. She succeeded in making the stiffened muscles of her face relax and managed to smile. In a bantering voice she expressed her pity for poor M. Derblay, who was condemned to the sad fate of marrying such a girl as herself, and who would hardly find sufficient advantages in the match to compensate for his wife's capricious and somewhat tyrannical disposition.

The Baroness was caught in the trap which her cousin set for her. She relied on the future to dispel Claire's melancholy dejection and calm her menacing irritation. She said to herself, in her own mind, that marriage has many surprises in reserve for a young girl, and that life in common generally softens the most violent characters. Alone with her husband —*en tête-à-tête*—the most recalcitrant wife is obliged to be reasonable. A man who is not a fool and who is very much in love may greatly modify a woman's ideas. And then, if a child is born, the situation is completely changed; the fury becomes as gentle as a lamb. With these reflections the Baroness quieted herself; besides, she was not the woman to follow the same idea for any length of time; and so, having devoted a whole day to gravity and penetration, she became frivolous for the rest of the week.

However, Philippe had returned from his journey, and had brought the betrothal ring with him—an admirable ruby of a dark tinge set round with brilliants. It was with a trembling voice that the poor fellow asked Mademoiselle de Beaulieu's permission to slip it on her finger. Claire only had a disdainful glance for this superb jewel. With mingled pride and indifference she held out her hand to M. Derblay, and did not give him a word of thanks. This ring was the symbol of her engagement, and as such it became odious to her. Indeed, on the morrow Philippe perceived, with a pang at the heart, that she no longer wore it. He did not dare to complain, for he was so timid in her presence. But his eyes gazed at Mademoiselle de Beaulieu's hand with such mute eloquence that she could not help saying to him, "You must excuse me. I never wear rings."

The ironmaster felt reassured on hearing this. Noting that the jewel had been laid aside, he had feared Mademoiselle de Beaulieu was moved by a feeling of repugnance for anything that might come from him. He was not unacquainted with the state of her heart. He had witnessed the crisis which Bachelin had predicted, and he was aware that he had only been accepted out of rancour and mortification. But he felt himself so imbued with passion and tenderness that he made sure of ultimately winning this wandering heart. How could a woman remain insensible to the attentive, delicate, devoted affection of every moment? Deceived in her hopes, Mademoiselle de Beaulieu had momentarily become callous, and distrustful of all men. But at twenty years of age the heart can hardly close for ever. Was it possible that in full youth she could decide on always remaining frigid and insensible, close her ears to all the appeals of life, shut her eyes to all the smiles of hope? Was it credible? Philippe, who was passionately in love with Claire, never doubted but that she would eventually reciprocate his affection. She thought that her heart was dead, but it only slept. By degrees it would recover consciousness and beat again. Beat again, and for whom, if not for the man who had roused it from lethargy? Would not Philippe have undoubted rights over this soul when he had saved it? And when Claire was restored to life, with her eyes opened, able to distinguish between the affection she had lost and the affection she had won—would she not reward Philippe for her deliverance by a whole lifetime of happiness?

These were the thoughts that occupied his mind during his long hours of silent contemplation. Forced at the dawn of manhood to devote himself to the all-absorbing toil attaching to weighty business matters, he had not had time to mingle in society. He had thus remained very timid, and was invariably agitated in the presence of women. As for Mademoiselle de Beaulieu, she made him tremble. His heart palpitated whenever he approached her, and Claire, so cold and grave, had only to turn her tranquil eyes upon him to put him out of countenance.

As Philippe climbed the slope, on his way from Pont-Avesnes to Beaulieu, he would often acquaint his sister with his plans for the future, mention the changes he intended to effect in the arrangements of the château, and finally begin to talk of how dearly he loved his betrothed. Suzanne listened to him with beaming eyes and a smile on her lips. She realised that he was rehearsing his part, training himself before appearing in Claire's presence, and whenever in search of approbation he exclaimed, "Don't you think so?" she maliciously answered, "But you ought to tell all that to her, Philippe, not to me. You see, I consider everything you say so right and proper, and everything you do so fitting, that I am always of your opinion. But Mademoiselle de Beaulieu——"

"Yes, I will speak to her this afternoon," cried the ironmaster resolutely. "Oh! I have so many things to tell her."

But all his courage vanished as soon as he reached the château and found himself in Claire's presence. He could not say "Good afternoon" without stammering. And then incensed with himself, he went and sat down in a secluded corner, regretting that no miracle enabled him to open his heart like a jewel-case, and show all the mysterious treasures it contained to the girl he loved.

As the cold weather came with the first days of November, and it was no longer possible to lounge on the terrace, the inmates of the château and their guests assembled in the grand drawing-room. In this closer circle Philippe found various occasions to speak advantageously—not of his love, for he was dumb on what was uppermost in his mind—but on general topics; and being skilfully seconded by Octave and the Baron, he was able to display the rectitude of his judgment and the sterling solidity of his knowledge. Listening more or less attentively, the Marchioness sat beside the fireplace, where a bright wood-fire blazed and hissed, whilst Claire, installed close by, busied herself with her embroidery, from which she never raised her eyes. Gusts of gay laughter were wafted through the open doorway of the billiard-room, where Suzanne and the Marquis were warmly contesting a game of in-door croquet. They were the only ones who lent a little animation to the scene. They had become friends at once, and amused themselves together like two children.

Furious at the failure of her artful combinations, Athénaïs returned to Paris with her father and the Duke. Previous to this, Moulinet had made a farewell call at Beaulieu, where the Marchioness had most graciously received him. At Claire's urgent request, indeed, Madame de Beaulieu assumed a smiling face, and welcomed the chocolate-manufacturer with all the cordiality due to the future father-in-law of a dearly loved nephew. Thus the mother herself consented to play a part in the comedy which the daughter had initiated, and the Moulinets and the Duc de Bligny were obliged to give credit to Mademoiselle de Beaulieu's haughty declaration, and dismiss all idea of having wounded her. The Duke was astonished to find himself so innocent, after fancying himself so culpable. Athénaïs admired her rival's strength of mind, and realising that she was vanquished after thinking herself victorious, vowed that she would have a terrible revenge. She had at first resolved that her own wedding should take place with great pomp at La Varenne, in the superb chapel attached to the château, but she ultimately decided in favour of Paris. She realised that the grandees of the Parisian middle classes, whom her father had invited to the ceremony, would scarcely journey into the provinces to swell her cortege, and she feared that the great families of the district, invited by the Duke, might also fail to put in an appearance. Naturally enough, she preferred not to expose herself to this rebuff. However, she promised to return for the wedding of her future cousin, "her dear Claire," as she was wont to say, and then started for Paris.

Claire felt greatly relieved by her departure. It seemed as if she breathed a purer atmosphere now that her rival was gone. Her beautiful face brightened up, and she became almost gay. Philippe had secretly set workmen to restore the apartments of the château of Pont-Avesnes, which time had somewhat injured, and he now profited by Claire's passing good-humour to ask Madame de Beaulieu to visit her daughter's future abode. The invitation was accepted, and on the morrow all the inmates of Beaulieu installed themselves in a roomy break, and set out for Pont-Avesnes.

The first impression was favourable. Claire was pleased with the broad courtyard planted with old limes, the sheet of water, and the deep moats full of fruit-trees. The park, with its long shady pathways, seemed to promise her a fitting spot for silent meditation. The solemn sadness of the vast rooms was in harmony with her own melancholy. In fact, although the château, girt round with tall trees, and literally without a view, would have seemed a tomb to any one else, it proved greatly to Mademoiselle de Beaulieu's liking. The Baroness inspected the reception rooms, indulging in cries of mingled delight and surprise as she admired the artistic treasures which Philippe's father had gathered together. The short-stitch tapestry of the Louis-Quatorze furniture sent her into a transport, and she remained in ecstasy before the Beauvais hangings depicting the battles of Alexander. Nowadays old china, old fabrics, and old furniture are so eagerly sought after that every one has become more or less of an expert. The Baroness constantly frequented art-sales, and it was at once entertaining and instructive to hear her value the carved credences set out with *gaudrons* of the reign of Henri III. and old Dresden *bonbonnières*. She rapped on the faïence dishes to make sure they were intact, in the most amusing style, and hastening from room to room she rattled on as vivaciously as a young parrot, fairly deafening her aunt, who did not understand a word of all this *bric-à-brac* parlance. Brigitte alone appreciated the Baroness's enthusiasm for the furniture which she had so long taken care of, accepting Madame de Préfont's praise as a tribute to her own cleanliness.

Suzanne and Octave had not even entered the château. Conversing together they had at first followed the pathways of the *parterre à la Française*, and then Suzanne darted off in the direction of the kitchen, whence she speedily returned with a huge hunch of bread, which was at once broken into bits and thrown to the carp in the sheet of water. For half an hour or so Suzanne and Octave amused themselves with watching the attempts of the gluttonous fish to swallow a big crust which floated on the surface. As for the Baron, he was influenced by the vicinity of the ironworks, and turning down a little path already well known to him, he at once started off for the laboratory.

Claire had remained behindhand whilst the Baroness took an inventory of the furniture of Pont-Avesnes, and whilst Philippe did the honours of the house to Madame de Beaulieu. Perceiving a glass door communicating with a flight of steps which led into the park, she opened it and went out. In the distance the hammers of the workshops resounded gaily on the anvils, the furnaces snorted and expelled thick smoke towards the sky; whilst in the park all was still, solemn, and mysterious. The contrast of the noise and the silence had a peculiar charm for Claire. The trees with their foliage already reddened by the winds of autumn formed a vault above her head, and, following the mossy pathways, she soon became absorbed in reverie. This dark deserted park seemed a fitting scene for her future life. The dead branches which crackled under her tread had fallen from the trees as her hopes from her heart. She must cast her dreams on one side, in the same way as she dispersed the withered leaves. Everything within her was inert and cold, just like this silent desolate wood. She went on, noticing the sad aspect of nature with bitter joy, but suddenly, as the path curved, she perceived through a large clearing, a far-stretching expanse of fertile plain, brilliant with sunlight. It came upon her as a picture suddenly discovered, and Claire experienced an acute impression. Her mind was all the more struck by this smiling scene, as she had just identified herself with the decay and gloominess around her. Thus joy followed sadness so promptly. After this black and gloomy park, these fertile plains so full of life; would it be the same with herself? Could the feelings she now experienced change? She turned with anger from the smiling scene, and retreating into solitude, sadness, and shade, disdained the promises of the future.

When the Baroness, Philippe, and Madame de Beaulieu, astonished by her absence and somewhat anxious thereat, went in search of her, they met her returning slowly along the silent pathway. She was calm and smiling. Her eyes, still moist with the tears she had shed in secret, alone gave evidence of the painful battle which had been waging in her heart. The Baron was at once recalled from his attractive scientific pursuits, Suzanne and Octave disembarked from the punt in which they had been navigating round the sheet of water, and the whole party took their seats in the break again, carrying off Philippe and his sister to dine at Beaulieu.

Only a week now separated Claire and Philippe from the day so anxiously awaited by the former's pride and the latter's love. As it grew nearer Mademoiselle de Beaulieu became more and more nervous and agitated. So great indeed was her impatience, that all those who saw her during this last week thought that the prospect of this marriage made her supremely happy. She seemed to fear that some obstacle would arise at the last moment. Packages were constantly arriving from the railway station, and fresh letters came with each delivery. The bell at the gate of the château seemed afflicted with St. Vitus's dance, and the servants almost went crazy, accustomed as they were to the light and casual duties of provincial life.

When the question of sending out the invitations was broached, Claire arrived at two decisions which stupefied everybody. First of all she declared that she wished the wedding to take place at midnight, without the least pomp, in the little church of Pont-Avesnes and, secondly, she expressed the desire that only the members of the two families should be present. On hearing this the Marchioness raised her arms to heaven, whilst the Baroness sank into an armchair and remained for ten minutes without speaking. Octave straightway asked his sister if she were going mad. Philippe alone remained impassive, without expressing an opinion, either by word or gesture. Claire gave no reasons, but she clung tenaciously to her determination despite all the efforts of her relatives. To be married at midnight! This was of itself passing strange, although the custom was still observed in some circles of the Faubourg St. Germain. And a black mass, too, as if Claire considered herself the Duke's widow! But even supposing the wedding took place at midnight, which might be conceded, it was preposterous that no one should be invited. It would look as if they all wished to hide themselves; as if Claire was ashamed of her husband. And besides it might bring misfortune. This last surmise emanated from the Baroness, but it had no more weight with Claire than any of the other objections. At last, however, Philippe was pressed to give his opinion, and he decided the matter by declaring that Mademoiselle de Beaulieu's wishes seemed all very proper to him, and that, for his own part, he saw no reason whatever why they should not be carried out.

As the person who was most interested in the matter raised no objection, all further opposition was abandoned. The Baroness, who was extremely vexed, for she had ordered a magnificent dress to be sent to her from Paris for the occasion, laughingly declared that the wedding would be like one of those melodramatic ceremonies on the stage, when the hero, under sentence of death, obtains the king's permission to marry the woman he loves in his prison before mounting the scaffold.

The marriage contract was signed on the eve of the great day. As Bachelin was obliged to choose between his two clients (for he was at the same time the notary of the Derblays and the Beaulieus), he secured the services of a Besançon colleague for Philippe, and personally represented the noble family for which his progenitors had officiated during centuries. The old lawyer skimmed the perusal of the contract with remarkable skill, and indeed even if Claire had attentively listened to Bachelin's mumble, she would hardly have realised her true situation. As it happened, she remained quite ignorant of the fact that she was ruined, and when Bachelin, who was certainly more agitated than herself, offered her the pen, she signed quite unsuspectingly the act which endowed her with half of M. Derblay's fortune.

As soon as the contract was duly signed Philippe felt less oppressed, but he subsequently acknowledged that he was not really at ease until he heard Claire answer "Yes" in a firm voice in response to the Mayor's inquiry, "Do you consent to take Monsieur Philippe Derblay for your husband?"

X.

It was nearly one o'clock in the morning when Suzanne, dressed in white, swept into the bridal apartments, having left the vestry before the register was signed. Kneeling in front of the tall carved sandstone chimney-piece in the little drawing-room, faithful Brigitte, with a pair of bellows in her hands, was vigorously endeavouring to facilitate the blaze of a large fire, the flames of which cast a glow over the iron plate studded with fleurs-de-lys at the back of the hearth. As she heard the door close behind her, she turned round, and still working with her bellows, gave Mademoiselle Derblay a hearty smile.

"What, have you already come from church, Mam'selle Suzanne?" she asked. "Is the wedding over, then?"

"Over, quite over, my good girl; and I left everybody with our kind curé, to come and give a last look round here. The house has a new mistress, Brigitte, and everything must be arranged to please her."

"Why," cried Brigitte, "how can she help being pleased here, with our Philippe beside her? And then, if the bird's a pretty one, the cage is a fine one too."

As she spoke the servant glanced admiringly at the severe and magnificent furniture, of Henri III. style, with which the lofty room was garnished; her eyes turning from the large carved arm-chairs and squat credences with rounded feet to the hangings of old Cordova leather, with tawny gilding that shone discreetly in the shade. A partially opened doorway allowed a glimpse of the adjoining bedroom, vaguely illumined by a lamp the flame of which shone back in the three glass doors of a superb Louis-Seize wardrobe.

"And in there, is everything in order?" asked Suzanne, pointing to the bedroom.

"Oh! everything, I'll answer for it. I did all the work myself. The wedding seems to have turned the heads of all the maids, and there's nothing to be done with the lazy bodies." Then approaching Suzanne, and looking at her maliciously, Brigitte added, "And when one thinks, mam'selle, that it'll be your turn to set the house topsy-turvy in a year or two!"

Suzanne blushed, and turning aside with some little embarrassment, replied, "There's no question of that, fortunately."

"Fortunately!" ejaculated the servant. "Ah, so much the better. But who was that nice-looking young gentleman who offered you his arm as you left and seemed so attentive towards you?"

"That was Monsieur Octave de Beaulieu," replied Suzanne, as she turned round the room, pretending to pass everything in review for the last time, "Mademoiselle Claire's brother——"

"Eh! eh!" said Brigitte, with a hearty laugh. "Well, for a best man he seemed to like the smell of your orange-blossom."

"Come, my good girl, you don't know what you are saying," rejoined Suzanne, flushing scarlet to the roots of her hair.

The noise of several vehicles rolling over the gravel in the courtyard appropriately brought Brigitte's chatter to an end. Suzanne hastened to the window. Flashing through the darkness a number of bright carriage-lamps lighted up the verdure of the trees.

"Here are our people," cried Mademoiselle Derblay; and opening the door she passed into the larger drawing-room just as the Baroness, clad and muffled up as if she were bound for an arctic expedition, swept in, followed by Octave and the Baron.

"Don't disturb yourself," she cried. "Ah! there's a fire here, thank heavens! I'm a perfect icicle." And so saying she drew an arm-chair up to the fire, installed herself in it, pulled up her skirts, and placed her tiny feet, encased in black satin shoes, on the fender. Then heaving a sigh of satisfaction, she threw her fur mantle off her shoulders and exclaimed, "Ah! I feel better already."

Fresh carriages now rapidly drew up in front of the steps, bringing Mademoiselle de Beaulieu's relatives, M. Derblay's witnesses, and a few intimate friends whom it had been absolutely necessary to invite. M. Moulinet, Athénaïs, and the Duke had been present at the wedding; and the chocolate-maker's famous gala barouche had been utilised, with the footmen in full livery. Unfortunately the night was a very dark one, and this splendid equipage had by no means produced its full effect. Moulinet would have given a hundred francs for a gleam of moonlight. But the orb of night disdained bribery and did not show itself. The ex-judge of the Tribunal of Commerce was altogether disappointed. He had arrived from Paris expecting to witness a great aristocratic wedding, but the ceremony had to his mind proved scarcely worthy of the middle classes. He had hoped to find a large number of noble families present, and now, in the drawing-room, whom did he perceive? Why, simply the notary who had sold him the estate of La Varenne, with the relatives and witnesses of the bridal pair. It was really ridiculous!

At one moment, it is true, he had experienced real emotion, and considered the ceremony a grand one. This was on the road from Beaulieu to the church, when the carriages defiled past the crowd of M. Derblay's workpeople, who stood in silence on the place. They had not been invited to the wedding mass, and yet they were unwilling that their dear master should go to the church without lifting their hats and caps to his bride. Accordingly, they arrayed themselves in their Sunday clothes, and assembled in front of the porch, waiting for the cortege. In the dark still night this solemn mass of a couple of thousand of human beings, men, women, and children, seemed enormous, and when every head was bared as the carriages passed by, Moulinet became strangely oppressed. He wished to smile and bow after the fashion of the functionaries he had seen on fête days, but suddenly moved and bewildered, he felt a tightening in the throat, and began to laugh without knowing why.

Recalled to consciousness of the situation by Athénaïs, who gave him an irritated glance, he promptly collected his scattered faculties, and alighted with great dignity, raising his head with an air of superb conceit, and smoothing his pearl-grey trousers. He found the church extremely small and dirty, and installing himself with a grimace on one of the wooden benches of the nave, he cast a commanding look around. There were not twenty tapers alight on the altar, and the worthy priest wore the same sacerdotal vestments that he had donned to marry a carpenter's daughter the week before. As an old subscriber to the *Siècle*, Moulinet had a dose of Voltairean scepticism in his nature,* and he felt in a humour for raillery. Leaning towards the Duke, he endeavoured to engage him in conversation; but Gaston raised his eyes and looked at him so strangely that he did not venture to insist. He turned his attention to the service, which was progressing with the same simplicity as would have been observed at a pauper's wedding. The organ, played by a proficient musician, alone accompanied the priest; there was no choir, no display of operatic vocalism, and under the cold, bare, vaulted roof the grave notes of the instrument resounded with melancholy effect.

The Duke, whose brow was contracted and whose face was pale, seemed to be absorbed in thought. Indeed the dreary music troubled him. Influenced by sudden recollection, he fancied himself once more in the gloomy church of Saint Germain-des-Prés at his father's funeral. The plaintive sounds of the organ seemed the same; the darkness, mitigated only by the burning tapers, was identical. There was the same smell of burning wax and vapoury incense, which affects the breathing and stifles one. But on the day long past he had had his aunt beside him—weeping as she looked at him—and Claire and Octave, clad in mourning like himself, had lovingly pressed his hands. Now, however, he was alone. He was separated and for ever from the dear ones who had surrounded him, comforted him, and been so kind. He had voluntarily severed the ties which bound him to them. The Claire whom he had adored was another man's wife, and he himself was about to become the husband of a girl to whose hateful schemes, as he fully realised, he had lent himself, unwittingly perhaps, but only too well. At this thought a

* The *Siècle* was formerly the most Radical and atheistical journal in Paris, but in these respects it has long since been surpassed.—*Trans.*

profound feeling of sadness came over him, and he bitterly deplored his weakness. How had he rewarded those who had adopted him and cherished him when he found himself an orphan? Had he not requited good with evil? Yes, that was how he had paid his debt. But was he not punished himself? For in abandoning Claire, had he not forfeited his own happiness?

He was thus led to compare Philippe's conduct to his own, and he could not help admitting that the ironmaster had proved as devoted and as generous as he himself had proved ungrateful and selfish. Philippe had married the woman he loved, dowerless as she was. He worked. The Duke bitterly regretted his own uselessness. Was he not a negative cipher in the world? Like a nought, he needed to be coupled with another figure to acquire any value. To turn himself to any account it was necessary that a rich merchant should take a fancy to his name. What could he do if left to himself? Nothing. He was a superfluity, and people purchased him just as they bought a high-stepping trotter.

He had never indulged in such thoughts before, and now that they presented themselves to him, they inspired him with perfect horror for Moulinet. He pictured himself as the chocolate-maker's slave, and furious at the idea, he determined to revolt and reduce his master to subjection. At the same time he saw Athénaïs as she really was, a young woman of the middle classes with no breadth of ideas nor any nobility of character, endowed merely with low-born envy and wickedness. He glanced at her as she knelt at her *prie-dieu*, yawning as if she were bored, and looking awkward and ill at ease in her superb dress, which was far too ornately trimmed for the toilette of an unmarried woman. Then his eyes turned to Claire, who bent forward under her white veil, and seemed absorbed in prayer. But by the movement of her shoulders the Duke divined that she was weeping.

Philippe stood erect and motionless beside her, with a grave expression on his face. Was that really the man she loved, the man she had preferred to the Duke? As Bligny thus reflected, a sudden light broke upon him, and he understood the meaning of Claire's conduct. For a fortnight the situation had seemed to him impenetrably dark, but it now became luminous. He realised what was the ironmaster's true position, and as he beheld Claire, so beautiful in her grief, there darted through his mind a thought which brought a fugitive smile to his lips. The sincere, regretful, tender-hearted Bligny of the last few weeks vanished for ever, and in lieu thereof there only remained the cold and sceptical *blasé* developed by Muscovite corruption. He decided that he would revenge himself very sweetly indeed on this M. Derblay, who was the chief accomplice in the humiliation to which he had been subjected. Was it possible that this iron-beater could become the undisputed lord and master of such an adorable woman as Claire? No; he, the Duke, would prove the contrary ere long. "She weeps," he said to himself. "She hates that man and still loves me."

After the service, the wedding party assembled in the humble little vestry, and the bride, raising her veil, met the gaze of her friends and relatives. Bligny now sought in vain for a trace of the tears which he had seen her shed in silence. The flame of pride, indeed, had obliterated all sign of sorrow from her face; she was calm and smiling and spoke with complete self-possession. The Duke was displeased; for he would have preferred to have found her overcome. And noting the change, he concluded that the proud young woman was bent on defending herself against him, and that a struggle would ensue. But no matter, he decided to fight the battle, and confidently looked forward to victory.

On resuming his seat in the gala carriage with his future father-in-law and Athénaïs, he had to listen to all the remarks which Moulinet had held in reserve during the ceremony. It was really gay, this midnight service in a sepulchral church with the cold air falling on one's shoulders like an icy mantle. The ex-judge of the Tribunal of Commerce had no taste for weddings of that kind. Three weeks later he meant to escort his daughter to the altar, and folks would then see what he understood by a wedding. The mass would be celebrated at the Madeleine; and he had ordered the most expensive ceremony that could be devised—"the whole nave illuminated, a lavish display of flowers and evergreens, chorus-singing and *solos*——"

"*Soli*," interrupted the Duke, whom this pictured magnificence was beginning to annoy.

"*Solos, soli*," resumed Moulinet, who attached little or no importance to the question which was the correct plural of the two. At all events there would be plenty of vocal music, chanted by the artistes of the Opera with M. Faure at their head. In fact, everything would be of the very best. The ceremony would cost fifteen thousand francs; but what did Moulinet care for that? He did not marry his daughter every day, and he was determined that her wedding should be long remembered and long spoken of.

"However little folks may speak of it, monsieur, they will always speak of it too much," interrupted the Duke, in a tone which was as cutting as the blade of a knife.

"But, my son-in-law," began Moulinet, who felt greatly vexed.

"Excuse me, monsieur," interrupted the Duke again,

"but to begin with, I am not your son-in-law yet, and in addition, you would oblige me by not using such a thoroughly vulgar expression, which is only worthy of shopkeepers.* Besides, here we are at Monsieur Derblay's, and I would urgently beg of you to speak as little as you can in the interest of all of us."

Thereupon slowly leaving the carriage, which had just stopped, the young man gallantly offered his hand to Mademoiselle Moulinet, so as to help her to alight, whilst the ex-commercial judge, who was altogether abashed, nervously asked himself if the Duke took him for an animal.

In the grand drawing-room of the Château de Pont-Avesnes, the Marquise de Beaulieu sat listening to Bachelin, who was talking to her in an undertone. That same morning she had requested the old notary to obtain M. Derblay's authorisation to acquaint Claire with her real pecuniary situation. The marriage being accomplished, the Marchioness had considered it was only right that the young wife should be informed of her ruin and her husband's loving disinterestedness. The ironmaster would thus receive a fitting reward for his delicacy of conduct. But Philippe, in his anxiety to spare his wife all worry and bitterness of feeling, had refused his consent. He did not wish that Claire should feel herself in any degree lessened on entering his house. Why cast a cloud over her delicate, sensitive mind? To satisfy his own self-esteem? To wring some confused and perhaps humiliating words of thanks from Claire? He considered it would be unworthy of him to employ such

* The French term *gendre*, for which the only English equivalent is son-in-law, is never used in good French society. Perhaps its etymology may account for this. At all events it has certainly been tabooed since the days when M. Poirier used it so frequently in M. Augier's masterpiece.—*Trans.*

means in view of gaining her affection. He was desirous of more than her gratitude. He wished to win her love.

"Well, my dear Bachelin, I will say nothing, as Monsieur Derblay desires it," remarked the Marchioness. "But I don't think I should show the same delicacy if I were in his place. At all events, I confess that he astonishes me. He has a surprising breadth of view and a wonderfully elevated mind. He is really an extraordinary man."

"So I had the honour of telling you, Madame la Marquise, when I first spoke to you of him," replied Bachelin. "He is a true nobleman."

"Yes, yes, we have been fortunate," rejoined the Marchioness. "And we are indebted to you for this happy result. Let us hope that my daughter will know how to appreciate her husband. She looks very pale, Bachelin."

The old notary turned round. Claire's face had the hue of death, and with her wreath of orange-blossom she looked as Juliet must have looked on rising from the marble slab in response to the loved voice of Romeo. The Duke had just approached her, and with a melancholy smile, "We are about to leave, Claire," he said, "but before retiring I wished to speak to you. My heart is very sad and troubled. A word from you would tranquillise me. Be good, and tell me that you forgive me."

Claire proudly raised her head, and giving the Duke a triumphant look she replied in a firm voice, "I have forgotten everything. I love my husband. Good-bye."

Bligny started, and answering bravado with bravado, "I trust you speak sincerely," he rejoined; and then, in an almost threatening tone, he added, "*Au revoir*, Claire, till we meet again." With a final bow he thereupon turned away.

"Ah, Duke, so you are going?" exclaimed the Baron, intercepting the young man as he crossed the room.

"Yes," answered the Duke coldly. "I've nothing more to do here. It's the husband's turn."

"Eh! eh!" said the Baron. "You speak rather bitterly. Come, confess it, now that Claire is married you are not without regret?"

With a sarcastic glance the Duke directed attention to Claire, who now seemed scarcely able to support herself. "Regret?" said he. "Is the regret on my side?"

"That's rather a pretentious answer, and a pretty ridiculous one too," rejoined Monsieur de Préfont. "But, as you consider yourself such a conqueror, pray do me a favour. Look at Monsieur Derblay, and tell me if he looks like a husband who would let his wife be taken from him?"

The Duke glanced at Philippe, who stood erect, at his full height, in a corner of the room. His face, bronzed by exposure to the sun, seemed symbolical of energy. Such a man's anger would assuredly prove terrible. But the Duke did not appear impressed; far from it. "Pooh!" said he, "blacksmiths have always been an unlucky set since Vulcan's time, you know."

"Indeed!" replied the Baron gravely. "Well, take my advice, and beware of the blacksmith's hammer."

The Duke shrugged his shoulders carelessly, and walked towards Monsieur Moulinet, who was standing alone near one of the doors. "We will go whenever you like," said Bligny.

"Oh! I won't detain you," muttered the ex-judge of the Tribunal of Commerce. "What a reception, my dear Duke! They haven't even offered us as much as a glass of water! That's what we folks of the middle classes call a dry wedding.

But you shall see how I'll manage matters. I mean to give a couple of dinners and a ball which will create quite a sensation. And when our guests leave my house they won't feel famished, I can promise you."

Moulinet might have continued enumerating all the splendid things he meant to do without fear of interruption, for the Duke did not listen to him. He was watching Athénaïs, who was just bidding the bride good-bye. She had taken hold of Claire's hands on approaching her, and was indulging in a noisy display of spurious affection.

"We shall be near one another all the summer," she said. "La Varenne is only a league off. But how I shall miss you during the winter! Paris will seem quite empty without you. Will Monsieur Derblay really be so cruel as to shut you up at Pont-Avesnes for good? Of course I know that you will lack nothing here, for you are loved, and you love in return. But promise me that you will think of me in your joys, and your *sadness*, if you have any. You know very well that I ought to share it."

Claire remained impassive on hearing these perfidiously cruel words. "You may be sure," she answered, "that I appreciate your friendship at its true value. But happiness, you know, needs no confidants. I shall be happy without talking of it."

Athénaïs despaired of conquering her intrepid enemy, and with rage at her heart she determined at least not to spare her any vexation. "Kiss me, dear," said she.

"Willingly," answered Claire without the least hesitation, and her soft burning lips touched Athénaïs's forehead. But her strength was now failing her, and hastily taking the arm of the Baroness, who stood close by, she drew her out of the drawing-room, saying, "Let us go. I am stifling."

The Marchioness, who felt somewhat nervous, rose and followed her daughter. Claire's face had at once changed. Her eyes had sunk into their sockets, her mouth was contracted, and she seemed about to faint. Once again, however, did the firmness of her spirit overcome the weakness of her flesh, and looking lovingly at her mother, who was leaning over her, she said, "It is nothing, a little fatigue and emotion, but I feel better already."

As she spoke a hectic flush suffused her face, and her eyes sparkled with fever. She had hitherto carefully concealed her sufferings from her mother, but Madame de Beaulieu now had a vague suspicion that she had been deceived. Would this marriage, with which, personally, she was so well satisfied, really make her daughter as happy as she deserved to be? Had Mademoiselle de Beaulieu contracted this engagement with a calm spirit and confident heart? For the first time during the last fortnight the Marchioness reflected seriously, and asked herself a number of questions to which she found no answers. Accustomed to yield, having formerly borne her husband's infidelity, and then given way to her daughter's gentle despotism, submitting in fact to everything, she never troubled herself about her responsibility. She was one of those women without a will, who put up with any situation, and fail to understand how any one can be bold enough to try and change fate. Thus she had allowed Claire to act as she pleased in reference to the marriage. And yet at this solemn moment she could not help asking herself if she had really behaved prudently; and in her trouble she looked searchingly into her daughter's eyes, anxious, as it were, for a glance of approbation. Then, taking Claire in her arms, "You are happy, my child, are you not?" she asked. "You see my maternal duties are over. You will now be mistress of your life. Tell me that I have done all that depended on me to ensure your happiness!"

Claire read her mother's anguish of mind in her eyes, and making a last effort to deceive her, she kissed her tenderly and exclaimed, "Yes, mother dear, you have made me happy. Have no care nor misgiving on that point." And as her mother burst into tears on hearing these words, she added in a stifled voice, "Don't cry, you will grieve me, and it might be thought——" She did not finish her phrase, but nervously clasping her mother in her arms for the last time, "Come," said she, "we must separate. Come, leave me now—until to-morrow."

Madame de Beaulieu felt reassured by Claire's apparent calmness, and she returned to the drawing-room with a weight off her mind.

At this moment Suzanne entered Madame Derblay's apartment, followed by Brigitte. Doubting the latter's dexterity, she had determined to accompany her and assist her in discharging her duties. As lightsome as a bird she turned round the room, carefully superintending the maid, whilst Claire looked on in silence, but with a gleam of suspicious displeasure in her eyes. She thought to herself that her husband's sister would be incessantly on the watch, and that her eyes, guided by affection for her brother, would note each fit of melancholy that overcame her. Claire thus looked upon Suzanne as a spy, and, carried away by the exaggeration of her feelings, she began to hate her.

However, the young girl had divested Claire of her veil and wreath, and was daintily fingering them, smoothing the creases of the tulle, and straightening the flowers—tormented plainly enough by some secret desire which she hesitated to express. At length, however, approaching Madame Derblay again, "It is thought in our province," she said, with a blush, "that a spray of orange-blossoms brings happiness when culled from the wreath of a bride one loves. I love you very dearly, sister, so will you allow me to take a few of these flowers?"

Claire looked coldly at Suzanne, and suddenly tearing away the garland which adorned her dress, she threw it at her feet, exclaiming, "If these flowers bring happiness I have no need of them. There, you can take them, take them all."

Suzanne stepped back in astonishment; the wreath fell from her hands, and turning her tearful eyes on Claire, "You don't seem to care for these flowers," she said. "And yet they were given you by my brother."

Claire was touched by this complaint, and for one instant she seemed about to soften. But her proud, obstinate nature swiftly regained supremacy, and she let the hand she was holding out to Suzanne drop to her side again.

"Leave her, my dear girl," said the Baroness to Mademoiselle Derblay. "She needs a little calm. Don't be grieved; take up the wreath again; it will serve you as a pattern one of these days." And showing Suzanne a smiling face, she led her—now reassured—to the drawing-room door.

Absorbed in her painful thoughts, Claire sat motionless and silent with her eyes fixed upon vacancy. "Well, my dear, what are you thinking of?" asked the Baroness, returning towards her. "You have sadly grieved that poor girl, and she really did not deserve it. Can't you manage to control your nerves?" And then in a bantering tone Madame de Préfont added, "Come, frankly now, you wouldn't look more overwhelmed if you were being led to execution to the tune of the funeral march in the fifth act of *La Juive*."

Claire replied with such a reproachful glance that her cousin at once became serious again. "Come," said she, "speak to me and tell me everything. What is the matter?"

Claire rose to her feet, took a few steps at hazard, and then pausing in front of the Baroness, and clasping her hands with a gesture of anguish, "Can't you see how I suffer?" she asked. "Don't you understand that I feel as if I were going mad? In a moment you will have gone, all of you—all those who love me—and I shall remain alone in this great unknown house. What can I catch at? whom can I turn to? Everything that bound me to the past is severed; everything that could have attached me to the future has disappeared."

"You are grieving and worrying yourself as if you were really abandoned," said the Baroness. "But come, you haven't lost the affection of your relatives. And besides, you have fresh affection awaiting you—sincere, devoted affection. Your husband is there; he loves you; be confident."

The Baroness stopped short, for as she pronounced the words "your husband," she saw Claire shudder. "Oh! if you only knew what is passing within me," muttered Madame Derblay. "I was bent on this marriage, no doubt; my pride urged me madly on; but now that it is accomplished it horrifies me. That man my husband! Ah! I should like to fly from him. Don't leave me yet, stay here; he will not dare to come to me as long as you are with me. Oh, that man! That man who inspires me with the first fear I have ever felt in life—ah! how I hate him!"

"Good heavens! you frighten me!" exclaimed the Baroness, who really felt alarmed. "Perhaps your mother has not gone yet. Shall I call her?"

"No, no!" Claire answered hastily. "I must hide the

truth from her more than from any one else. You saw how I restrained myself when she was here. She must never know my fears; she must never suspect my despair. Poor dear mother! It was for love of me that she helped me to conclude this marriage. If she only thought! Oh, no! 'Tis enough that I should suffer. It was I that willed it, and I alone must bear the burden. My weakness is inexcusable, unworthy of me. Rest at ease, I will not give way like that again."

The Baroness looked at Claire, alarmed by the bitterness of her tone and the violence of her words; but nothing could be read in the expression of the young bride's face. "Go and join your husband," she added. "Don't worry yourself, or think about it. Kiss me, and promise me you will forget what has happened here as soon as you leave the room. Will you promise it?"

"Yes, dear, I will," replied the Baroness. "Come, till to-morrow." And thereupon, with a stifled sigh and a last sad glance at her cousin, Madame de Préfont left the room, murmuring, "Poor Claire!"

XI.

CLAIRE remained alone in the spacious room, and her eyes strayed vaguely round her. The aspect of the apartment was solemn and severe. The lamps cast a soft light over the old tapestry hangings, which depicted the adventures of Renaud and Armide. Under a tent all gold and purple the knight was stretched at the feet of the enchantress, and smiled as he languidly raised a large drinking-cup of precious metal. Farther on came the two knightly liberators riding through the enchanted forest and warding off the monsters that tried to bar their way by means of the magic shield. Finally appeared the battle fought by the Christians against the troops of the Soudan under the walls of Jerusalem, and here Armide was shown, standing in her chariot drawn by white unicorns, and aiming with bow and arrow at Renaud, all gory with the blood of the infidels. A marvellous Renaissance cabinet, in ebony, incrusted with polychromatic marble, stood in a recess, facing a handsome colonnaded bedstead of carved pear-wood, which had a canopy of Genoa velvet, with bunches of flowers woven on a maize ground. An admirable Louis XIII. coffer, in ebony with brass ornaments, served in lieu of the usual commonplace chest of drawers. A superb mirror, in a bronze frame of detached foliage daintily chiselled, reflected the subsiding glow of the fire now smouldering in a lofty sandstone chimney-piece, above which, set in the wainscot, there appeared a remarkable oil-painting of the Spanish school, depicting a fair infanta, rigid in her stiff costume, with her chin resting on a lace ruff, and with a melancholy smile playing over her face as she inhaled the perfume of a rose. Broad brass fillets fastened to the walls, and a Flemish chandelier hanging from the panelled ceiling, completed the decoration of the room, at once so rich and simple in its aspect.

But Claire cared little for the surroundings. She was thinking. Carried away by her desire to avenge herself on the Duke and Athénaïs, she had deceived herself as to the situation in reserve for her. She had dismissed all thought of what would happen when the marriage was accomplished. She had fervently hastened the wedding, anxious that society should believe it was she who had jilted the Duke, and not the Duke who had forsaken her. But now, all on a sudden, she found herself face to face with the cruel reality. The necessities of married life appeared to her, revealed by this room, which would belong to her husband as to herself, by this couch, which she must share with a man who was almost a total stranger to her.

Her feminine delicacy revolted at the thought. She held Philippe and herself in horror. She must have been mad when she decided on this marriage, and he had acted most unworthily in lending himself to her plans. Her ideas became confused and whirled despairingly through her brain. She went to the window, and opening it, inhaled the fresh night air, which made her a little calmer. The moon had passed through the clouds, and shone over the lofty trees in the park, with its pale disc mirrored in the sheet of water. All was silent and solemn, and Claire asked herself if it would not be better for her to disappear for ever in the midst of this pure deep peacefulness, rather than struggle against the shameful and repugnant difficulties of life. She thought, for one moment, of hastening to that shining, unruffled water, and of confiding herself to its keeping, like Hamlet's pale Ophelia, in the immaculate virginity of her first and only love.

But she was deterred by concern as to the opinion of society, by the same anxiety as to what other people might say that had influenced her so fatally in her earlier resolutions. She smiled bitterly at the thought that Athénaïs would probably say she had killed herself for the love of the Duke. She shrank from the commotion which this romantic death would cause among all who knew her. She did not wish to rend the hearts of her relatives, and leave them as a legacy the almost degrading shame of the suicide. She glanced for the last time at the luminous, quiescent water, and closing the window, went and sat down near the fireplace. It was settled, she realised it; she no longer belonged to herself. She must live, live bound to a man who was on the point of coming to her armed with his rights and privileged to enforce his will upon her—upon her, hitherto so free and invariably obeyed. She experienced mingled fear and anger at the thought. Her pride protested against subjection, and eager for revolt, she asked herself how she might best wring her liberty from her husband.

She dreamt of a form of wedlock in which husband and wife would both remain free. She cared little whether Philippe remained faithful or not, provided he were respectful and submissive. He might do what he pleased on condition that she remained her own mistress. Would it be so very difficult to induce this ironmaster, an ambitious man, no doubt, to show some amount of deference to the wishes of a wife who placed a large fortune and high family influence at his disposal? She had divined that he loved her, but she could not take his feelings into account. With the despotism of a woman accustomed to see everything bend to her fancy, she waived this embarrassing question of his love aside, and determined to stand her ground if he showed himself exacting. She was proud and energetic, capable of fighting and struggling if need be, and she felt confident that she would triumph over all resistance, however serious. In her implacable selfishness, she did not once think of how grievously she was about to wound the heart of the man who adored her.

The noise of footsteps sounding in the adjoining room made her suddenly start. The blood rushed to her face, and too nervous to remain seated, she rose, and leaning on the mantelshelf murmured, "It is he!"

Philippe had remained alone after doing the honours of the house to his friends and relatives and superintending their departure. As the last of them drove away he betook himself almost mechanically to his bachelor's bedroom. The apartment he was to occupy with his wife had formerly belonged to his father and mother. With delicious perturbation he reflected that close by, separated merely by a few doors, the woman he loved was awaiting him, in her white bridal robe, and even more a prey to emotion than himself. He had often thought with yearning of the happy hour when this beautiful girl would become wholly his, but now it seemed as if all desire were quelled. He was grave, preoccupied, and greatly touched. His love for Claire was blended with a kind of protective tenderness. He felt for her almost the same affection as he had felt for his sister when she was a child. In his heart he thanked Providence for granting him possession of the treasure he had so ardently coveted; and he vowed that he would show himself worthy of the favour conferred upon him and do everything in his power to make Claire truly happy.

Half an hour after the last guest had gone off he was still in his bachelor's room, seated in his arm-chair and thinking. As he suddenly realised the flight of time, he smiled and considered himself rather foolish. Then springing to his feet he hastened into his dressing-room. He caught sight of himself in the cheval-glass, and on noting his wedding attire it occurred to him that it would be supremely ridiculous to appear before his wife in a dress coat and a white necktie. He accordingly donned a dark blue morning suit, and then with a palpitating heart, with inexpressible emotion pervading his whole being, he took the way to Claire's apartment. After crossing the little drawing-room he rapped lightly at the door, but obtained no answer. Considering, however, that he had sufficiently announced his coming, he turned the handle and went in.

Claire, who still wore her bridal dress, was standing silent and grave beside the chimney-piece, with her arm resting on the mantelshelf. She did not look at him, but merely lowered her head, and Philippe could see her fair hair scintillating in the lamplight. He took a few steps forward and speaking with effort asked, "Will you allow me to approach you?"

Claire made a gesture of assent, and profiting by the authorisation, Philippe glided to the sofa, where he sat down, or rather crouched, bending forward at such an acute angle that he seemed to be almost at his wife's feet. He looked at her attentively, and her contracted features and their harsh expression astonished him. He was already acquainted with that wild threatening gleam in her eyes; he had noted it when she was in the presence of the Duc de Bligny. He felt anxious on seeing her thus drawn together, as it were, as if she were preparing for a struggle. He could not divine her projects, but he instinctively foresaw some form of resistance. However, he was determined to try and penetrate that heart which remained so obstinately closed, determined to endeavour to solve this living riddle, and thus he at once became as calm and as collected as he had been nervous and troubled a few moments before. This change in Philippe's mind was ominous for Claire. She might easily have subdued a troubled, hesitating husband, but by putting him on his guard she revived all his penetration and energy.

"We are now for the first time alone," said Philippe in a low voice, "and I have many things on my heart which I wish to tell you. So far I have not dared to speak—I should not have expressed my feelings properly. All my life has been spent in work. And I must beg you to be indulgent. Believe me, what I say can give no idea of what I feel. You have often seen me approach you, stammer a few words, and then lapse into silence. I was afraid of appearing either too bold or too timid. And this fear paralyzed me. I contented myself with listening to you, and your voice seemed like music to my ears. I forgot everything while looking at you and watching you as you walked along the terrace in the sunlight. Thoughts of you absorbed me and I began to adore you. Now indeed you have become my only thought, my hope, my life. And thus judge of my happiness when I see you there, near me and wholly mine!"

As he spoke, Philippe took hold of Claire's hand and pressed it passionately to his burning brow. But she stepped back and disengaged herself. "I beg you, monsieur——" said she in a tone of weariness.

Philippe hastily raised his head, and looking in astonishment at Claire, "What worries you?" he asked. "Am I so unfortunate that my words displease you?"

"Do not speak them now, I beg of you," answered Claire, gently. "You can see that I am deeply distressed."

Philippe was touched by his wife's sorrowful tone, and shaking his head sadly he exclaimed, "Yes, you are pale and trembling. Am I the cause of it?"

Claire averted her face to hide the tears which were trickling down her cheeks and then in an unsteady, quivering voice, she answered, "Yes."

"Set your mind at ease, I beg of you," rejoined Philippe. "Can you not realise that my first and foremost wish is to avoid displeasing you? What would you have me do? Tell me. The task will be an easy one, for I love you so."

The young wife started joyfully. It seemed as if a ray of hope shone through the darkness in which she was struggling. Noting her husband's passionate ardour, she realised what boundless power she might exercise over him, and she pitilessly decided to abuse her position. She became coquettish, and looking at the ironmaster for the first time, with an insidious smile, "If you love me," she said, "then——"

She finished her phrase with a gesture which Philippe fully understood.

"Do you wish me to leave you?" he asked submissively. "Is that the trial you are pleased to impose on me? I will resign myself to it if such be your will."

Claire breathed again with a delightful feeling of relief. She realised that she was the absolute mistress of this man who had so frightened her at first. The expression of her face at once changed, and she looked at Philippe with a radiant brow. "Yes," said she, "I should feel grateful to you. The day's emotion has upset me. I need calm; I need to think. But later, to-morrow, when I am more self-possessed, more mistress of myself, I will explain to you——"

Philippe remained for a moment silent. Certain of Claire's words did not ring clearly. This postponement, suggested with so much embarrassment, seemed to him suspicious. There was some mystery in all this, and he must solve it. "What will you tell me to-morrow, or later on, that I cannot hear to-day?" he rejoined. "Isn't my life henceforth inseparable from yours? Our road is traced already. It is for you to be confiding and sincere, for me to be devoted and patient. I am prepared to be so, I assure you. Are you of the same disposition?"

Philippe's language was clear and firm, and he looked his wife full in the face whilst speaking. She feared she had advanced too rapidly, and accordingly retreated. "Let me tell you that confidence is not acquired in a moment," said she. "I have only been married for a couple of hours. And alas! my life dates farther back than that. My life was a happy one. I had the right to think aloud. I was free to remain silent when I chose. I have never been compelled to prevaricate. My troubles—I was not without troubles, as you know—were readily guessed, and those about me understood that the recollection of them could not fade away at once. I was greatly spoiled—never asked to smile when I felt sad at heart. But if I must resign myself to dissimulation with you, I beg of you to grant me time to grow accustomed to such constraint."

Claire had skilfully shifted the question, so as to avoid a frank reply. She set herself up as a victim, and insistence would have seemed cruelty on Philippe's part, as he well realised. "Pray don't add another word," cried he, hastening as it were to the sacrifice expected of him. "You wrong me with those suppositions. You will never have a more tender and devoted friend than myself. In marrying you I took my share of your troubles, and my ambition is to efface them from your memory. Rely on me; I am responsible for your happiness. If you have had deceptions in the past, hope for something better in the future. Far from me be the thought of imposing my love upon you. All that I ask of you is to allow me to try, by dint of care and tenderness, to win you from yourself. That is all my ambition; and since you need repose and solitude, remain here as free and as confident as you were yesterday. I will retire, for that is what you wish, is it not? Well, let it be as you desire."

These words had not merely irritated the young wife, but made her apprehensive as well. The ironmaster showed himself so proud and so magnanimous that it seemed as if all the combinations she had devised in view of regaining her liberty would result in miserable failure. Philippe hastened to satisfy her wishes with such unexpected alacrity that she asked herself if it would be possible for her to live apart from him? He adored her, and he declared that his ambition was to win her love. How could she for ever repel such a loyal, generous man, without showing herself unjust or cruel. Her husband's gentleness and tenderness would prevent her resisting on the morrow, unless downright brutality was had recourse to. She realised the danger she ran, and determined to escape it by resolutely severing the ties that united her to Philippe.

As she remained silent and motionless, her husband approached her. He leant forward, and his lips touched her forehead. "Till to-morrow," said he; but as he inhaled the perfume of her golden hair, as his mouth came in contact with her quivering brow, he was seized with a wild, mad, passionate longing. Forgetful of his promises, oblivious of the susceptible feelings of the troubled heart which beat so near his own, conscious only that he was beside an adorable woman whom he passionately loved and who belonged to him, he caught her in his arms in an irresistible transport, and looking at her with burning eyes exclaimed, "Ah! if you only knew how much I love you."

Surprised at first, Claire promptly turned livid. She threw herself back, and setting her hands on her husband's shoulders, she tried to escape this contact which was so odious to her. "Leave me!" she cried in an angry voice.

Philippe unlinked his arms, and drew back in turn; then, looking at his wife, who stood before him with trembling limbs and her face convulsed as it were with anguish, "What!" said he in a troubled voice, "you do not even allow me to touch your forehead with my lips. You repel me with violence, almost with horror. What is passing in your mind? This is not the mere timidity of a maiden. It is repugnance. Do you hate me, then?—and why? What have I done to you? Ah! the words you spoke a little while ago return to me; now, I fear, I understand them only too well. Since the deception you experienced, something more than bitterness has remained in your heart. There is regret, perhaps——"

"Monsieur!" protested Claire in a husky voice.

But Philippe had become excited. Surging anger had brought colour to his cheeks, and walking nervously up and down, "Madame," said he, "this is no time for vague protestations. The moment has come for a frank, full explanation between us. Your attitude has inspired me with suspicions that you must dispel. A woman does not repulse her husband without a motive. To treat me as you do, you must——"

Philippe stopped short. His voice died away in his throat. He had become extremely pale and his hands trembled nervously. However, he drew a long breath, and then taking his stand in front of his wife, so as to carefully observe the play of her features, he resumed, "That man who forsook you so cowardly—that man, do you still happen to love him?"

Claire realised that a certain, decisive opportunity for the rupture she desired was now at hand, and yet she hesitated to profit by it. Philippe frightened her with his powerful, lucid anger. She remained in suspense before him, with her heart leaping in her bosom, and understanding well enough that her fate now hung on a mere thread. Her silence brought Philippe's anger to such a pitch that he caught her by the arm, and looking at her with flaming eyes exclaimed, "You have heard me. Answer me. You must do so. I am determined on it."

The grasp of his hand on Claire's arm was as the touch of a finger on the trigger of a loaded firearm. Her answer sped forth like a bullet. The haughty young bride, wounded by his violence and actuated by resentment, looked her husband full in the face. "Well, and even if it were so?" she answered audaciously.

Scarcely were these words spoken than she regretted them. The ironmaster drew himself up to his extreme height. He seemed to increase in stature, his face assumed a terrible expression, and he raised his fist as though he held one of the heavy hammers with which his workmen beat the raw metal. "You unfortunate woman!" he cried.

Claire did not retreat a single step. She lowered her head and let her hands fall listlessly beside her, as though she were a martyr prepared for death. Philippe noticed her attitude, heaved a heartrending sigh, and took a few steps up and down, forcibly clutching hold of his right hand with the left one, as if he wished to crush it for having dared to threaten the woman he loved so well. Then regaining some amount of self-possession, "Come," said he to Claire, "measure your words. What you have told me cannot be true. It is impossible. I am dreaming, or else you have meant to try me. It must be that, is it not? Oh, don't fear to confess it. I forgive you beforehand, although you have made me suffer sadly. You must not trifle with a heart like mine, as you will know some day. It is a cruel pastime, I assure you."

He tried to smile, but a bitter twinge clung to his lips. Claire's brow remained obstinately overcast. She seemed insensible, gifted, as it were, with the inert strength of a block of stone. "But speak, come," said Philippe, entreatingly. "Tell me something. You are silent. It is true, then?"

She did not answer a word, but abandoned herself to the fate she had prepared; vaguely conscious that she was committing a crime, and yet determined, in her unconquerable pride, to carry matters to the bitter end. Philippe, who was overcome with painful stupefaction, approached the window, and leaning his burning forehead against the cool glass, strove to regain his self-possession. He realised that the painful explanation he had provoked was only commencing, and he wished to learn how far Claire had decided to carry her audacious revolt. He approached her again. "And so," said he, "it was with your heart full of another that you consented to marry me? And despite the unworthiness of his conduct, despite the affront he exposed you to, you still love him! And you dare to tell me so! You gave me your word that you would prove a faithful, loyal wife, and this is how you keep your engagement! Without a blush of shame, you placed your hand in mine. Ah! to what point of moral turpitude have you fallen then!"

"I do not defend myself, monsieur," said Claire. "Is it generous on your part to make me suffer?"

"You suffer!" cried Philippe. "And I, do I not suffer also? I, who love you with all the strength of my soul—I, who was ready to do anything to please you, and who only asked for a little indulgence and affection in exchange. But you have sacrificed me, speculating on my confidence, laughing at my blindness, perhaps, in order to satisfy your wounded pride and hide your mortification! Do you know such conduct is atrocious?"

"Ah! Have you not perceived that I have been mad for the last fortnight?" cried Claire, ceasing to restrain herself. "Can you not understand that I am struggling in a circle from which I find no outlet. I was impelled to act as I did by irresistible fate. I must seem to you a miserable woman, but you will never judge my conduct as severely as I judge it myself. I have deserved your anger and contempt, no doubt. Come! take everything belonging to me except myself. My fortune is yours. I give it to you. Let it be the ransom of my liberty!"

"Your fortune! You offer it to me? *To me?*" cried Philippe. He was on the point of revealing the truth, of acquainting her, in his indignation, with everything that he had hitherto hidden with such scrupulous delicacy and care. What a vengeance to wreak on haughty Claire! And how sure, swift, and crushing it would be! But he cast the idea far aside. He considered it unworthy of him; and calmed now by the satisfaction he felt on finding himself so morally superior to his wife, he was able to look at her without a vestige of anger. "Do you really take me for a man who sells himself?" he asked coldly. "Do you think that I merely looked upon my marriage with you as a speculation? You are mistaken, madame; you fancy that you have still to deal with the Duc de Bligny."

The thrust reached home, and Claire bounded as if this sneer at the Duke were an insult for herself. "Monsieur!" she cried with a crushing glance at Philippe. But instead of speaking further she relapsed into silence as if ashamed of herself.

"Well, why do you pause?" rejoined the ironmaster bitterly. "Defend him, come. It is the least you can do for him. You are perfectly fitted to appreciate his merits. Your conduct is similar to his own. 'Calculation and deceit,' that is your motto, is it not? Oh! I see things clearly now. You wanted a husband who would be your dependant, and you chose a very confident one, one very much in love. Marriage with me was a *mésalliance*, no doubt, but my docility would compensate for my low birth. And if I chanced to think of revolting and asserting my rights, why you had all that was needful to close my mouth. A bag of gold, forsooth! And indeed what could I urge in answer to such an argument? The husband of such a noble and wealthy wife! I, such a vulgar, mercenary being! That is what you planned! And when do you come and reveal it to me? Honestly, no doubt, an hour before the wedding? In time for me to refuse the bargain if I choose? Nothing of the sort! You only enlighten me when I can no longer retreat, when everything is finished, signed, and irrevocable,—when I am irremediably your dupe, and when you no longer need fear my escaping you! And I, blind that I was, not to have seen the trap! Simpleton, not to have suspected this smart intrigue! I, who came here but a little while ago—palpitating and trembling

—to tell you my love! Wasn't I more than mad, more than grotesque? Wasn't my conduct cynical and ignoble in the extreme? For, after all, I have your fortune, of course. I'm paid! I have no right to complain!"

As he uttered the last words Philippe burst into a frightfully bitter laugh, and falling on to the sofa hid his face with his quivering hands. Claire had listened to him without protesting, and yet she felt more hurt by her husband's reproaches than troubled by his grief. She had discarded all rules of equity, and the truth irritated her without enlightening her. She did not hear Philippe's cry of anguish; she only thought of the irony of his words.

"Monsieur!" she said haughtily, " let us finish this. Spare me useless raillery——"

Philippe hastily drew his hands aside, and showing his face, down which the tears were streaming, " I am not railing, madame," he replied. " I am weeping—mourning my deceptive hopes, my happiness for ever lost. But this is enough weakness. You wished to purchase your liberty a little while ago. I give it to you for nothing. Believe me, I shall never seek to trouble it. Between us each tie is severed, and henceforth we can have nothing in common. Still a public separation would cause a scandal which I do not deserve and which I must ask you to spare me. We shall live side by side, but not together. As I do not wish that there should be any equivocation between us, I must beg you to listen to what I am about to tell you. You will some day learn the truth. You will realise that you have been even more unjust than cruel, and perhaps you may then think of trying to undo what you have done. But I now warn you that it will be useless. If I saw you on your knees at my feet begging my forgiveness, I should not have a word of pity for you. I might have been indulgent as regards your anger, but I can never forget your selfishness and the callousness of your heart. Adieu, madame; we shall live as you have willed it. This is your room. I have mine. From this moment you will cease to exist for me."

Claire did not reply a word, but simply bent her head in token of assent. Philippe, with a pang at his heart, gave her a last glance, hoping for some softening, some return of sensibility that would restore her to him at the moment when he was about to lose her for ever. But she remained inert and frigid. Not a gleam shot from her eyes, not a word escaped her lips. He crossed the room, slowly opened the door, and closed it, as if regretfully, pausing again in the little drawing-room to listen if a cry, a sob, or a sigh would give him—wounded and humiliated as he was—the pretext for returning the first and offering to forgive, whilst there was yet time. But all was silent; he did not hear a sound.

Then confronting the door behind which the implacable young woman remained alone, "Proud creature," said he; "you refuse to bend, but I will break you."

And passing out into the passage which he had followed so hopefully but an hour before, he regained the solitude of his bachelor's room.

XII.

The lamps now only gave a feeble light, and the fire had gone out, so that the spacious room remained in semi-obscurity. Claire still stood beside the chimney-piece, spell bound as it were, and striving to collect her scattered thoughts. She had triumphed in the struggle, and yet she felt as crushed as if she had been vanquished. A sensation of extreme torpor oppressed her, and her head seemed so heavy that she was obliged to support it with her hand. There was a ringing in her ears which deafened her, and everything seemed to whirl madly round and round before her dazzled eyes. Her heart leapt to her lips, an icy perspiration overspread her brow, and she remained distracted, inert, suffering horribly, feeling as if about to faint, and having neither the strength to move nor the will to call for help.

She allowed herself to sink on to the sofa, but was compelled to rise again at once. Sharp pains twitched the muscles of her limbs, and she was unable to remain seated. To procure some relief she had to walk up and down, despite the heaviness of her head, which seemed to her at once swollen and empty. She felt an acute pain above the left eyebrow, as if some one had hammered a nail into her forehead. Fever dilated her arteries. She walked to and fro, and bent almost double, moaning, so great was her suffering, and ever revolving in her troubled mind the same harassing, unbearable ideas. Although she was awake she seemed a prey to a kind of nightmare; and she came and went muttering confused words, interrupted from time to time by the convulsive grating of her teeth.

She suffered like this for hours, obstinately determined not to call for help, and imagining that if she merely so much as opened the door her husband would return in the belief that she was anxious to obtain his pardon. And yet, confident in his loyalty, she had not even turned the key in the lock nor pushed the bolt of the door. She would in truth have been a sorry conquest, a conquest calculated to frighten Philippe, for under the influence of the fever which consumed her she had so greatly changed that she could inspire no other feeling than one of pity.

The first glimpse of dawn surprised her still pacing to and fro, trying to quell by dint of motion the swelling pain in her limbs. She dragged herself along, with a pale face and dim eyes, with her temples beating now as if struck with a pair of hammers. Her strength was failing her. She glanced at the sky, which was tinged with the rosy hues of daybreak, and, hoping that the pure morning air might refresh and calm her, she approached the window to open it. But she had not strength enough to turn the handle, and suddenly a cry escaped her, and she fell back fainting on the carpet.

At about nine o'clock, when Brigitte approached the door on tiptoe to ascertain if her mistress were still asleep, she heard a melancholy moan. The faithful girl was alarmed, and without hesitating she entered the room. Claire was stretched motionless in the position in which she had fallen. She was speaking incoherently. Her face was red, and her feet were perfect icicles. Brigitte did not ask herself how it happened that Madame Derblay was lying there, still arrayed in her bridal robe, but caught her up in her sturdy arms, undressed her, and put her to bed as if she had been a child. Then, noting that her mistress appeared calmer now that she lay between the fresh cool sheets, the faithful girl hastened to fetch her master. He was dressing in his room. At a glance Brigitte noted the tumbled bed, and read the sadness on Philippe's face. Taking up a handkerchief which lay all moist with tears beside the pillow, she shook her head gloomily, and exclaimed, "Ah, Monsieur Philippe! What a sad misfortune! You have been crying, and she——"

The ironmaster turned livid and began to tremble. The idea came to him that Claire had given way to some fit of despair and was dead. "And she?" he repeated with an expression of frightful agony.

Brigitte divined his thought. "No," said she, "not that, but so very ill."

Philippe did not wait to hear another word; but, without even taking the time to put on his coat, he hastened like a madman towards Claire's room. The bridal dress, the tumbled petticoats, the tiny shoes with daintily curved heels, the perfumed white satin stays, lay here and there in disorder on the carpet. Claire was stretched in the large colonnaded bed with a purple face and scintillating eyes but partly opened. The grave-looking warriors on the tapestry, with their lances at rest, seemed to be watching over her. Philippe approached the bedside. She did not recognise him. She was smiling softly with parted, discoloured lips, which disclosed her pearly teeth. He took hold of her hand, and found that it was burning. After passing such an agitated night, it now seemed as if deep torpor were stealing over her. Philippe was seriously alarmed. He hastily wrote a note to the best doctor at Besançon, and despatched a servant with a vehicle and a fast horse to fetch him. At the same time he sent word to Beaulieu.

These first duties accomplished, he sat down at Claire's bedside, and abandoned himself to his desolating thoughts. Would she die? was it all over? She remained motionless, but her eyes were fully opened now, and he noticed that they squinted. A painful contraction seemed to compel them to look askance. Her brow, moreover, was contracted as if with pain, and from time to time she moaned and raised her hand to the nape of her neck. It was evident that she was suffering terribly, and her delirium became more and more intense each minute. All the husband's rancour died away in presence of this sad sight. Feeling superstitious for the first time in his life, Philippe was seized with the idea that if Claire recovered it would be a sign that happiness was ultimately in store for them, and from this moment his only desire was to save her. He loved her madly yet, despite all the sufferings she had caused him; perhaps—who knows?—positively on account of them.

The two hours Philippe spent at Claire's bedside were perhaps the most cruel he had ever known; and yet his life had already been full of trials. He felt greatly relieved when Madame de Beaulieu and Octave arrived, for it seemed to him that he had now a lesser weight of responsibility to bear. Stupefied and frightened as the Marchioness was, she gave no expression to her feelings. She did not shriek, nor shed a torrent of tears, nor invoke Providence with frantic gestures. She simply asked her son-in-law a few discreet questions, prescribed a few elementary remedies, and then, pale and grave, sat down beside her daughter, who was wholly unconscious of her presence. Octave, who was boiling over with impatience and alarm, had ordered a horse to be saddled, and galloped off in view of meeting the doctor and hastening his arrival.

It was nearly noon when the practitioner whom Philippe had sent for reached Pont-Avesnes. He was a man still young in years, who had had considerable experience in hospitals, and who was well acquainted with the progress of therapeutics and quite competent to arrive at a serious diagnosis. Besides, no particular penetration was needed to specialise the complaint from which Claire was suffering. It was easily determined by her delirium, the pain she felt in her forehead and at the nape of her neck, and by the bi-lateral contraction which caused her eyes to squint. The doctor felt his patient's pulse, and counted one hundred and twenty pulsations to the minute, and when the thermometer was placed under her arm-pits it recorded a heat of no less than 85°. The fever was thus extremely intense, and the doctor could not help shaking his head and murmuring, "Very serious." Then, as the mother, the brother, and the husband gave him an anxious questioning look, he added, "Meningitis." Next, applying his ear to Claire's white bosom, which rose and fell with a painful and oft-repeated effort at breathing, he listened attentively for several minutes. "Some commotion at the heart," he said, as he drew himself up again, "the result of a very severe nervous attack. You must procure some ice and a dozen leeches at once."

Suzanne, who was listening on the threshold, made a sign to Brigitte, and the faithful maid immediately started off.

For the last two hours Mademoiselle Derblay had been waiting in the drawing-room, nervously trembling, suspecting that something very strange had happened, but not daring to enter the bedchamber. Now, however, she glided towards the bed, not venturing to speak for fear that she might be sent away, but holding her breath and gazing with a look of terror at Claire's flushed face and colourless lips. The atmosphere of the spacious room seemed to her weighty and oppressive, and without a question, guided in fact merely by the instinct which makes women such admirable nurses, she walked on tip-toe to the window and opened it. The doctor glanced at her, smiled, and exclaimed, "Very good." Philippe, who was so absorbed that he had not even seen his sister, now turned towards her with a loving grateful look, and unable to restrain himself, opened his arms to her and burst into tears. His nerves had been too forcibly strained during the last four-and-twenty hours. Suzanne mingled her tears with his, and leaning on his shoulder murmured, "Come, don't be afraid, Philippe; with us to nurse her, she will surely recover. We will save her between us!"

But if Claire were to be saved it could not be by Suzanne's care. Philippe asked his sister, as a great sacrifice, to consent to return to her convent. The ironmaster was afraid of his wife's delirium. She spoke with increasing animation and the name of the Duc de Bligny incessantly rose to her lips. She called to him with mad rage as it were, overwhelming him with reproaches, and openly displaying the cruel wound he had inflicted upon her by his desertion. Philippe also appeared to her in her hallucinations, and always under a threatening aspect. He came armed to kill her, having already killed the Duke. She could see the blood on his hands, and she begged him to strike and slay her so that she might join the man she loved. Philippe had to listen, quiet and motionless, to these delirious words, but he did not choose that Suzanne should hear them. He had sufficient confidence in the future to spare his sister all grief as to his misfortune. He trusted that the painful present would some day fade away like a bad dream, and he was desirous that there should not be even the shadow of a painful recollection to estrange Suzanne and Claire. Mademoiselle Derblay wept bitterly, but obedient as usual to her brother's behest, she started for Besançon under the charge of faithful Brigitte; and Philippe remained to watch over his suffering wife. From the very first, when the Marchioness perceived how resolutely, sagaciously, and attentively her son-in-law grappled with the disease, she left him free to act as he judged fit, and contented herself with assisting him in his endeavours. She spent the greater part of the daytime in her daughter's room; and at night-time Philippe installed himself in an arm-chair at the bedside, and remained watching his wife by the subdued light of a lamp standing in a retired corner.

The delirium still continued. With a pale face the ironmaster had seen Claire's blood trickle drop by drop down her lovely neck, leaving a ruddy trace on her white skin; but all in vain; the madness which had seized hold of her poor weakened brain continued to disturb it. Days and nights elapsed and still the fever subsisted, and its ravaging effects increased. The young woman's face had become extremely thin, her cheeks were sunken, and the outline of her jaws became each day more defined. Her limbs were ever restlessly on the move, rubbing painfully against the sheets, and a murmur of indistinct words—indistinct since her weakness had become so great—could be heard in the gloom cast by the bed-curtains. On one question alone had Claire's brain retained a semblance of lucidity. She was conscious that Athénaïs's wedding was taking place whilst she lay stretched on her bed of suffering. She awoke as it were from her trance on the day when her rival triumphantly mounted the steps of the Madeleine, profusely adorned with flowers, thanks to M. Moulinet's lavish magnificence; she was gifted, so to say, with second sight at the precise moment when the crowd flocked into the church, in the wake of the bride and bridegroom. A gleam of lucidity flashed from her eyes and she raised herself up, and, in a distinct tone of voice exclaimed, "They are being married now, and I, I am going to die."

The Marchioness approached the bedside and spoke to her trying to reassure her, but she would not listen. Besides, delirium had already resumed possession of her mind. She had a frightful nervous attack, shrieked and wrung her arms, while her lips were blistered by the intensity of the fever and the perspiration saturated her tangled hair. Philippe was so alarmed that he at once sent for the doctor, who had not intended calling until the evening. As soon as he arrived he remarked a fresh rise in the heat of Claire's body. Like steam-pipes put to too hard a test, her arteries seemed on the point of bursting. A degree higher and the end would come.

That day was a horrible one. Philippe waited for the result of the crisis in mortal agony. He realised that his life was being decided during these interminable hours, and ever and ever through his mind, overcome with weariness and grief, there revolved, as imperiously as a sentence, the thought, "If she lives, we shall end by being happy." He believed in the truth of this presentiment, and would willingly have given a part of his own life to prolong Claire's existence.

The evening came at last, but there was no sign of the passing calmness which usually came over Claire at nighttime. With knitted brows and grating teeth she lay on the tumbled bed, incessantly calling for the Duke in a frantic, heartrending tone. Philippe had risen and was leaning over her, thinking she could not see him. But suddenly her eyes dilated and gazed at him with a look of horror. She made an effort to raise her arm, and in a husky voice said, "You have killed him; what are you waiting for—to kill me as well?"

Philippe, whose heart was rent at finding himself still so cruelly misunderstood, and who was worn out by so many stupendous efforts, became for a moment as feeble as a child. Leaning forward, he rested his forehead on the carved woodwork of the bedstead, and shed bitter tears. His tears fell slowly one by one on to Claire's burning brow. They came like some refreshing dew; it seemed indeed as if these tears, springing from Philippe's heart, were a sovereign remedy. The contraction of Claire's features relaxed. She sighed gently and raised herself on one side to listen. Philippe was sobbing in the gloom without restraint, believing that his wife was still senseless. But suddenly a hand was laid on his, and at the same time the sufferer murmured in a weak voice, "Who is crying like that? Is it you, mother?"

The ironmaster raised his head and saw that Claire's eyes were turned towards him. He approached still nearer, and at last she recognised him. A cloud seemed to pass before her brow, as if she remembered the past. A tear sparkled in her dilated eyes, and holding out her hand to the man whom she had made suffer so cruelly, "Ah, it is you," she said; "always you—generous and devoted. Oh! forgive me, Philippe, forgive me!"

The ironmaster fell on his knees and passionately kissed those eyes which for the first time looked at him without a gleam of anger. His wife smiled sadly; then a powerful contraction lent a harsh expression to her face again; delirium resumed its hold, and she once more began to stammer disconnected words.

For three weeks she had remained between life and death, but this crisis was the last. After that night the malady entered into a new phase, and violent agitation was followed by increasing torpor. "The comatose period," said the doctor quietly. "So far we have done all we could to send Madame Derblay to sleep, but now we will do all we can to keep her awake."

As Philippe realised well enough, this meant that Claire would be saved, providing she had no relapse, and providing no unforeseen complications set in. But with the hope of her surviving there came the knotty question of arranging their future life. As long as she had been in danger he had only thought of saving her from death, but now he would have to contend against life itself. On recovering Claire would probably relapse into her former repugnance for her husband. Oppressed by disease, she had been momentarily touched; she had had a minute's weakness, and had implored his forgiveness. But on regaining her self-possession, would she still show herself so humble and submissive? Philippe had learned to know his wife's proud character. He feared a return of her uncompromising pride. He trembled at the thought that she might imagine he had determined to profit by her convalescence to set aside the pact they had made on that frightful wedding-night. If in undignified fashion he broke the engagement which he had himself suggested and enunciated, he would lower himself, and perhaps for always, in Claire's eyes. Thus it seemed to him that rigour was necessary, and, with the strength of character that he possessed, he had no fear of weakness turning him from his course. He had sworn to himself that he would break his wife's pride, and he prepared to keep his oath.

It was now January, and the winter had so far been a

severe one. The ironworks, where labour had been suspended during the height of Claire's illness, were now again in full activity. The noise of the hammers sounding on the anvils enlivened the young wife. Her long convalescence proved very pleasant to her. She found something delightful in this resumption of life, and gazed joyfully on the objects surrounding her. She was greatly pleased with her spacious room, severe in aspect and somewhat dark, with its old furniture and costly tapestry hangings. There was nothing noisy about it; everything seemed blended in the same quiet harmony. Glancing from her bed to the hangings, she could see a nymph with streaming hair, who carried a vase whence water gushed, spreading over the plain and flowing on like a river. The design appeared an allegory to Claire, and it seemed to her as if this nymph were pouring out life from the vase she held. Through the high windows she could see the trees, still white with flakes of snow and shining in the wintry sunlight. The birds often flew to the window as if in search of shelter. She looked at them with delight, and was careful to have crumbs of bread scattered on the window-sill in readiness for her feathered visitors. She took interest in everything. Strength gradually came back to her, and it was with genuine pleasure that she felt herself return morally and physically to life. She would lie for hours idly in her bed, listening to the ticking of the clock without an idea in her head, but lost as it were in a delicious sensation of vacuity.

Her days were spent *en tête-à-tête* with the Marchioness, Philippe only coming to see her in the morning and the evening. He was careful to inquire after her health, and invariably asked her if there was anything she fancied which he could procure. Then, after remaining seated for five minutes at the foot of her bed, he gravely took his leave. She listened

to his footsteps as they died away. She looked forward to
his visits, found that they were too short, and began to feel
slightly irritated with him. Finding an opportunity for a
little quarrel, she took advantage of it with childish pleasure.
She was anxious to have some flowers in her room. The conservatories of Beaulieu were full of floral treasures, and one
day the Marchioness brought her daughter a superb bouquet
of white lilac. Philippe happened to enter the room and found
his wife inhaling the flowers. He gently observed that their
perfume might do her harm, and, taking the bouquet from
her, he was about to carry it into the drawing-room, when
Claire vivaciously exclaimed, " But I feel very well, I assure
you, and you really might leave me those flowers."

"You are like all convalescents," rejoined Philippe with a
smile. "You think yourself stronger than you really are.
But we must act reasonably for you."

"A proof that I'm quite well is that you venture to displease me," retorted the young wife, with a coquettish pout.
"You were very different when I was really ill."

Philippe became very grave, and, without replying, he gave
Claire a sad, severe glance. She heaved a sigh, and then in a
changed voice, "You are right," she said; "take those
flowers away, and thank you."

For the rest of the day she was pensive. By degrees the
faculty of reflecting returned to her, and recollection of the past
came back. She found courage to question herself, and was
astonished to find in her heart no trace of the love she had
borne the Duke. Indeed, her love for him had left her, like
a blighted fruit falls from a tree. Nor did she feel any more
hatred for Athénaïs; she rather pitied her, divining that s h
was destined to suffer from incurable envy. She made no
inquiries about her rival's wedding; she presumed it had

taken place. In point of fact, all mention of the Duc de Bligny was carefully avoided in her presence, but the precaution was really a superfluous one, for she would have heard Gaston spoken of without the least emotion, so thoroughly had her heart changed.

Her convalescence proved a very long one. The first time she wished to get up she fainted from weakness, and had to be put to bed again. Philippe, who showed great anxiety, at once returned to her bedside, and resumed nursing her with his usual impassive, silent devotion. Her forehead still troubled her, and it seemed as if there were yet something the matter with the coating of her brain. Whenever she moved her head she declared that she felt her brain sway to and fro like a pendulum. "I was somewhat mad before my marriage," she added with a smile, "but what will it be now?"

Five months had elapsed since the wedding, when one fine April afternoon she was able to venture into the garden, leaning on her mother and Brigitte. She walked slowly round the sheet of water, pausing from time to time to regain strength, seated on one of the stone benches which the springtide sun had warmed. On seeing her as she trod slowly over the gravel walk, no one would have recognised the proud and haughty maiden, of whom her mother had so often said, "She ought to have been a boy." Her features seemed to have a softer outline, and her eyes beamed with a more gentle light. She had altogether become more feminine, and she appeared shorter, now that she no longer carried her head haughtily erect.

From that day forth Philippe's manner did not change. Gentle, amiable, and most attentive towards Claire in the presence of strangers, he showed himself cold, grave, and but strictly polite when they were alone. So correctly was his conduct varied that he passed for a model husband among his friends. The Marchioness never once suspected the truth. Besides, she was accustomed to the quiet, correct gallantry of aristocratic society, and moreover the defunct Marquis de Beaulieu had never shown himself effusive. She accordingly decided that everything was for the best in her daughter's household, and that watchfulness was altogether uncalled for. Quite at ease, moreover, in reference to Claire's health, she now announced her intention of starting for Paris, where Octave had been installed since January. Faithful to his theories of equality, the young Marquis evinced a decided disposition to cast his escutcheon on one side, and cater for clients as a simple advocate.

Claire thus remained alone with her husband, whom she mainly saw at mealtime. After dinner he escorted her into the drawing-room, sat down for five minutes or so, then rose again, wished her good night, and retired to his study. One evening she felt curious to know what he did there, and wrapping herself in a mantle she went into the garden in view of watching him. She could see his shadow, to which the play of the lamplight lent gigantic height, passing incessantly to and fro on the curtains of the study window. He was walking up and down in a thoughtful attitude. Claire went in-doors again, and glided on tiptoe into the room next the study. She sat down in the dark, looked at the ray of light under the door, and listened to Philippe's measured tread, which had a solemn, muffled sound as he passed to and fro over the thick carpet. He continued walking up and down till midnight; and then, just as the clock finished striking, she heard him open the door on the other side of the study, and at once the ray of light disappeared.

What could he be thinking of during this prolonged perambulation? What thoughts absorbed him during the long hours he spent in solitude? Claire would have given a great deal to have known. She was a woman, be it remembered, and women who are inquisitive can never restrain themselves for long. Thus it happened that one evening, as Philippe was taking leave of her as usual, she suddenly asked him, "What do you do so far into the night, shut up in your study alone?"

"I attend to accounts that are behindhand," answered the ironmaster quietly. "And, in fact, it just happens that I have some money to give you." So speaking he drew a bundle of banknotes from his pocket.

"Some money?" exclaimed Claire in astonishment. "For me?"

"Yes, the income of your fortune during six months." And laying the banknotes on the table, Philippe added coldly, "pray see if the amount is correct."

Claire stepped back; her face flushed, her hands trembled, and she felt a pang at the heart. "Take it back, monsieur," she cried; "take it back, pray—I cannot accept this money."

"But you *must* take it," rejoined the ironmaster; and with a disdainful gesture he pushed the notes across the table to his wife.

She drew herself erect as if preparing for a struggle. Philippe's gesture and tone of voice had wounded all her feelings. Her eyes sparkled, and in a moment she became once more the proud and violent-tempered Claire of other times. "I won't——" she began, looking at her husband audaciously.

"You won't?" he rejoined with irony.

Their eyes met, and Philippe's gaze was so firm, so direct,

and so powerful, that his wife could not bear it. Her resistance suddenly gave way, the hand she had proudly raised fell to her side again, and she relapsed—conquered—into painful silence. Without another word the ironmaster bowed to her and left the room.

For the first time Claire's will had clashed with Philippe's. She felt stunned and broken by the shock. She was obliged to admit that her husband's character was superior to her own, and she experienced mingled irritation and delight at the discovery. She began to esteem him in all sincerity, and attracted, as it were, by his energetic nature, she studied it attentively. In the first expansion of her return to life she had decided she would be amiable, and frankly grant her friendship to Philippe; and she now observed with no little mortification that she was disposed to grant more than was asked of her. Whilst she was ready to go as far as friendship, her husband contented himself with remaining indifferent. He did not sulk. There is a means of dealing with the sulks. But no; he simply refrained from paying any attention to her; he let her live as she chose, as she had asked him to do, and treated her with icy coldness. This indifference, which was not without a tinge of disdain, sorely humiliated Claire, and she strove to overcome it. Her nature was an essentially militant one, and she was always in search of some difficulty to vanquish.

Whenever Bachelin came to dine at Pont-Avesnes, Philippe spent the evening in the drawing-room. Accordingly Claire invited the notary regularly twice a week. She learned to play whist, and took "dummy" like a dowager. As long as Bachelin was there the ironmaster certainly talked and played, but as soon as his guest withdrew he became grave and silent again. Despite all her efforts Madame Derblay was quite unable to soften her husband's will. The power Philippe possessed over himself at last exasperated her, and at times, in the solitude of her own room, she gave way to violent outbursts of anger. She quivered at the thought that she was enthralled. This man was her master. He led her as he pleased, and whenever she tried to revolt, a glance from him sufficed to reduce her to obedience. He seemed to her as cold and as hard as the iron he hammered out. He was fashioning her character, and plainly enough he would be able to give it whatever form he pleased. Claire wept with shame as she realised how powerless she was; still a last vestige of pride enabled her to hide her sufferings from Philippe, and she showed herself such as circumstances required—resigned, not bitterly despondent, and dignified, but not haughty.

Although she now took but little interest in what happened away from Pont-Avesnes, her relations in Paris did not allow her to forget them. When the Baroness learned that her cousin had recovered she began with intermittent affection to write her long epistles, which were full of incoherent but curious details. It was through Madame de Préfont that Claire received news of the Duke, the Duchess, and M. Moulinet. Athénaïs had made a noisy entry into society. She had generally pleased the men, but on the other hand all the women railed against her free, careless, masculine habits. The Duke paid little or no attention to her. Three months after the wedding it was reported on all sides that he and his wife virtually lived apart. He was now paying court to the lovely Comtesse de Canalheilles, a beauty of Irish birth, whose eyes were as deep and as troublous as the sea. As for the Duchess, she flirted with half a dozen young fops, with curly hair and irreproachable shirt-fronts, and who followed her about wherever she went. She called this little squadron

of lovers her "six-in-hand," and skilfully tooled the reins
without any fear of a spill. In point of fact her selfishness
and dryness of heart guaranteed her against all surprises.

In the meantime M. Moulinet, now that he had provided for
his daughter, seemed bent on maturing some important plans.
He had engaged a secretary, and for several hours every day
he shut himself up in a room which he called his library,
although the only book it contained was a treatise on political
economy laid open on his writing-table. His daughter pretended that he conscientiously went to sleep over it from two
till five each afternoon. On the other hand, the Baroness
declared in her letters to Claire that the ex-judge of the
Tribunal of Commerce was supposed to be planning some
political candidature. He had been seen about, she said,
with various shabby individuals, who could only be journalists.
He had, moreover, made several excursions to the Jura. He
was building a strictly laical school at La Varenne, and on
the other hand he was secretly restoring the village church.
With his left hand he fondled the Radicals, whilst with the
right one he petted the Conservatives. In point of fact, the
chocolate-maker was becoming Machiavellian. To tell the
truth, ambition had stung him, rather late in the day, perhaps,
and yet none the less surely. Having managed his own affairs
so well, he considered that he was admirably adapted to
manage other people's, and he asked himself if there were
a single man in the Chamber of Deputies who could prop
up a political situation with a fortune larger than his own.
He frankly confessed to himself that there wasn't one, and
having bought his daughter a husband of the highest rank in
the market, he saw no reason why he should debar himself
a constituency.

For some little time he hesitated between the Senate and

the Chamber of Deputies. Senator! The title seemed to him a majestic one. He retained a kind of worship for this legislative body which once comprised all the more eminent men in the country. On the other hand the title of Deputy had by no means a disagreeable ring; and, besides, the Chamber seemed to be livelier than the Senate. Moulinet possessed a certain amount of common-sense, and he realised that he should find a sufficient number of dolts and dullards in the lower assembly to acquire promptly enough the reputation of being a remarkable man himself. Accordingly he commenced his campaign, and prepared for every sacrifice in view of securing success. The first thing he did was to start for La Varenne, which was the centre of an electoral district, bordered on one side by that of Besançon, and on the other by that of Pont-Avesnes. M. Derblay possessed great influence throughout the Department, and Moulinet determined to try and secure his good graces. He called on the ironmaster, and cunningly flattered him, with an air of consummate simplicity. He did not breathe a word concerning his political plans, but he mentioned that he intended sojourning at La Varenne during the summer, and he contrived to make Claire believe that he was simple rather than malevolent, and that in the matter of his daughter's marriage he had unconsciously served her revengeful designs.

At the same time Moulinet founded a halfpenny newspaper called the *Courrier Jurassien* at Besançon, in view of advocating his claims to a seat in the legislature. The editor was one of the shabby individuals whom the Baroness had spoken of in her letters. Moulinet had chosen the cleanest among them, and the journalist having offered him a stock of political opinions to select from, he had decided on a moderately Republican line of politics, something that was neither meat nor fish; deep enough in colour to please advanced folks, and yet sufficiently light to suit the timid. It was like the words of the "Marseillaise" set to the tune of "Partant pour la Syrie." After all, he cared but little about a precise tint of political opinions; he relied on his purse as a decisive argument, and he was not wrong in doing so. It must be mentioned, however, that his plans were by no means to the liking of the Duc de Bligny, who considered that, as M. Moulinet had amassed so fine a fortune, he ought only to think of letting his son-in-law enjoy it. In fact, at the first opportunity that presented itself, Gaston spoke his mind in the semi-impertinent, familiar style which he habitually adopted when addressing his wife's father.

"What wasp has stung you, that you want to plunge into politics?" he asked. "Don't you think that public affairs are bad enough as it is? It is really most singular that quiet folks always want to rush into a scuffle? Do you know the electors might be fools enough to return you?"

"But, my dear Duke, I hope they will."

"Well, we'll see what it will cost you."

"What can that matter to you?"

"It matters a great deal to me. I married an only daughter, and now you give her a sister."

"A sister?"

"Certainly; a sister called Politics, and a sister who will have a great many children, too—all your touters, agents, assistants, protectors and defenders, without counting the electors, who will vie in squeezing money out of you. Heaven knows where it will stop!"

Moulinet made a majestic gesture, and clapped his hand to his waistcoat pocket, a deplorable habit he was never able to get rid of. "My means allow me to have whatever fancies

I choose," said he. "I am only sixty years old, and I might keep ballet-girls if I pleased——"

"Oh! I shouldn't consider it a crime. That's a folly I can understand. A little foot, a dainty ankle, a slim waist in a golden circlet, like the gipsies wear in the ballet in *Faust*, and a pair of black or blue eyes looking over the stalls in search of you—all that's very nice and pleasant. If you would like me to introduce you into the dancing *foyer* at the Opera, I'll do so. But the idea of paying court to Marianne,* offering her flowers and making her an allowance! Come, you positively distress me, Monsieur Moulinet! You had far better choose the ballet-girls."

"I'm sorry to displease you, my dear Duke, but I'm a man of moral principles. I profer politics——"

"Well, I wish you joy; but tell me, if you are elected, do you mean to speak?"

"Very probably I shall."

"Indeed! It will be amusing. I shall take my friends to hear you. But, at all events, try not to become a minister. You would end by compromising me."

However, Moulinet treated his son-in-law's banter with contempt, and steadily proceeded with his plans. In fact, early in the spring he arrived at La Varenne, and at once began working the electors vigorously.

At about the same time that the Marchioness returned to Beaulieu Suzanne came home from the convent. Claire had had some little influence in this latter respect. Mademoiselle Derblay's arrival imparted more animation to the house, and the relations of husband and wife improved, at least in appearance. Philippe had to act a part in Suzanne's presence and show himself affectionate towards his wife. He accom-

* The slang name by which French Royalists designate the Republic.—*Trans.*

plished this most skilfully, so that not even the faintest suspicion was aroused in his young sister's candid mind. She thought that her brother was completely happy. As for Claire, she did not recognise her. So proud and morose as Mademoiselle de Beaulieu, she was now simple and lively. Suzanne began to love her sister-in-law very dearly, and Claire treated the young girl with the solicitude of a mother and the gentle affection of a friend. Claire's youth, which had momentarily suffered from the effects of anxiety, care, and grief, now started off afresh, as vigorously as the sap of a young tree. The two sisters did not leave each other. As soon as Suzanne returned to Pont-Avesnes she resumed her visits to the workmen's dwellings, and Claire accompanied her like some good fairy. Taking the money which Philippe had left with her, she expended it in relieving the poor folks of the district. She and Suzanne were constantly to be met on the highways round about Pont-Avesnes, both of them simply attired and followed by Philippe's big brown dog, and every one who met them bowed to them. In a few months Claire became the idol of the labouring classes. At the time of her marriage there had been considerable talk of her in all the surrounding cottages. She was in fact well known to the workfolks of Pont-Avesnes. They had often seen her ride by on horseback, indifferent to surroundings, absorbed in thoughts of the Duke, and carelessly touching her veiled hat with the knob of her riding-whip whenever she was bowed to. It was said that she was very proud, and among themselves the workmen, somewhat spitefully, perhaps, called her "The Marchioness" like her mother. And "The Marchioness" she remained, though in another sense, even when she had become Madame Derblay. To these rough miners and iron-forgers she seemed to come of a superior race. Her skin was so white, her figure so refined, and she looked so elegant even in her plain dark woollen dress, that when she passed through Pont-Avesnes or stood on the threshold of some homestead, she seemed a young queen to all who saw her. However, she was not only worshipped: she was loved as well.

In the month of July Octave arrived at Beaulieu, and then some delightful excursions began. The two sisters-in-law installed themselves in a little basket carriage, which Claire drove skilfully enough. The Marquis followed on horseback, and they wended their way through the woods of Pont-Avesnes. The tall trees formed a dark verdant vault over their heads; on each side sprang the fresh green grass interspersed with briars and dotted with woodland flowers. The vehicle slowly followed the ruts caused by the heavy carts of the wood merchant who had bought the "cut" of the year. At times it was necessary to alight. Octave pushed the chaise from behind whilst Suzanne led the horse by the bridle; and the young man's mare followed Claire like a pet lamb, looking at her with big moist eyes, and extending her neck as if to ask for the customary lump of sugar.

These were happy days, and Claire forgot her sadness. But at night-time when she found herself alone in her spacious room, a feeling of discouragement came over her again. She had broken her life and beyond all remedy. She was now sufficiently acquainted with Philippe to understand that he would never return to her. He was faithful to the pact concluded between them. He had given her back her liberty, and she disposed of it as she pleased. Ah! how joyfully she would have sacrificed it to him. Proud and impulsive as she was, she had met with more than her match, and it was with a kind of bitter pleasure that she acknowledged she was mastered. A man had come who had laid his hand on her shoulder and bent her; and he it was whom she loved now, for the very fact that he had made her feel the power of his will.

During the long hours she spent alone she bitterly reproached herself for not having been able to discern prior to her marriage what a superior man Philippe really was. She now saw what a high position he occupied. She was constantly discovering with astonishment some fresh source of his wealth. Before Suzanne returned to Pont-Avesnes she had been quite ignorant of the existence of the foundry he owned in the Nivernais. But having skilfully questioned her sister-in-law, she learnt with surprise that her husband was on the high road to becoming one of the princes of industry—that great power of the century. She felt ashamed of herself. What! she had offered her fortune to a man like him, as a compensation for the wrong she had done him? What was her fortune absorbed in the ironmaster's huge capital? A drop of water in a lake. She realised how odious and ridiculous her pride had been. She judged that Philippe could only feel contempt for her, and at this idea she was oppressed with bitter sorrow. Still she managed to hide it, following her husband's example with admirable strength of mind.

On the other hand, the love she now felt for Philippe became apparent in many little things. Her face lighted up whenever he approached her. She constantly looked at him, and invariably did whatever she thought would please him. Suzanne proved a precious auxiliary in this, the by-play of love. One afternoon, on the terrace, just after lunch, as Mademoiselle Derblay was amusing herself by passing a blade of grass across Claire's neck, the latter caught her by the shoulders and drew her towards her. Philippe was seated hard by, sipping a cup of coffee and carelessly watching some starlings who pursued each other with shrill cries. Claire took her sister-in-law's head in her hands and looked at her with beaming eyes. Then suddenly she heaved a sigh, and pressing her lips to the curls which fell over Suzanne's forehead, "Dear girl," she murmured, "how like your brother you are."

Philippe heard her and started. This was the first time that anything so much to the point had sped from Claire's heart to his own. He remained for a moment motionless, and then, abruptly rising, he walked off without saying a word. Madame Derblay wiped away a tear which was pearling in her eyes, while Suzanne threw herself into her arms with frenzied affection as it were. "You are crying," she said, "you are crying! What is the matter! Come, tell me! You know how much I love you. Has Philippe done anything to hurt you? It must have been unconsciously, and a word, no doubt, would—— Come, shall I speak to him?"

"No, no," answered Claire, trying to smile. "I am only a little out of sorts. But Philippe is perfect. And I, I am very happy," she added seriously, looking into Suzanne's eyes, as if to convince her all the more. Then rising to her feet, "Let us go for a stroll," she gaily said. And they went off into the park, running after each other like two mad schoolgirls and laughing as if nothing had happened.

This was one of the last relatively happy days that Claire spent. On the morrow the Duke and Duchesse de Bligny arrived at La Varenne. Claire felt annoyed on hearing of their presence in the neighbourhood. She had hoped that she would never see them again. She remarked that Philippe looked at her more attentively than usual, and she at once endeavoured to retain a calm, impassive countenance. That same evening, as soon as Suzanne had retired, the ironmaster spoke to his wife respecting the connection they should keep up with the inmates of La Varenne.

"The Duc de Bligny is your nearest relative after your brother," he said quietly. "There has been no apparent rupture between him and your family. At the time of our marriage you even endeavoured to keep the connection on a good footing. I don't think it would be wise to alter that line of conduct now. My opinion is that if the Duke and Duchesse de Bligny call here we ought to receive them as your relatives—that is, as well as we can. If we close our doors to them we shall expose ourselves to all sorts of commentaries, which for my own part I should like to avoid. Still I don't presume to *impose* my views on you. You are more interested in the question than any one else. Pray tell me your opinion, and I will act in accordance with it."

Claire remained for a moment silent. It seemed to her as if the return of the Duke and Athénaïs betokened some great peril. She had a presentiment that complete irremediable misfortune would enter the house in their train. At one moment she was on the point of speaking, of opening her heart to Philippe, of begging him to spare her, perhaps; but her courage failed her, and she blindly accepted his decision.

"You are right," she said. "They must be fittingly received. I must thank you for accepting this constraint. The Duke's presence will be as painful to me as to you. I trust you will not doubt it."

Philippe made a sign which meant neither yes nor no, and the conversation ended.

XIII.

The Duke did not instal himself at La Varenne of his own accord. He detested the country like a true Parisian, and all the verdure he cared for was furnished by the plane-trees on the Boulevards and the chestnut-trees in the Champs-Elysées. His chief attraction was his club, where he passed his afternoons and the better part of his evenings. He was in nowise of a contemplative nature and he hated reading.

When his father-in-law proudly led him into the conservatories of La Varenne and showed him the superb collection of orchids which his gardener, a man whom he treated with deference, had begun to form at great expense, the Duke glanced carelessly at the symmetrical rows of flower-pots and just muttered, "Very pretty." Then plucking one of the marvellous flowers from its stem, he set it in his button-hole. The gardener was thunderstruck when he saw this flower culled so unceremoniously, for it had only been produced at great cost and by dint of great care, and in his amazement he let a pot of begonia he was about to show slip through his fingers on to the tiles. Then giving Moulinet a stern glance, he walked out of the conservatory.

"Do you know that flower has cost fifteen louis?" remarked the ex-judge of the Tribunal of Commerce with a smile.

"Ah!" said the Duke quietly. "Well, all the same, I don't find it too dear for me."

Moulinet looked askance at his son-in-law, but he did not dare to say anything. The fact is, he feared the Duke. He was always put out of countenance by the manner in which Gaston seemed to take his measure whenever he looked at him. One evening in Paris, now long ago, he had said to young Maître Escande, the notary, "Do what we will, the nobles will always be our superiors." And in point of fact, although he had tendencies towards equality especially since beginning his electoral campaign, he by no means felt on a level with the Duke.

As the conservatories had produced no effect, he trusted to succeed better with the stables, where he had a dozen saddle and carriage horses installed, which his head coachman pronounced to be perfect, and for which he had paid accordingly. The stables of La Varenne are really magnificent. They are built of brick in the Mauresque style, which proved particularly pleasing to the ex-commercial judge. Whenever he spoke of them he was in the habit of remarking, "They are very like the Alhambra and the new College Chaptal in Paris," thus grotesquely establishing a parallel between the marvel of Granada and a nineteenth-century educational establishment. But to return to La Varenne. The courtyard, which is more than a couple of hundred yards across, is surrounded on its four sides by a range of buildings comprising the stables proper, the coachhouse, the harness-room, and the forage-store. A monumental entrance, with stone pillars adorned with horses' heads in bronze, conducts into the courtyard. Arcades run round the buildings, forming a paved promenade three yards wide. A wooden palisade, painted white and of a convenient height for leaning against, separates these arcades from the central space, where the horses are turned out and trotted up and down.

The Duchess, who was arrayed in a robe of *foulard*, with a collar of Venetian point, and who carried a large red parasol in her jewelled hand, accompanied her father and her husband on their visit to the stables. She set her little shoes on the plaited straw borders of the litters and looked at the horses, installed in separate boxes, above which a plate had been fixed for inscribing each animal's name. The stables met with the Duke's approval, but he looked very coldly at the horses themselves. The head coachman touted in vain for compliments. At the first glance the Duke noted each animal's defects, and the result of his remarks was that M. Moulinet indulged in some very serious reflections. In the evening there was a thorough explanation, from which it resulted that M. Moulinet's son-in-law was too good a judge of horseflesh for animals worth eighteen hundred francs to be palmed off henceforth by the coachman on his master at the price of six thousand. The Duke expressed his opinion in a manner which won him the coachman's full esteem. "Rob your master, my good fellow," said he, "it's only natural; but for heaven's sake let him have decent animals."

Having shown the Duke his conservatories and his stables with equal failure, the ex-judge of the Tribunal of Commerce found that he had nothing more to entertain him with. In the society of his wife and M. Moulinet Gaston soon began to feel intensely weary. He preferred solitude to their company, and each afternoon, as soon as lunch was over, he shut himself up in the smoking-room, where, stretched on the broad leather divan, he slept at ease. After a week of this life, feeling he could support it no longer, and conscious that if he remained at La Varenne he should end by treating his wife and father-in-law with unbecoming impertinence, he had just resolved to tell them that a pressing engagement summoned him to Trouville, when Athénaïs suddenly suggested calling on the Derblays at Pont-Avesnes. The proposal surprised the Duke, and at the first moment it displeased him. He had gradually forgotten Claire, but he remembered the ironmaster well enough. He cared little or nothing for the wife, but he harboured highly vindictive feelings against the husband. Why so? it may be asked. He would have been greatly embarrassed to reply. Perhaps it was because Philippe had assisted Claire in publicly inflicting an affront upon him. Perhaps because the ironmaster was just the reverse of himself. At all events he instinctively disliked the man whom he still familiarly called "the blacksmith."

On the other hand he felt some little curiosity as to the result of this marriage which had been decided on in so strange a fashion; and after all it did not need much pressing to induce him to accompany his father-in-law and his wife on the occasion of their visit to the Derblays. He said to himself, "My journey to Trouville will only be postponed for a day, and I shall be able to show some deference to poor Claire. I at least owe her that." He pitied her; and he had indeed formed a very strange idea of the life which the woman he had intended to marry now led. He pictured her to himself as having become narrowminded and precise, entirely absorbed in business cares. A little more and he would have imagined his proud cousin keeping her husband's books, with black *percaline* sleeve-protectors on her arms.

He had only seen Pont-Avesnes in the darkness of the night, and he was astonished when in the full sunlight he now beheld the spacious court of honour with its elegant *parterre à la Française*, and noted the severe and imposing aspect of the château. The servants seemed to him remarkably well mannered, with nothing provincial about them. The drawing-rooms displayed themselves in all their luxurious splendour, and he was obliged to confess to himself that M. Derblay's household was mounted in first-rate style.

He felt disturbed when Claire appeared. She seemed no longer the same. Not that she was more beautiful than when he had known her, but she was so very different: simple and grave, with an imposing gleam in her eyes which impressed him. On the other hand M. Derblay was too prepossessing not to displease the Duke, who for the first time noticed that the ironmaster wore the ribbon of the Legion of Honour. Bligny suddenly became thoughtful. He spoke but little, though appropriately enough, and it was owing to this unintentional reserve of his that he did not on this occasion awaken Philippe's suspicions. On the road back to La Varenne the Duke was remarkably taciturn; but at dinner he proved exceedingly gay, talking with febrile loquacity, bantering M. Moulinet in a good-humoured style, and altogether showing himself the best son-in-law in the world. His apathy had suddenly left him, and on the morrow he no longer thought of speaking about the pressing engagement which called him to Trouville.

On the contrary, he secluded himself more than ever in the smoking-room, only he no longer fell asleep there. Stretched on the divan, he passed his afternoons smoking a number of those Oriental cigarettes which are so conducive to reverie. He watched the smoke rise slowly in blue spirals towards the ceiling as if he were looking for some ethereal vision in the midst of the revolving circles. In the subdued light of the room he fancied he could perceive the face of Claire, just as he had recently seen her. He closed his eyes, and yet he saw her still.

The vision disturbed him, and, to escape it, he tried outdoor exercise. He selected the best of the horses which M. Moulinet had paid such a high price for but which were worth so little, had it saddled, and letting the reins fall loosely on the animal's neck, he rode into the park. It was four o'clock in the afternoon, and vague sounds began to pervade the wood. The rabbits bounded through the underbrush, making the leaves rustle, and from time to time some frightened magpie flew screeching from the summit of a lofty oak-tree, beating the air with its short wings. The day had been a very hot one, but now the delicious freshness of evening settled over the wood. Delightful perfumes rose from the grassy ground, and as the sun sank to rest on the western horizon it darted golden rays through the forest foliage. The Duke shook off his growing torpor and spurred his horse into a gallop. Without noticing it he had passed the boundary of the park, and he was now careering through the forest. Still and ever the charming vision which haunted his mind seemed to fly before him, impelling him onward. At last he reached the edge of the cultivated plain. Beyond, he perceived a long low wall, on which rested the weighty drooping branches of thickset trees, with a spacious clearing, bounded by a deep ditch, in their midst. The Duke mechanically turned in this direction. A large expanse of grass was stretched before him, and beyond it rose up a vast white pile. He started: he had just recognised the château of Pont-Avesnes.

Thus fate brought him back to the woman whom he sought to fly from. Could it be that destiny really meant to unite those whom it had separated?

Bligny began to smile. He recollected what he had said to the Baron on the wedding-night: "Since Vulcan's time blacksmiths have been unlucky," though, on the other hand, he forgot Préfont's warning anent the blacksmith's hammer.

But, after all, fear was scarcely calculated to turn the Duke from one of his fancies. He set his horse at a trot again, and having taken a final decision, he returned to La Varenne with his mind eased.

The Duke's new intentions were eminently calculated to disturb the ironmaster's peace. Between Philippe's frigid gravity and Gaston's insidious attentions Claire would find herself greatly embarrassed, if not in a situation of serious danger. It was evident enough that the ironmaster had an afterthought when he treated Gaston with such quiet cordiality. It would have been easy for him to have gradually kept his wife's relatives at an increasing distance, and to have limited the intimacy which declared itself during the first days to a simple neighbourly good understanding. Philippe was not easily influenced, and, as a rule, whatever he decided upon was rigidly carried out. Thus if he gave way so unresistingly to the insinuating amiability which the Duke and the Duchess displayed, it must have been that it suited his plans to let them have the run of his house. During the long hours which Philippe had spent at his wife's bedside when she was in peril of her life, he had carefully examined the many events which had preceded his marriage. He realised how mercilessly Athénaïs had revenged herself on her rival, and he allotted the Duchess her due share of responsibility. The more guilty he found her, the more disposed he was to excuse Claire. Still he considered it was necessary that he should not abandon the rigour with which he had so far treated her.

The struggle they had engaged in must end by his victory. He must expose proud Claire to some decisive trial, so as to wash away for ever the undeserved affront she had inflicted upon him. He foresaw that Athénaïs was destined to play a part in this dangerous game. The battle would be fought on the one side between the Duchess and Claire, on the other between the Duke and himself. He realised that it would be a bitter, desperate warfare, replete with perfidious ambuscades and redoubtable surprises. Maybe its only issue would be a man's death—his own or Gaston's. Still Philippe did not hesitate. After all, what had he to lose? His future was compromised; his happiness was already lost. It was to his advantage to risk the game. Only he was prudent as well as resolute, and he determined to take every precaution in view of assuring success. He could not ostensibly defend Claire, and as it would be dangerous to leave her to her own resources, he thought of providing her with a faithful ally. He invited the Baronne de Préfont and her husband to come and spend a few weeks at Pont-Avesnes. The respective forces being thus balanced and the parties in presence of each other, one had only to wait for the engagement.

Almost as soon as the Duchesse de Bligny arrived at La Varenne, it was easy to see that she intended to revolutionise this quiet little provincial district. La Varenne became the joyful scene of the numerous fêtes which Athénaïs gave by way of signalising her presence. Although she was but a newcomer in the district, she had the ambition of becoming its uncontested sovereign, by dint of lavish display, vivacity, and eccentricity. She brought two of her usual followers from Paris—fat La Brède and little Du Tremblays, the two most brilliant trotters of her famous "six-in-hand." "La Brède and Du Tremblays," she said with a laugh, "will be quite enough for the country. I'll harness them in posting fashion, and with plenty of bells to jingle folks will fancy that they are more numerous."

In point of fact these bosom associates were tame enough when taken separately, but combined they met with surprising success. They reminded one of the saying that two negatives make an affirmative. They had arrived from Paris with all the necessary paraphernalia for a *cotillon*, lawn tennis, and polo among their luggage, and, as if the demon which possesses the Parisians had journeyed down in one of their portmanteaus, they had no sooner reached La Varenne than life became extremely "hot" and fast there. Besançon provided the Duchess with an orchestra of ten musicians, for every Saturday there was dancing at the château. The young bloods of the Jura learned with mingled stupefaction and delight that Madame de Bligny intended to amuse the whole province. Berlines and britzkas and *chars-à-bancs*, the most singular specimens of the carriage-builder's art, often dating from the times of the Restoration, poured forth from all the neighbouring châteaux and rolled with a wonderful creaking of wheels along the road to La Varenne. The ruddy-faced petty nobles, whose muscles were as hard as their mountain rocks, eagerly took to propelling the tennis-balls, to galloping over the lawns at polo, knocking each other on the head with their sticks, and to waltzing far into the night with indefatigable vigour.

"I say, Duchess, your provincials come of a good stock," cried fat La Brède. "They lift their dancers like feathers, and never rest. I've half a mind to take a few of them to Paris for the winter season; they'd put some spirit into our *cotillons*, and I fancy they'd be eagerly sought for in the market."

"Yes," said little Du Tremblays; "but the misfortune is, that these muscular, full-blooded provincials generally don't get on in Paris. After six months or so they lose their colour and have less strength left than the Parisians themselves. They are not a race to be acclimatised."

Whilst the two friends thus gravely studied the rearing of provincial dancers, the ten musicians filled the drawing-rooms of La Varenne with harmony. Careless of other people's opinions, and disdainful of criticism, the youth of Besançon danced with a fervour that made Moulinet's very heart rejoice. The ex-judge of the Tribunal of Commerce became radiant when he saw his daughter throw the aristocratic society of his electoral district into such commotion, and in his capacity as a candidate he remarked to himself, "So many guests, so many electors." Accordingly he urged the Duchess on by opening an unlimited credit in her favour. And while the wives and daughters danced, he undertook to win the fathers and husbands. One thing certainly worried him. Neither the Prefect nor the General commanding Besançon had showed themselves at the evening parties of La Varenne. Perhaps the representative of the Home Office found the society too aristocratic. As for the commander of the troops, he had just been reprimanded for having allowed the garrison to present arms to the Bishop at a public procession, and he no doubt considered it prudent not to show his uniform in the Duchess's drawing-rooms.

"What does it matter if the Prefect doesn't come, providing the people he is set over vote for you," said Athénaïs to Moulinet, who had expressed his anxiety. "Have him attacked in the *Courrier*, papa; have some stupid story told about him. Shall I get La Brède to concoct an article? It would be rather funny. As for the General, he's a nullity; his troops don't vote."

Athénaïs had an annoyance of her own, and a far more serious one than her father's. Madame Derblay had asked to be excused from attending the Saturday receptions. She declared that she was not yet well enough to sit up late.

Now in point of fact, the Duchess had only given these fêtes with the view of compelling Claire to witness them, and she could ill conceal the rage which her rival's absence caused her. She had fits of petulance and ill-humour which affected the gaiety of those about her. She had promised herself such delightful pleasure, but it was all lost since she could not crush her rival with her magnificence, stab her with a thousand daggers by appearing on the arm of the man she was to have married, or see her shiver each time that she—Athénaïs—was addressed as "Madame la Duchesse." Madame de Bligny's hatred would perhaps have been quieted by the spectacle of Claire's humiliation, by the spectacle of the tortures she endured; but it increased in the presence of her resistance and at sight of the haughty calmness of her brow.

Claire came on one occasion to dine at La Varenne, and conducted herself most skilfully. The petulant, imperious Duchess appeared as she really was by the side of this dignified, elegant woman—that is, as an unmannerly young person, who said and did whatever came into her head with the vulgar audacity of an opulent parvenu. The difference between the two was at once apparent, and all the advantage rested on Claire's side. Athénaïs divined that such was the case, and swore that she would have a terrible revenge. This young woman, with such glossy black hair, such a charming face, such bright eyes, and such an engaging smile, was in point of fact one of the most perverse beings to be found on earth. If she could only have been sure of impunity, she would have been quite capable of throwing vitriol in Claire's face, so as to permanently disfigure her, and burn out those lovely eyes so soft and pure, but in which she herself read so much disdain. The Duchess was especially irritated by the good understanding which apparently prevailed between Monsieur and Madame Derblay. The husband showed himself gracious, loving, and attentive; the wife gave every token of deference and affection. There was no mistaking Claire's smile when Philippe was near her and gave her the protection of his presence: she loved him, and no doubt she was loved in return. How could the ironmaster help adoring such a perfect being, uniting in her person so much physical grace and moral beauty? And, besides, had he not married her for love?—overriding all the humiliating strangeness of the situation, accepting a woman who was ruined, and who had been forsaken by the Duke? Yes, he had done all that, simply and quietly, happy to be able to possess her as if she were some rare and precious treasure!

So thus it was Claire's destiny to be always loved, whilst fate had decided that Athénaïs should never inspire a man with real affection. She was courted, no doubt, but what was drawing-room gallantry, flattery, and flirtation, what were the passing caprices she kindled, in comparison with the sincere, deep, unchangeable love which Claire had the power of inspiring?

In her jealous rage Athénaïs began to devote particular attention to M. Derblay. With the view of pleasing him she put on a serious face, and managed to monopolise him for a part of the evening. She found him really very good-looking. With his brown face tanned by the sun, his black hair cropped very short, and his big dark eyes, he was not unlike an Arab. Athénaïs suddenly felt very much disturbed; no man had ever inspired her with such feelings before, and she thought to herself that if she were really capable of falling in love with any one it would certainly be with Philippe. At the thought of the grief that she might thus cause Claire her eyes brightened, and she allowed her usual coquettish tendencies full play, with a readiness and a vivacity that surprised even herself. She was filled with diabolical joy when she saw Claire become gloomy and restless, and watch the little game she was playing with a look of anguish. Athénaïs could read on her rival's brow how much she suffered, and she realised that she had found the flaw in Claire's armour which would enable her to deal a mortal blow.

In point of fact, Philippe's attitude was that of a well-mannered man who finds himself flatteringly distinguished by the mistress of the house. He met the Duchess's marked advances with perfect ease, let her take his arm to stroll through the drawing-rooms, and talked to her gracefully and pleasantly. He was just sufficiently attentive to seem an agreeable companion, and just cold enough to prevent any one from saying that he had conducted himself with the Duchess differently from what he would have done with any other woman. And yet, despite all his power of self-control, an attentive observer would have detected that he was really much upset. Whilst the Duchess, curvetting like a young peacock, took possession of him and showed him the drawing-rooms and the conservatories, he had seen Bligny glide gently towards Claire, lean over the back of her arm-chair, and speak to her with a smile on his face. It was the first time he had seen Gaston and Claire together, exchanging their thoughts beyond hearing. He quivered, and a burning flush rose to his brow. For a moment he suffered so cruelly that his arm stiffened, and he involuntarily pressed the Duchess's hand to his side. She looked at him with astonishment. They were in a little conservatory which M. Moulinet called "the tropics," and where numerous deadly plants of Africa and the Indies were reared in a moist heated atmosphere.

"What is the matter?" asked the Duchess, as she lightly pressed her cavalier's arm with her fingers by way of return; and as she spoke she smiled.

"The strong scent of these plants and the heat of the conservatory have oppressed me," answered the ironmaster, who was already calm again. "Let us return to the drawing-room, if agreeable to you." And, with the Duchess still on his arm, he walked slowly back to the drawing-room, keeping his eyes on the Duke and Claire, who were still conversing together.

Immediately after dinner Gaston had taken most of his masculine guests into the smoking-room, where he had placed a varied collection of cigars and cigarettes at their disposal. At the end of half an hour, however, he declared that he must attend to his duties as a host, and abandoned the smokers to themselves in the midst of a thick cloud. He was anxious to approach Claire, but being acquainted with her impulsive, quick-tempered character, he did not venture upon a front attack. Besides, he felt ill at ease with her, and audacious as he was, he hesitated to speak, for he realised that the first words he addressed to her would have decisive influence on their subsequent relations. Perhaps abstention would have been the better policy, so as to have allowed time to consolidate the ground before venturing upon it; but Bligny had reached such a degree of cynical egotism that he could not delay satisfying whatever fancy seized him. So he stepped forward, talking to his friends, pausing for a short time near the different ladies who were present, and gradually lessening the circle which he described round Claire, as if he had been some bird of prey. At last he found himself just behind her. He took a step forward, and leaning towards her and inhaling the warm perfume of her person, "Do you feel quite well to-night?" he asked in a caressing voice. "I come in trembling to inquire after you, for I fear it is my misfortune that you cannot see me without displeasure."

Claire turned quickly round and looked the Duke full in the face. "And why should I see you with displeasure?" she boldly asked. "Should I have come here if I were influenced by the feelings you ascribe to me."

The Duke shook his head in a melancholy manner. "This is the first time since your marriage that we are able to speak freely," he rejoined, "and I can see very well that we are not going to tell each other the truth. Having behaved so badly towards you, it will be the grief of my life not to be able to explain to you the reasons which might perhaps induce you to absolve me."

"But you have no need of absolution, believe me," said Claire quietly. "Have I ever reproached you? And do you really think that you deserve reproaches? Let me tell you that it would be a sign of strange conceit on your part."

"You ease my conscience of a very heavy weight," rejoined the Duke. "My marriage was one of the fatal consequences of Parisian life. I found myself one day in such a situation that I had to choose between my happiness and my honour. I had two debts to pay, but in acquitting myself of one of them I had to leave the other outstanding. I sacrificed my love to save my name. That is what I wished to tell you, Claire."

"In other words, Monsieur Moulinet helped you out of embarrassment, and in your gratitude you married his daughter —with a dowry of several millions! Come, Duke, that is pleasant penitence, as the song says; and besides, if I understand you rightly, you were sustained in this trial by the consciousness that you had done your duty. So you must be very happy, and I am delighted to hear it."

The Duke started, as if stung by these ironical words. "And you," he asked abruptly, "are *you* happy?"

"You are the very person who has no right to ask me such a question," Claire answered proudly.

At the same moment the Duchess re-entered the drawing-room with Philippe. The Duke jerked his head, as if to call Claire's attention to Athénaïs, who was leaning on the ironmaster's arm, and seeing how pale and perturbed she became, he gave her an ironical look, and exclaimed, "You deserved to have been better loved." Then, having bowed, he slowly turned away.

Claire shuddered at the thought that the Duke had been able to divine her secret. Thus he doubted of the happiness she had endeavoured to make him believe in by dint of dissimulation. She foresaw what dangers she would be exposed to if the Duke made love to her. How could she continue her task of winning her husband's affection? How could she prevent her husband from resenting the Duke's attentions? And with this dangerous assailant to contend against, how would she be able to fight the Duchess, whom she already pictured as subjugating Philippe with her audacious coquetry? She resolved to fly from the house, and making a sign to her husband, who at once came to her, she asked him to have the carriage sent for. Then, curtailing Athénaïs's caressing protestations and bowing coldly to the Duke, she led Philippe from the drawing-room as precipitately as if the château had been on fire.

When they were in their brougham, rolling along the road in the clear, balmy night air, Claire fancied she was saved. She did not fear to question Philippe, and turning towards him, she asked, "How did you find the Duchess?"

"Charming," answered Philippe carelessly.

The young wife shrank back into her corner with a gesture of mortification which was hidden from her husband by the darkness. The word alone had struck her; she had not noted the tone of utter indifference in which it was uttered. "We'll not go to La Varenne again," thought Claire to herself, "I should suffer too much."

At the same moment Philippe, who was absorbed in reverie saw—vision-like, as it were—the Duke leaning forward near Claire, and with a perfidious smile whispering tender words in her ear. The ironmaster's throat became dry, a threatening light gleamed from his eyes, and he clenched his strong fists with very rage.

They did not go to La Varenne again; but a fortnight later they returned the dinner they had partaken of, inviting M. Moulinet, the Duke, and the Duchess to Pont-Avesnes; after which they constantly declined their neighbours' repeated invitations. In her exasperation Athénaïs began to consider that there was no "go" left in La Brède, and no inventive power in Du Tremblays. It was without the least pleasure that she waltzed with the gentlemen-farmers of the neighbourhood. In vain did Moulinet distinguish himself at the flower-show of La Varenne, whereof he managed to obtain the chairmanship, by delivering a speech which sent more than half of his audience to sleep, and provoked discreet merriment among everybody else. There were fireworks, a joust with lances on the river, and a solemn crowning of *rosières*,* the whole enlivened with the sonorous strains of a Besançon society of musicians called "La Lyre." The gay, noisy, tiring life which Athénaïs usually appreciated so much was still led; but now nothing could satisfy her.

* Young girls who are rewarded for their virtue and good conduct with crowns of honour and modest marriage portions.—*Trans.*

Madame Derblay was not there to be crushed by the sight of her triumphs.

The old Marchioness, perched on the heights of Beaulieu like a lonely, forlorn turtle-dove, had not once set her feet in the abode of her niece by marriage. People were, moreover, beginning to remark the continued absence of M. and Madame Derblay. Considerable tittle-tattle was indulged in, and when the Baronne de Préfont, who possessed such a long tongue, arrived at Claire's residence, Athénaïs foresaw that the neighbours would soon begin to believe that La Varenne and Pont-Avesnes had quarrelled. The ice, which was accumulating in threatening blocks between the two households, must be broken at any cost; and the only thing that could draw them in a measure together again was some general entertainment, some almost public gathering, to which all the good society of the neighbourhood would be invited.

It was La Brède who, like all inspired men, unintentionally furnished the Duchess with the occasion she was longing for. He suggested a mounted paper-chase through the woods of La Varenne and Pont-Avesnes. The civil and military authorities should be asked to attend. The officers of the garrison of Besançon would receive invitations, and everybody would follow the hunt on horseback or in carriages as they pleased. A monster lunch would be provided at the Rond-Point des Etangs; in one word, the whole affair would be such a fête that even the newspapers of Paris would talk about it.

The scheme was worthy of a man of genius, and in her delight Athénaïs almost embraced La Brède. Setting the whole household to work tearing up bits of paper, and bidding her father attend to the general invitations, the Duchess betook herself in person to Pont-Avesnes, whence she returned with a radiant face, for she had obtained a favourable reply.

XIV.

The Rond-Point des Etangs lies at the edge of the woods of Pont-Avesnes and of those of La Varenne. A succession of meres, full of rushes and waterplants, with large leaves and shiny stems, which stretch over the surface of the water like serpents asleep, extends for five or six hundred yards around, and has given the spot its name. The lower branches of the oak-trees droop as if thirsting for the freshness of the water, and the leaves which have fallen each autumn, decaying and rotting on the banks, have formed a thick slime wherein the wild-boars roll with delight at early morning. A high palisade, painted white, and shutting off the forest roads in ordinary times, encloses an open space some two hundred yards across, which is covered with grass as soft as velvet. Huge beech-trees with thick foliage rise up round about and cast their refreshing shade over the grass. Here meet eight roads edged with ruddy heather, each more than twenty yards broad, and extending in a straight line as far as the eye can reach through the woods. It is a spot full of silence and mystery. The sun plays over the water which, though it be somewhat ruffled by the breeze, serves as a mirror for the tranquil azure sky. On occasions of forest sport the site is excellent. Tired by the pursuit of the dogs, the deer come here to bathe their quivering limbs in the meres and imbibe fresh vigour. A skilful marksman, stationed on the bank behind one of the oaks, can readily find the coveted opportunity for crying, "Hallali!"* Sad to say, however, M. Moulinet was such a passionate admirer of nature that, impressed by the beauty of the site, he dishonoured it by erecting there a Chinese kiosk.

In the midst of the open space behold now a series of tables where footmen in full livery serve, and which are spread with every delectable dainty likely to stimulate the Duchess's guests for their long ride. For an hour or so La Brède, coupled with his faithful Du Tremblays, has been making way through the underwood, scattering scraps of paper to indicate the scent, extending his advance, constantly changing his direction, and preparing any number of false scents in the most conscientious and fatiguing manner. Cavaliers and dames and damsels on horseback, with breaks and caleches full of people, are arriving by all the roads conducting to the Rond-Point. The light toilettes of the ladies, who shade themselves with many-coloured parasols, the blue dolmans and the red trousers of the hussar officers from Besançon, stand out gaily against the dark foliage of the trees. The horses held by the green-coated keepers greedily stretch their necks towards the fresh grass; the stirrups clink as they strike against each other whenever the horses move; a clear neigh bursts forth from time to time, and the champagne corks pop gaily as the foam falls into the glasses.

Attired in a tight-bodied, short-skirted habit, and waving her riding-whip, the knob of which was adorned with a huge cat's-eye, in her gloved hand, Athénaïs was doing the honours of the forest to every new arrival with surprising gaiety, ease, and grace. The cushions of the Duke's mail-coach had been laid on the grassy banks, and here sat many of the ladies.

* The French hunting shout, whereby the death of the stag is announced.—*Trans.*

Moulinet, who was arrayed in a blue dress coat and pearl grey gloves, although it was only ten o'clock in the morning, was monopolising the Baron de Préfont, for whom he seemed to have conceived a most tyrannical affection. The Duke wore the English scarlet hunting coat, with buckskins and a black velvet cap adorned with a green bow—his colours, the field of his escutcheon being sinople. Philippe, as usual, wore a black coat, but he had donned a pair of grey velveteen breeches with leggings of the same tint. Claire and the Baroness were both attired in riding-habits of blue cloth, with felt hats adorned with black feathers, and they looked particularly charming—Madame de Préfont elegant, if somewhat short, and Claire tall and superb, with the outlines of her finely curved shoulders and perfect bust showing to great advantage ; Suzanne, whom Octave had served, was dipping a biscuit into a glass of Malaga and watching her mare, which her brother was paternally attending to, tightening the girth and examining the bit ; whilst Bachelin, having quietly unharnessed his horse, which served both for driving and riding purposes, was assisting his own keeper in fastening the saddle, which he had brought with him in his gig. The sun gilded the forest foliage and cast dazzling lustre upon the brilliant scene. The atmosphere was light and fresh. It was the kind of weather that makes life enjoyable.

"Monsieur Derblay!" suddenly cried Athénaïs, turning away from the much-desired Prefect, with whom she had been talking ; and as Philippe quietly approached her, without in the least degree hurrying himself, she added, "Don't you think it is time to start. Messieurs La Brède and Du Tremblays went off at least an hour ago with their scraps of paper, and if they have kept up a good pace, we shall need a hard gallop to catch them."

"*Mon Dieu*, Madame," answered Philippe, "I must own to you that I am but little acquainted with the rules of paper-chasing. I would rather not give an opinion. You would do better to apply to Pontac, who, as a master of wolfhounds, is no doubt well informed on the matter."

As he spoke, Philippe pointed out a tall young man, clad in a silver-braided hunting coat, with a three-cornered hat on his head, a dirk at his side, and a Dampierre horn over his shoulder. As if he had been only waiting for an opportunity to bring himself into notice, the Vicomte de Pontac at once advanced into the centre of the open space, and, bowing to Madame de Bligny with English-like stiffness, "Duchess," he said, "I am at your orders; and if you will grant me the management of the hunt, I will engage to finish with Messieurs La Brède and Du Tremblays before a couple of hours are over. Shall we sound to the saddle? I have my *piqueur* there—— Here! here! Bistocq!"

A big fellow in a braided coat and brown leather gaiters, with a red nose which was as conspicuous on his tanned face as a strawberry on dark soil, emerged from a group of servants, shambling over the ground and dragging after him a big, badly groomed, vicious-looking roan, whose bridle was passed over his arm. On arriving at half-a-dozen paces from M. de Pontac he stopped short, drew himself up in military fashion, saluted by raising his hand to the peak of his cap, and waited to be asked for his report.

"Do you wish to question him?" asked the Vicomte turning to the Duchess.

"Of course I do," replied Athénaïs, who was delighted with the solemnity of the scene.

"I say, dear," murmured the Baronne de Préfont to Claire, "just look at her. She gives herself the airs of a queen! And

Pontac plays his part as if it were all serious, though we are only going to follow a lot of scraps of paper. It's really amusing."

In the meantime Bistocq was giving his report. "The start will take place at the Héronnière," said he. "That's where the scent begins. There's a bit of paper there as large as my hand. We shan't need any 'find!' The gentlemen are no doubt afraid they won't be found easily enough. They might have left a whole newspaper while they were about it. The animals—I beg pardon, the gentlemen—went off straight through the wood, jumped the Pavé Neuf, took to the plain at the Vente-au-Sergent, came back into the forest at Belle-Empleuse, struck fresh ground at the foot of the hill of La Haie, started a false scent at La Boulottière——"

"Halt!" cried M. de Pontac with a laugh. "If we let you go on, you will give us the whole line of route from beginning to end."

"Perhaps I might," replied the *piqueur* with a knowing wink. "It isn't so easy for human beings to imitate stags except in a respect I won't mention."

The Duchess smiled and turned to Pontac. "He's a funny fellow that man of yours," said she. "Papa, give this good fellow a louis. Thanks to him, La Brède and Du Tremblays will have to cover a good deal of ground if they don't want to be speedily caught."

"Death on the run!" said Pontac. "Duchess, shall I sound the start?"

"Yes, please, Vicomte."

Pontac turned his horn round with his left hand so as to have the mouthpiece placed conveniently, stationed himself in the centre of the clearing, and puffing out his cheeks as if he wished to blow down all the trees in the forest, proceeded to awaken every echo with his deafening strains.

"My compliments, Vicomte," said the Duchess. "You possess a remarkable talent——"

"It is hereditary in my family," replied Pontac with dreamy gravity. "From father to son, for the last three centuries, we have all known how to play on the horn." And jerking his head as if he considered himself a superior being, the Vicomte walked towards his horse.

In a moment the whole gathering was in motion. The riders set their feet in the stirrups, while the sightseers who meant to follow in vehicles installed themselves on their cushions. A general impulse led the great mass of the throng to make at once for the wide avenues near the Héronnière. The horses started at a gallop, and the dull thuds of their hoofs over the moss and turf were already becoming more distant, like the triumphant horn-tooting which Bistocq indulged in as he guided the hunters with his big bony horse at a fast trot.

"Monsieur Derblay," said the Duchess with a smile, "as you know the district so well, would you be kind enough to be my guide? Let us allow the crowd to go on in front. You have a strong horse, and I also; we can cut through the forest and gain an advance."

"But, Duchess, haven't you Pontac, who would be able to escort you much better than I could?" replied Philippe.

"No, no," rejoined Madame de Bligny gaily. "You're the guide I want, unless you refuse to accompany me. But I don't think you capable of doing so."

The ironmaster bowed without replying. Claire, who was standing a few paces off, quivered with anger as she witnessed Athénaïs's audacity. Tears of anguish started to her eyes, and she convulsively pressed the arm of the stupefied Baroness.

"You will come with us, won't you?" asked the Duchess, turning towards Claire.

Madame Derblay gently lowered her head, and in a calm voice replied, "No, I presumed too much on my strength in thinking of following the hunt on horseback. I shall go with the carriage——" And at the same time Claire gave her husband a beseeching look, as if to induce him to remain with her.

"Shall you be displeased by my carrying your husband off?" asked Athénaïs with feigned solicitude. And then with a laugh she added, "Do you happen to be jealous, dear?"

"No," replied Claire, who was unwilling to acknowledge her grief and her helplessness so openly.

"Then to horse!" joyously cried Athénaïs, who was eager to complete her victory.

With a pang at her heart Claire watched her husband turn away, and at one moment she thought of calling to him and retaining him. "Philippe!" she cried.

The ironmaster at once turned round and came towards her. "What is the matter?" he asked. "Don't you feel well? Is there anything you wish for?"

No doubt, if the young wife had only spoken a single word, her husband would have remained with her, and perhaps many torments might thus have been spared them both. But Claire's pride, still stronger than her love, repressed the words of entreaty which were rising to her lips. She shook her head, and with a stern air, twitching lips, and a gesture of disdain, replied: "No. There is nothing the matter with me. I need nothing. You can go!"

Philippe turned away. At this moment Claire included him in the surging hatred she felt for Athénaïs. She was seized with one of those fits of rage which impel human beings to murder.

Setting her foot on the bank of the ditch, the Duchess had

raised her skirt so that her dainty boot was fully visible. Making a sign to M. Derblay, she showed him that her spur-strap had become unfastened. The ironmaster bent forward, and without a word re-affixed the leather strap garnished with little silver chains, and buckled it near the heel. As the Duchess leant upon him, she touched his shoulder with the knob of her riding-whip in a bold, provoking manner, as if to indicate that he belonged to her.

"Dear me, what does this mean?" muttered the Baroness. But on glancing at Claire, she saw her trembling so acutely and looking so pale that she did not dare to follow up her question.

With the assistance of Philippe's strong arms the Duchess sprang into her saddle. She caught up the reins, waved her hand proudly to her discomfited rival, and starting her horse at a gallop, made him leap the ditch which separated the clearing from the wood. Philippe followed, and a moment later they disappeared in the depths of the forest.

"Shall I remain with you?" murmured a soft voice near Claire, who stood rooted to the spot, overwhelmed as it were, as she gazed after the two riders until they vanished like her happiness. But on hearing these words she swiftly turned her head and found the Duke behind her. She stifled a cry of anger, and tearing off her gloves, "Leave me," said she, with a heavy brow and lowered eyes. "I wish to be alone." Then taking the Baroness's arm, she walked towards the meres, whilst the Duke turned his horse in the direction of the main body of his guests, being guided by the notes of the horn which resounded in the distance.

Careless of the chase, Octave and Suzanne were conversing as they strolled along the green bank of one of the meres. Their horses, tethered to the same tree, rubbed their necks

s

together in sympathising fashion, or tugged as well as their bits would allow them at the young green shoots. The Baron, abandoned to himself, had sat down in a secluded corner, and with a little hammer was breaking some mineralogical specimens he had picked up.

Meanwhile the Baroness and Claire reached M. Moulinet's Chinese kiosk, and sat down on one of the benches in front of it without exchanging a word. After all the noise and motion deep silence was now spreading through the wood. A light breeze shook the reeds, among which the dragon-flies scintillated as they passed and repassed in their uncertain flight. The Baroness raised her eyes and looked at her friend. Claire had recovered her self-possession, and such nervousness as remained was only indicated by a slight trembling of her lips. Fearing, however, that the sad truth had been divined by the Baroness, she had lowered her head and averted her eyes, and she sat there stirring the gravel with her foot, and striving to assume an air of indifference.

"Well! What does all this mean?" exclaimed Sophie, who was unable to restrain herself any longer. "I arrive at your house expecting to find biblical tranquillity, and I tumble into the midst of discussions and worries. Your husband gallops off with Athénaïs, and the Duke comes and humbly offers to keep you company——"

"It's like in a quadrille," said Claire, with a nervous laugh. "There is a change of partners."

The Baroness became grave, and taking hold of her cousin's hand, "Why do you try to deceive me?" she asked. "Do you think that I am so frivolous that I can't understand what is passing in your mind? Claire, you are not happy."

"I? Why, how can I help being happy? I live in the midst of luxury, noise, and animation. I have relatives who dearly love me, friends who surround me, a husband who leaves me my liberty. You know that this is what I dreamt of. So how can I be unhappy?"

"Ah, my dear, what you used to dream of now drives you to despair. Your husband leaves you your liberty, but he takes his own. And when you see him near anyone else, there is a pang at your heart. With your pride, you would like to deny it, but your grief betrays you. No, you are not happy; and you can't be happy, for you are jealous."

"I!" cried Claire in a tone of rage; and she burst into a painfully nervous laugh, which ended in a sob. Her eyes filled with tears, and, as her face flushed with shame, she threw herself into her friend's arms and wept most bitterly.

The Baroness let her ease her heart, which was so full of grief, but when she grew calmer, she wrung from her the sad secret of her rupture with Philippe. Madame de Préfont was stupefied. She realised how cruelly Claire was tortured, and she suspected as much concerning the ironmaster. She divined the horrible contrast which existed between their public and their private life. In presence of society a display, a semblance of gaiety and love; and then when there was no one to watch, silence, coldness, and solitude. These unfortunate beings played a part in public, and they were obliged to play it well. On thus becoming acquainted with the situation the Baroness had but one thought—that of trying to reconcile this husband and this wife who were so sadly estranged. First of all she was desirous of finding out everything that Claire had on her mind.

"But when your husband nursed you with such devotion," said she, "didn't you ever think of going to him and trying to unite the severed ties again?"

"Yes," answered Claire with a blush. "I don't know

what was passing in me, but I no longer felt the same. Was it gratitude for his devotion, or a better appreciation of his character, that drew me to him? At all events, when he was not there I involuntarily looked for him. When he was near me I did not raise my eyes to his face, and yet I saw him. He seemed so stern, so sad, that I did not dare speak to him. Oh! if he had only encouraged me!"

"And didn't he?"

"No; he is as proud as I am, and more resolute. Ah! There is nothing to hope for, and we are separated for ever."

"At all events, as far as I see, he doesn't seem to worry himself; and our charming little Duchesse Moulinet——"

"Oh! don't accuse Philippe," Claire interrupted hastily; "it is she who impudently throws herself at his head. She pursues me without relaxing. After my betrothed, my husband! What a triumph, is it not? And how can I tear him from her? What can I do to defend myself? Have I a right to do anything? Is he really mine?"

"Well, frankly, he's rather more yours than hers."

"Oh, let her take care!" exclaimed Claire in a violent tone. "I have suffered too much from her already. The longest patience has its limits; and if she drives me beyond these I don't know what I shall do, but it will be some act of madness which will prove the ruin of one or the other of us."

"Come, my dear, calm yourself. Now that I'm here to assist you, I promise you we'll master that delightful Athénaïs. She's a monopoliser, you see; it runs in the family. Her father used to lay his hands on all the sugar in the market, and her specialty seems to be husbands. She wants them all. Ah, how I should like to see her take it into her head to fascinate the Baron; how I should amuse myself!"

So saying, the Baroness called Claire's attention to M. de

Préfont, who was still at the same spot, delightfully employing the hours of waiting for the hunting party's return in picking up little stones and filling his pockets with them. Claire could not help smiling. A vision of Philippe passed before her eyes. Ah, he was no docile and patient retainer like the Baron, but an imperious and redoubtable master.

"We mustn't deceive ourselves," resumed the Baroness; "the situation is a serious one. If there could be an explanation, reconciliation would come easily enough; but by speaking you expose yourself to an unfavourable reception, and then good-night, there's no more hope; so we must proceed diplomatically. However, nothing will rid me of the idea that your husband adores you, but won't let you see it. Men like him only love once, and then for all their life. Have you ever looked at Monsieur Derblay attentively? I am sure that his nature is an obstinate one. He has a head to batter a wall with. With such a character as that you can only disarm him by humiliating yourself."

"Ah! I sha'n't hesitate to do so. I shall spare no effort to win him. But perhaps he would only look on my overtures as some fresh fancy?"

"For that very reason you must wait for a favourable opportunity before venturing to risk such an important engagement. If no opportunity shows itself, we'll devise one. But, for Heaven's sake, don't look so mournful and despairing. Our dear friend Athénaïs would only be too glad to see you looking like that. Recollect that other people consider you happy, so put on a semblance of happiness till you secure it in reality."

Claire heaved a sigh. She who was once so indomitable, who so flattered herself that she could overcome every obstacle, now doubted her power of will and strength of mind.

"It seems to me that we have been talking very seriously during the last half hour," said the Baroness. "This conjugal psychology has made my head feel heavy. If you are willing, we will have a little gallop; it will do us good. And besides, I should like to see what our lovely Duchesse Moulinet is doing with your husband. Will you come?"

"No," answered Claire gloomily. "I feel weary. I shall stay here. My brother and Suzanne don't seem any more disposed than myself to follow the hunt. They will keep me company."

Octave and Mademoiselle Derblay were now slowly returning together. They were no longer talking to each other. The Marquis seemed somewhat more serious than usual. Suzanne was looking down and smiling, as it were, to happy thoughts. At last they reached the spot where their horses were tethered. The young man detached the bridles, and turning to Suzanne asked, "You will allow me to tell my sister?"

Suzanne nodded her head in token of assent and said, "Tell her, I wish it. You know how much she loves us. She will be joyful."

"Well, go with the Baron and the Baroness, and I will stay with Claire and tell her our secret."

Then presenting his hands crossed, so that Suzanne might poise her tiny foot upon them, he speedily put her into the saddle. The young girl raised her eyes and gave Octave a rather longer look than was necessary perhaps, and exchanged a shake of the hand with him, in which she expressed all that she dared not say. Then touching her mare with her whip, she reached the centre of the clearing at one bound.

The hunting-horn resounded through the forest, coming nearer and nearer, and lending wings to La Brède and Du

Tremblays. "Come, Baron, to horse!" said Madame de Préfont to her husband.

"I'm at your orders, my dear," replied the amiable man of science, tearing himself away from the contemplation of his mineralogical specimens. "It's very curious," he added. "Do you know, I shouldn't be astonished if these rocks contained alum. I must speak on the subject to Monsieur Derblay. One might, perhaps, start a competition to the alum-beds of Italy— you know, near Civita Vecchia. I showed them to you during our wedding tour. It would be a first-rate affair, and a good business could be done in sulphates with the papermakers."

"Yes, Baron, yes," said Madame de Préfont, suddenly softening. "You are an angel, you are! And what is more, a learned angel. Come, kiss my hand."

"With pleasure," said the Baron, in nowise departing from his bland tranquillity, and he raised his wife's daintily gloved hand to his lips.

The Baroness glanced round her, made her horse paw the ground, and waved her hand to Claire and Octave; then, turning to Suzanne, she asked, "You are ready? Yes? Then start!" And followed by her husband and the young girl, she went off at a full gallop.

Octave and Claire watched the trio as they rode away. There was a moment's silence. The young man was solemn, and seemed somewhat oppressed by emotion, as if he had some very serious revelation to make. On her side the young wife was thinking of what the Baroness had told her, and was weighing, with vague anxiety, the chances she had of succeeding in her difficult enterprise. Her brother's voice at last roused her from her meditation.

"Claire," said he, "I have some great news to tell you." And as his sister made a gesture of surprise, and looked at him questioningly, he added in an undertone, "We love each other, Suzanne and I."

Claire's sad face brightened up like a stormy sky suddenly traversed by a ray of sunlight. She held both hands out towards her brother, and drawing him quickly towards her made him sit down at her side. Her nerves were delightfully agitated, her heart dilated; she longed to learn everything, and it seemed to her as if a favourable occasion for a reconciliation with Philippe might now present itself. Then, in the stillness, Octave rapturously told her the simple and yet already long story of two hearts which had gradually taken possession of each other—candid and truthful love, full of pure delights, which had come gently into being without an effort, without a throe, like a beautiful flower under the blue sky.

"You have so much influence over Philippe," said the Marquis to his sister. "Speak to him for me, and obtain his consent. He has long been well acquainted with my ideas. He knows that I count the advantages of birth for nothing, and that I wish to make my position myself. And be eloquent and strive to convince him, for you have my happiness in your hands."

Claire had suddenly become very grave again. Alas! she did not possess the influence which her brother attributed to her. Never, since that fatal night, the starting-point of so much grief, had she exchanged a single serious word with Philippe. At Pont-Avesnes they only saw each other at mealtimes, and in presence of the servants they talked but little, and merely on indifferent subjects. And yet now, without preparation and encouragement, she must lay this weighty matter before her husband. Still she didn't hesitate; all her old confidence had come back to her. She seemed to have a presentiment of victory.

Claire's silence, however, had already made the Marquis feel anxious, for like all lovers he was prompt in espying difficulties. "At least you don't refuse to plead my cause?" said he.

"Certainly not," replied his sister with a smile, "and be at ease; I will plead it as if it were my own."

"Oh, how I thank you!" cried Octave; and taking his sister by the shoulders he kissed her tenderly.

"Is that my honorarium?" said she, with a gaiety she had not shown for a whole year. "One can see that you are confident; you pay in advance. Come, go in search of her, now that you have confessed your crime. You know that I don' fear solitude; and besides, I need to reflect over all that you have told me."

The Marquis was already hastening towards his horse. He vaulted into the saddle, and kissing his hand to Claire, who was looking at him with a smile, he started off with all the impetuosity of a man who knows that the girl he loves is at the end of the road.

XV.

Left to herself, Claire forgot where she was, what was passing around her, and began to think. A distant hum rose from the forest, mingled with the notes of the horn, which was now sounding "full cry," and in the direction of the paved highway a loud rumble of vehicles could be heard. But the young wife was blind and deaf to everything unconnected with Philippe. She took a bitter pleasure in picturing to herself her life as it might have been. She dived back into the past, and counted the days of happiness which she had voluntarily deprived herself of. Far now from the fatal epoch when she had wrecked her life, she could hardly understand the feelings which had then swayed her. She could not comprehend the delirium of pride to which she had been a prey. Her all-absorbing preoccupation had been that her wedding should at any cost take place before the Duke's, but now it seemed to her so petty and trivial that she positively blushed for it. Was it possible that she had risked her whole existence for the sake of yielding to such a vulgar impulse? She said to herself that Philippe, although most outrageously treated, could not show himself inexorable for ever. And yet his stern and haughty profile was still before her eyes, and she could hear him saying, "One day you will learn the truth. You will discover that you have been even more unjust than cruel. But though you may drag yourself at my feet, imploring forgiveness, I shall not have a word of pity for you." But was it not anger that had dictated this terrible resolution? Was he a man to cling to it without ever wavering? She saw him again, with his brow resting on his hands, as if he were crushed with grief, and then rising up and showing her his face, down which the tears were streaming. He had certainly loved her, and on that fatal night he would have given his life for a word of hope or a tender look. But eight months had since elapsed, and maybe all his love had oozed forth and utterly flowed away through the wound she had inflicted on him.

With the tip of her foot Claire listlessly stirred the gravel. "When a man has deeply loved," said she aloud, as if she wished to submit the question which disturbed her to the woods, the wind, and space—"when a man has loved as he loved me can he ever forget?"

"No, a man never forgets when he has deeply loved," replied a mocking voice which seemed to descend from above. Claire sprang to her feet at once, and on raising her head she perceived the Duke, who had entered the kiosk a moment previously, and now stood leaning over the balustrade, looking at her with a smile on his face. "You will agree that I have arrived appropriately enough to answer you," he gaily remarked. "But come, were you thinking of me?"

Claire looked at him through her half-closed eyelids with an air of superb contempt. "Indeed, no," she replied.

"So much the worse, then, for me."

"And you?" asked the young wife. "What are you seeking for here?"

The Duke came down the steps and approached her. "I was seeking for you," he answered with a bow.

"And why so, pray?"

"Because I wished to speak to you frankly. You gave me a bad reception when I offered you my company an hour ago. But I thought you might perhaps have become more sociable. So here I am. Are you in a humour to answer me?"

"But, my dear Duke, I don't think we have anything to say to each other?"

"Are you really sure of it? I am sorry to see that you are such an adept in practising dissimulation. You have a great many things to grieve you, and you won't admit it."

Claire shrugged her shoulders disdainfully. "And I," said she, "see that your faculties are clearly on the wane. You are always returning to the same subject with a lachrymose air, which is really painful to witness. Set your soft heart at ease. I have no grief, and I am not at all disposed to worry myself to please you."

"Maybe," rejoined the Duke, with seeming simplicity. "I shall be delighted to learn I have been so mistaken in my surmises, and yet they appeared to me to be correct. However, as you say, I must have lost some of my intellectual lucidity. This morning it seemed to me that you were nervous and disturbed. This paper-chase was very attractive, but you would not take any part in it. You spent your time in watching your husband."

"Well?" asked Claire, as she repressed a gesture of irritation.

"Well," continued the Duke, "the singular thing is that Monsieur Derblay didn't seem to pay any attention to you. He busied himself with the Duchess, who had chosen him as her *cavaliere servente*, and on your side, instead of looking pleased when he discharged his duties gallantly, you kept on giving him crushing glances."

"And what did you conclude from that?" asked Claire coldly.

"Why, I concluded that the good understanding which you told me prevailed between him and you did not really exist. I concluded that he did not rightly value the treasure which chance, or rather my ill-luck, has given him. And then—what shall I say?—a thousand little things, which I had forgotten, returned to my mind. I remembered how strange you looked on your wedding-day. I thought of your sadness and analyzed your anger, and having weighed the *pros* and the *cons* I came to this conclusion, that despite all you say to the contrary, you are really not so happy as you deserve to be."

The attack was sudden and direct. In a moment the Duke had turned the defensive works which Claire had raised so patiently. He audaciously let her understand that, like a fortress which can expect no succour from outside, she must resign herself to a regular siege. The young wife disdained to make an effort at retreat. In fact she sallied forth to the battle, and with unrestrained bitterness replied, "And so you, with your generous commiserating heart, you thought that the moment was perhaps a favourable one to offer me some consolation."

The Duke had too much experience of this kind of warfare to take up the position which Claire so boldly offered him; at least for the present. His cause would have been irrevocably lost if he had at once acknowledged that she was right in her surmises. He wished it to seem rather as if he were impelled by an earnest, serious feeling, and so, setting aside the bantering tone in which he had hitherto spoken, "You judge me wrongly, Claire," he said with assumed sadness. "Believe me when I tell you that I have done all in my power to forget you. When I arrived here I thought I loved you no longer. I thought I should be able to see you again without the least danger for my heart. I was told that you were happy and I rejoiced to hear it. Ah! madman that I was! I thought my heart dried up and dead after so many trials and deceptions; but to my bitter grief I felt it revive and palpitate again. When I saw you, you looked, alas! so very careworn—despite all your efforts to conceal your worry and sadness. But then your face cannot hide anything from me. Had you been happy I should merely have adored you from afar, and no word of mine should have ever disturbed your peace. But you suffered. Ah! when I saw that, I was no longer my own master. An irresistible power seemed to impel me towards you, and I realised that only one woman existed on earth for me—yourself."

Claire listened with astonishment to these passionate words. Not a fibre of her heart throbbed. Was this man, who spoke to her so tenderly, really the same one she had loved to madness? His voice, which once had made her palpitate with passion, now left her cold and somewhat irritated. She saw that he was one of those skilful actors who disturb the minds and trouble the senses of women, whose natures are deficient in equilibrium. She did not for a moment imagine that he was sincere. She looked upon his attack rather as some low desire to gratify a sudden fancy.

"Do you know that you are not wanting in impudence?" she said bitterly. "When you had to choose between a woman you pretended to love and a fortune that tempted you, you did not hesitate. You closed your heart and opened your hands. But now that you have the money safe, you would perhaps like to have the woman as well. And so you come and make advances to me. Ah! my dear Duke, you are too ambitious. One can't have everything, you know. It would be cumulation!"

The Duke jerked his head in a melancholy manner. "How harshly you speak to me," said he. "I knew that you still harboured vindictive feelings against me."

"Vindictive feelings!" she cried. "You flatter yourself too much, my dear Duke! If I had any feeling towards you at all, it would surely be one of gratitude; for it is thanks to you that I am the wife of Monsieur Derblay, who is as useful as you are useless in the world, as devoted as you are egotistical, as generous as you are selfish, who, in one word, has all the qualities you don't possess and none of your failings."

The Duke bit his lips. Each word of this violent outburst had been a slap in the face for him. "Monsieur Derblay," said he, trying to subjugate Claire with his glance, "is no doubt perfect. But there is one little point that greatly detracts from his perfection, at least so far as you yourself are concerned—he does not love you! He has only been your husband a few months, and if he appreciated you at your worth he would have remained beside you, attentively and affectionately. But where is he? Why, he has gone off with the Duchess."

"Your wife!" cried Claire, in a tone of violence. Then making an effort and regaining composure, "Well, after all, why should I be disturbed when you yourself are so unconcerned?"

"Oh! as for me, I'm not jealous," answered the Duke gaily. "And besides, I know the Duchess. She is a charming doll, covered with lace and brave with jewels; but under all this adornment there's neither a head nor a heart. So where could passion lodge? But your husband——" He stopped short and came nearer to Claire, as if he feared that the venom of his words might lose some of its poisonous effect as it passed through the air, and then added, "Well, you saw him with her, only a little while ago. Ah! the ungrateful fellow, who fails to recognise his happiness. The imprudent fellow, who risks losing it! Come, leave him with the Duchess. They are worthy of each other. But let me remain with you—I who appreciate you, I who understand you, I who love you."

Claire took a step back, as if to place a greater distance between herself and the Duke; and then, oppressed as it were, and trying in vain to appear calm, she answered, "Come, as for all that, I can only laugh at it——"

"Yes, like Figaro, so as not to be obliged to cry," rejoined Bligny. "For in point of fact it is very sad. You are bound to a man who will, morally at least, always be a stranger for you. Everything in you and him is contradictory and antagonistic. He is a plebeian and you are a patrician. I am sure that he is biassed in favour of equality; but you, you are an aristocrat to the tips of your finger-nails. He is rough, like everything that pertains to the people, and that is distasteful to you. You are proud, like all members of the nobility, and that wounds him. The races from which you have sprung, you and he, are born foes. This gentleman's forefathers cut your grandparents' heads off, my dear. In a word, there is every reason why you should hate each other, but there is nothing to induce you to love one another."

Claire proudly raised her head and looked defiantly at the Duke. "And yet I love him," she said, "and you know it."

"You imagine that you love him," rejoined Bligny softly,

as if he wished to convince a child. "And why so? Because you are jealous. But there are all kinds of jealousies. There is the jealousy born of love and the jealousy born of pride, and I would not mind swearing that you are troubled with the latter sort. Your husband neglects you, and though you care very little for him, it irritates you. That's quite natural. And so out of a spirit of contradiction you attach yourself to him. All women are the same; and as to the crisis you are passing through, why, I know it by heart."

Full of astonishment and disgust, Claire silently listened to the Duke as he developed his audacious analysis. Bligny mistook her stupefaction for curiosity, and was eager to pursue the work of demoralisation he had, to his fancy, so well commenced. "Come, I'll be frank with you," he resumed, laughing, "and lay my cards on the table. The crisis comprises four phases, like the course of the moon. At the present moment you are in the first phase, otherwise the phase of resistance. Your husband is beginning to neglect you, and you are obstinately striving to win him back. It is a fixed idea on your part. But he resists, and you will soon find that all your efforts are useless. This gallant man, after contenting himself with flirtation, will at last come to downright infidelity. Then you will reach the second phase. You will have lost all your illusions and your peace of mind as well. You will be altogether overwhelmed, and at first you will turn for comfort to the Divinity, who alone can console great griefs. But as your husband will continue the course of his successes, your further resignation will give way to bitterness. Your happy husband will be too gay, and you will find yourself too sad. After all, you are only two-and-twenty, and you have a right to claim a share of love. One cannot live alone for ever. Irritation will seize hold of you, and you will reach the third phase, called the phase of anger. A veil will have fallen from your eyes, and you will see your husband as he really is — clumsy, vulgar, and foolish. You will feel astonished at having regretted his loss for a single moment, and you will feel a vague longing for certain compensation. Ah! now let the fickle husband take care, for the end of the crisis approaches! Still blushing and yet resolute, you will step into the phase of consolation. Look before you; everything is gay and rosy. Here the past may be forgotten in the most charming style! Come, another step and there you are. Do you hesitate? Well, madame, allow me to offer you my hand to do you the honours of this last phase, which I wait for with a little hope and a great deal of love."

As he spoke the Duke tried to take Claire's hand, but she abruptly repulsed him with a dark and threatening look. "Your calculations are ingenious," she said "and they show that you have studied women. Only I regret to see that if you have conscientiously noted the conduct of those who are mad or depraved, you have neglected to take the honest ones into account. There are, I am proud to tell you, some unfortunate women who do not lose their heads, who decline to avenge themselves, and who find themselves sufficiently consoled when they preserve their own self-esteem and deserve the respect of others."

"Very good, very good!" exclaimed the Duke. "You are playing your part: this is the phase of resistance."

"If you persist, I can only hate you."

"I persist because I can only love you."

"But what you call your love is a shameful persecution! What manner of man are you, to expose yourself to my hatred after winning my contempt?"

For a moment the Duke remained silent, looking at Claire who stood before him, quivering but defiant. A tress of her fair hair had become loosened and was waving over her shoulder. Her bosom heaved under her blue cloth riding-habit, and with a clenched hand she brandished her tapering plaited leather riding-whip as if it had been a weapon. She looked more beautiful than ever in this attitude, and furious desire seized hold of Bligny. He turned pale, his eyes became clouded, and walking towards Claire with open arms, "There is nothing I will not risk to win you," he stammered.

He touched her. She could feel his burning breath pass over her face. She drew herself back, and with lowered brows and contracted lips, "Have a care!" she cried. "If you take another step forward I will treat you like the coward that you are, and slash you across the face." He saw that she had raised her arm with threatening energy, that she was ready to strike, and he retreated. Then, proud of her triumph, drawing herself erect and yet trembling nervously at the thought of the resolution she had shown, "Have matters come to such a pass," she asked, "that you dare to insult me like this? Am I so publicly abandoned that I can be subjected to such affronts with impunity? Would you dare to attack me like this if I had a man near me to defend me? No; I am alone, and so you are brave; but you see I am quite able to defend myself."

The Duke, who had become calm again, now bowed. "You will change," said he. "The future belongs to me. I am patient; I can wait."

This cool, audacious reply exasperated Claire. She gave the Duke a wild look, and in a voice that shook with violent emotion said, "Learn that even if I were the most unhappy of women—even were I destined to become the most unworthy of my sex, which is impossible—even if I were to ruin myself—well, you inspire me with so much aversion and disgust that I would take no matter whom, a stranger, a passer-by, for my lover rather than take *you!*"

This cry of fury did not seem to make any impression on the Duke. With the cool, confident smile that habitually exasperated Claire, he quietly exclaimed, "We shall see."

The young wife made no rejoinder. She turned away from her persecutor, and proceeding in the direction of the clearing, whence she was merely separated by a wavy veil of aspens and alders, she drew near to the spot where M. Moulinet's footmen were preparing an appetising lunch for the hunters. In reality the Duke's sudden aggression had made her apprehensive. She had seen him with a pale face, sparkling eyes, and quivering hands eager to seize hold of her. Thanks to her energy, she had this time escaped the struggle, but a feeling of horror and loathing came over her at the thought that the attempt might be renewed. And thus, no longer having any confidence in the honour of this nobleman, whom she had once worshipped as a god, she came in deep grief to place herself under the protection of lacqueys.

"Come, look sharp," said the head butler to his assistants. "Here are our people arriving!"

In a perfect stream the vehicles were now coming back along all the forest roads, rumbling less noisily as they rolled over the green sward. The horsemen followed along the side paths, and all these young folks, heated by their mad gallop, were calling gaily after one another. They were still five or six hundred yards from the clearing, and yet their voices could be distinctly heard. This beautiful day was fraught with complete enjoyment for them, for they were free from care and entirely intent on present pleasure. Claire could not help comparing their gaiety with her sadness. She felt angry that all nature should be *en fête* when she herself was so gloomy; forgetting, alas! that she alone was responsible for her woe.

She was aroused from her distressing thoughts on seeing a carriage drive into the open space. The Marchioness de Beaulieu, with a little lace shawl over her shoulders, was ensconced inside, just as if she were seated in her cosy arm-chair at home. Claire went towards her as towards salvation. The atmosphere seemed purified by the presence of this noble woman, and by her mother's side the young wife at once regained her peace of mind. Madame de Beaulieu, habitually indolent, had reached the forest rather late. It was mainly in view of seeing her daughter on horseback that she had shaken off her usual apathy and ordered the carriage. "What?" cried she as she perceived Claire. "You are here all by yourself? But where is your husband, then? And what is Sophie doing?"

"The Baroness has just left me," answered Claire with perfect composure. "And as for Philippe, I insisted that he should follow the hunt. A husband mustn't hang about his wife in public; it would make people talk."

She was calm and smiling, and her mother looked at her with thorough satisfaction. A shadow of a suspicion had never once crossed the Marchioness's somewhat superficial mind. "You are happy enough to allow yourselves to hide your happiness," she said. "Ah! Philippe is the paragon of sons-in-law."

At this moment the arrival of the main party of horsemen at a sharp trot interrupted Madame de Beaulieu, and enabled Claire to conceal the embarrassment which her mother's praise had caused her. Foremost came La Brède and Du Tremblays on horses white with foam, the former fairly purple, and looking as if about to burst, and the latter extremely pale, and seeming as if he were on the point of fainting. They were at once surrounded by the joyous hunters, and properly complimented on the vigour with which they had kept their pursuers at a distance. Pontac was sounding the "hallali" on his Dampierre horn with all the strength of his lungs, while his *piqueur*, Bistocq, who looked altogether out of sorts, was shambling along on foot, leading his big bony roan by the bridle, and mumbling some scarcely complimentary remarks concerning the amateurs who played at hunting and tired out poor horses for the mere sake of rushing after bits of paper, as if "with your permission, sir," they had been so many *chiffonniers*. At the same moment Claire perceived Philippe, who was returning with Suzanne and the Baroness. Sophie outpaced her companions, and approaching her cousin the first, whispered these words, which at once brought roses to the young wife's cheeks: " When we got there he was no longer beside Athénaïs; he had left her to that fool of a Pontac, who only knows how to bray on a horn. A nice talent the simpleton has, and a truly delightful one in company."

So saying she began to laugh, and blinking her eyes with the unintentional air of impertinence common to shortsighted people, she looked at Athénaïs, who now came up fairly deafened by her companion's horn, but not daring to say anything, for fear people might think she was deficient in power of endurance. However, on perceiving Claire, the Duchess put her horse to a canter, and made an ironical gesture to her husband, who was standing with an air of careless indifference near Madame de Beaulieu's carriage.

"Ah, Duke!" she cried, "so I've found you at last, at the same time as Madame Derblay, eh? It was really amiable on your part to keep your cousin company."

As she spoke Athénaïs gave Philippe a diabolical glance, as if to instil some poisonous supposition into his mind. She wished by this to revenge herself upon him for the humiliation she had experienced when he abandoned her so promptly during the hunt. Scarcely had the gleam shot from her eyes when the ironmaster came forward with a firm step and an almost threatening look. Claire turned pale. Would the Duchess's implacable hatred impel these two men against each other?

But the Duke was speaking. "I was not fortunate enough to keep my cousin company, as you so appropriately remarked," he said to his wife, bowing respectfully at the same time to Madame Derblay. "My aunt was already here when I arrived."

"Then you must have a bad horse, my dear; you had better change it," rejoined the Duchess; and grinding her teeth, enraged that her malevolence should have been so promptly foiled, she cut her mare so severely across the ears with her whip that the animal bounded on one side and reared, furiously shaking its bit all white with foam.

The Duke quietly advanced, caught the horse by the bridle, at once reduced it to submission, and assisted Athénaïs to alight. "Nothing could be more unseemly than to make a horse rear like that, my dear," said he with an impertinent air. "And besides, you are by no means a first-rate rider, and you might easily come to the ground, which would scarcely be a pleasant contingency. Take my advice, and rid yourself of such manners as soon as possible; they are 'shoppy' all over." Thereupon, leaving the Duchess pale with rage, Bligny quietly walked off to join his friends, and drink with them to the success of the day.

Claire, who shuddered and felt icy cold, had taken a seat in her mother's carriage, requesting her to drive her back to Pont-Avesnes. She felt a weight on her heart. It seemed to her as if the Duke's answer to Athénaïs—which so appropriately prevented Philippe's perilous intervention—had made her in some measure his accomplice. She was on the point of telling everything to her husband, preferring his blame and anger to this odious connivance with the man who had so outrageously insulted her; but at the decisive moment her courage failed her, she did not dare to speak. And sighing bitterly, she pictured herself condemned for ever to falsehood, despite all her loathing for it, and compelled to practise deceit everywhere and always; to show, indeed, a smiling face, even when her heart was full of despair. She glanced timidly at Philippe, who was cantering by the side of Bachelin's gig. The ironmaster's features wore an expression of composure, and there was not the least sign of emotion in his voice as he quietly talked with the old notary. Claire thought to herself that perhaps she had been mistaken in fancying she had detected a gleam of anger in his eyes as he approached the Duke. Still she was aware of Philippe's wonderful power over himself, and perhaps at the present moment he was merely forcing himself to look careless.

Claire hoped that he was jealous. At the risk of her life, she began to wish he would break out in threats and raise his hand to strike her as he had done on that fatal night. She could no longer remain in this terrible suspense. She resolved that on the morrow she would speak to him about her brother, and do all in her power to penetrate his mysterious intentions. Then, having come to this decision, she determined to try and be gay; she made an effort to dispel the clouds that hovered over her brow, and, like an actor on the stage, she composed herself a smiling face.

Through the trees in the distance one could still hear the joyous laughter of the hunting party, while Pontac's horn still awoke the echoes of the forest, as it sounded the death of the stag, incarnate in those dissimilar beings, fat La Brède and little Du Tremblays.

XVI.

Philippe was working in his spacious, staidly furnished study. His writing-table was covered with papers which he glanced at rapidly. With a stroke of the pen he initialed each of them that proved to be satisfactory, and then without a pause turned to another one. It was ten o'clock in the morning. The burning sunrays fell direct upon the front of the château, and one of them darting through the window-pane suddenly played upon the ironmaster's forehead, and induced him to interrupt his work. He rose, approached the window, and looked out into the garden.

Under a striped sailcloth tent installed at the edge of the sheet of water, Suzanne, attired in a white dress, was fishing absentmindedly. Her line dipped into the basin, and the float, stirred by the tugs of a fish which had taken the bait, was bobbing up and down, making the water undulate in shiny, expanding circles. But the young girl failed to notice this. Her gaze was lost in vacancy, and seemed to be following some happy thought. She sat there motionless with a radiant face, fully absorbed in her dream.

A smile curved Philippe's lips, and softly opening the window, he exclaimed, "Eh! Suzanne, you have a bite!"

The young girl started, and turned towards her brother with a graceful pout, "Oh, Philippe!" she said, "how you frightened me!"

"But draw in your line," rejoined the ironmaster. "A perch has been struggling at the end of it for the last ten minutes. It is really not right to make fish suffer like that."

Suzanne instinctively raised her slender rod, and as it bent she hoisted from the water a wriggling perch which gleamed with the brilliancy of silver. With her gloved hand she at once unhooked it and dropped it into a netted bag which was immersed among the waterplants near the bank.

"I've a dozen!" cried Suzanne, proudly showing her brother how full the bag was.

"They will make a dish," gaily answered the ironmaster. "They show themselves willing, and no mistake."

For a minute longer he stood gazing at his sister, who was gravely baiting her line again. In the shade of the tent, under the blue sky, she looked so fresh and rosy that a sudden feeling of emotion overcame him. His chest heaved with a sigh, and he mentally sent his pretty sister a kiss. Then closing the window again, he drew down the blind so that it might protect him from the sun. Refreshing shade now pervaded the study, and Philippe, returning to his writing-table, was on the point of sitting down, when a tap at the door made him pause. "Come in," said he in a careless tone.

The door opened, and Claire, with a blush on her face, but resolute despite her emotion, appeared on the threshold. "Am I disturbing you?" she asked as she entered the room, whilst Philippe, extremely surprised by this unexpected question, courteously offered her an arm-chair.

"Not at all," he answered quietly, and leaning against the mantelpiece, he waited for her to speak again.

Claire sat down, and leaning back in her chair glanced for

a moment around her. She never entered this room, which was set aside for Philippe's private use. Its somewhat cold and solemn aspect pleased her, as symbolical of the character of its inmate, and she examined everything with great complacency. In reality she was not sorry to be able to defer the moment of speaking, for her heart was beating quickly, and it seemed as if a band compressed her temples.

Philippe stood on his guard watching her. He was the first to break the silence. "Have you anything to ask of me?" said he.

Claire turned her eyes towards her husband, and with a touch of sadness in her voice, "We live so much apart from each other," she said, "that if I had not something to ask of you I should not have risked disturbing you."

Philippe made a deprecatory gesture, and bowing to his wife as if to encourage her, he rejoined, "I am listening."

Claire bent her head as though she wished to collect her thoughts. She was trembling, and her throat was dry. Never had she engaged in battle with such an acute feeling of anguish. "What I have to speak to you about," she said at last, "is most important, and interests you as much as it interests me."

"Let us see."

Claire gave her husband a look so full of mute supplication that any other man would have fallen on his knees; but he remained standing, in the same expectant, circumspect attitude.

"Before anything else," said the young wife, "you take some interest in Octave, I believe?"

"Well, I don't think," answered the ironmaster with astonishment, "that your brother has so far had any reason to doubt it."

The reply was somewhat ambiguous, and Claire slightly

frowned. "And if you had occasion to show that you took an interest in him?" she asked.

"It is probable that I should avail myself of the opportunity."

It was to this precise point that Claire had wished to bring her husband, and she no doubt fancied he was caught in the network of her questions. It now only remained for her to indicate the point at issue, and carried away by the fever of the battle she had engaged in, the young wife did not hesitate. "Well," said she, "such an occasion now presents itself. Do you wish to know what it is? I must tell you that it is a serious matter, and one which does not merely concern my brother."

"What a deal of digression!" interrupted the ironmaster. "Does what you have to ask of me seem so *very* difficult to obtain?"

Claire looked her husband full in the face, as if to lose nothing of the play of his features, and then boldly replied, "Judge for yourself. Octave loves your sister, and has requested me to ask you for her hand."

A muffled exclamation escaped Philippe, and his face became gloomy. To hide his perturbation he approached the window, and standing there in silence, he gently raised the blind. Unconscious of what was happening in the study, Suzanne still sat dreaming beside the sheet of water, with her line dipping in the rippling mirror. The ironmaster gazed at her. She looked so gentle and so candid, surely she was born for happiness.

Such was Claire's anxiety that she impatiently rose to her feet and approached her husband; then, seeing how pensive and absorbed he looked, she exclaimed, "You do not answer me?"

Philippe turned round, and speaking slowly, as if he regretted having to give such a reply, "I am sorry for your brother, but this marriage is impossible," he said.

"You refuse?" cried Claire, a prey to horrible torments.

"I refuse," repeated the ironmaster coldly.

"Why?"

Philippe looked fixedly at his wife, as if he wished his answer to penetrate into her very heart. "Because," said he, "because there is already one unhappy person in my family through the fault of yours, and I consider that enough."

"Take care," rejoined Claire, swiftly, "you may all the more surely make Suzanne unhappy by refusing my brother her hand."

"How is that?" asked the ironmaster with sudden animation.

"She loves him."

In the garden Suzanne's joyous voice could now be heard, as she set her fishing paraphernalia in order, with Brigitte's assistance.

Philippe paused for a moment to listen to her. "She loves him," he repeated. "That is no doubt a great misfortune, but it will not alter my decision. If, on the eve of the day fixed for my marriage with you, some one had prevented that marriage from taking place, even by breaking my heart, he would have rendered me an immense service. My cruel experience shall at least serve for something, If my sister has to weep, she shall at least weep in liberty; she shall not see her future irremediably lost like mine."

This was such a blow for Claire that she was unable to retain her composure. "You are seeking for revenge!" she rejoined in an excited tone.

"Revenge?" said the ironmaster, haughtily. "Do you

think I need it? No; I am taking a precaution, and everything advises me to take it."

Claire sank into her arm-chair. She could detect such disdain and such resolution in her husband's words that she renounced the contest. She now only thought of entreating him. "Come," said she, "I beg of you, don't render me responsible for the unhappiness of these children. I am sufficiently crushed myself. What can I do to mollify you. I know that I acted very wrongly towards you."

Philippe began to smile bitterly. "You acted very wrongly towards me?" he said. "Really? And you deign to own it? But it seems to me that that is a very great concession on your part!"

Claire took no notice of her husband's irony. She was determined not to let anything repel her; she was resolved to go on to the end, bitter as it might be. "Yes, I did you a grievous wrong," she rejoined; "but you have cruelly punished me for it."

"I?" interrupted Philippe, "And how? Have I ever reproached you, ever spoken a wounding word to you? Have I been wanting in politeness towards you?"

"No. But how much I should have preferred your anger to the haughty indifference with which you treat me. I hear everyone around me talking of my happiness. I am envied and congratulated wherever I go. But I return home and where is my happiness then? I seek for it, and in its place I only find solitude, abandonment, and sadness."

Philippe drew himself erect, and looking down on the poor woman who, as he felt, had fallen so completely into his power, "It did not depend on me," he answered, "for matters to be different. You decided your life yourself. It is such as you made it."

"That is true," rejoined Claire, in a broken voice. "But at least I had a right to count on repose, and even that has been denied me." She rose, half sobbing, with clenched hands and a wild look in her eyes. "That miserable woman who hates me pursues me even into my home, and you suffer it, and lend yourself to her manœuvres! She openly flirts with you; she compromises you! But you have not even enough pity for me to spare me her outrageous bravado. Oh! but my patience is at an end; this situation shall not last any longer. I will not have it!"

"You will not?" rejoined Philippe; and as Claire repeated with furious obstinacy, "No, no! I will not!" he sternly added," You forget that there is but one person here who has a right to say 'I will not.'"

His proud young wife's blood mantled over her face. She revolted; and, blinded by anger, carried away by jealousy, "Take care!" she cried, "my endurance has its limits. I can bear your indifference; but such insulting disdain, such public abandonment— No! I will never consent to it!"

Philippe paused in front of her, and looked at her with ironical curiosity. "That is so like you!" he said. "Always the same, always influenced by pride! You are concerned as to what the people about you may think. Public opinion —that is your foremost care. It was simply for the sake of your position in society that you plunged so madly into our marriage adventure. And again to-day, exasperated at the thought that people may deride and taunt you, you are fairly carried away, and forget yourself even to the point of threatening me."

"Oh, no! I do not threaten," interrupted Claire, no longer able to restrain her tears, "I beg. Take pity on me, Philippe. Be generous—— Will you never weary of striking so harshly at my heart? You have had a full revenge, be sure of it; you can be indulgent now. If you will make no change in our mode of life, at least let me have some peace; deliver me from the Duchess. Keep the Duke away from me."

She spoke these last words in a low voice, as if she were ashamed that they should fall from her lips.

"What do you complain of?" rejoined the ironmaster. "Don't I have to support them both myself? They are your relatives. What would society say—that society whose opinion is your first concern—if we closed our doors to them without a reason? One must wait patiently, and put up with the evils of our sad situation. Life cannot be changed to suit the fancies of a spoilt child. Everything is grave and serious in life, and misfortune comes only too easily. There is no need of courting it; you know it now. Cast out of the beaten track, both of us—and by your fault—our duty is to march onward since we have no right, since we are unable, to retreat."

"So I have nothing to await from you, nothing to hope from you?"

"Nothing," replied Philippe coldly. "And remember that you yourself decided it should be so."

Claire looked at her husband. The expression of his features had greatly changed. His eyes had receded under his brows, and he was extremely pale. Still he spoke in a firm voice. For one moment she thought of throwing herself at his feet, of opening her heart to him, of confessing that she loved him. She walked towards him, half stifling, with a heaving bosom and outstretched hands; but a lingering vestige of pride restrained her. She heaved a deep sigh and stopped short.

Philippe now approached. "I am obliged to go to the works," said he, as calmly as if no such distressing scene had occurred between him and this woman he adored. "Excuse me for leaving you."

"What answer shall I give to my brother?" asked Claire timidly.

"Tell him that I rely on his honourable feeling not to breathe a word of my refusal to Suzanne. In a week from now I will arrange to send her away for a short time." And gliding like a shadow through the dim study, he nodded with seeming indifference to Claire and went out.

For some minutes the young wife remained alone in the spacious room, and gave way to her grief without restraint. Stretched on the divan, she measured the full extent of her love. Thus it was irrevocable. In vain had she displayed the gaping wound in her heart to Philippe; he had merely given her a careless look. She no longer existed for him. He had told her so; and he kept his word. Such was his implacability that he would not forgive her for her passing error, and he harshly repulsed her when she came to him. She accused herself of having ruined her brother's future. It was because her husband distrusted the hot blood of the Beaulieus—the full and fatal violence of which she had revealed to him—that he refused to let Suzanne become Octave's wife. How would she ever be able to break this sad news to her brother?

The sound of Suzanne's voice in the next room made her spring to her feet, like a hind alarmed by the baying of the hounds. She was fearful of being found weeping in her husband's study, and she at once hastened to her own room and locked herself in. At luncheon time she sent word that she was poorly and need not be waited for. Finally, at two o'clock, when from her window she had seen Suzanne disappear among the shady trees of the park, she furtively tripped down the stairs, and leaving the château by the little side gate in the courtyard, set out for Beaulieu on foot.

The Marquis, who was impatient to learn the result of the mission which he had entrusted to his sister, was walking up and down the terrace, fully expecting that Claire would not keep him long in suspense. He espied her from afar as she came up the steep road leading to the château, and her attitude impressed him painfully. Madame Derblay was walking slowly along the grassy embankment which fringed the roadway. She was leaning forward, looking on the ground, and often forgetting to shade herself with her parasol from the burning sunrays which constantly darted through the clouds. There was a touch of weariness in her attitude that seemed to presage defeat. She did not approach with the alert, triumphant footstep of a messenger bearing good news. However, the young man hastened forth to meet her and speedily reached her side. They exchanged a long look; the brother's was a troubled and anxious one, the sister's very mournful.

"Good heavens! what has happened?" murmured Octave, as he convulsively caught his sister by the arm and led her towards an open space where several benches had been installed in full view of the lovely valley. Claire was already enervated, and the delicious scent of the blooming lime-trees, which rose around, affected her so grievously that she began to tremble, and, with her eyes full of tears, remained in front of her brother without saying a word.

"Come, Claire, for heaven's sake," resumed the Marquis; "what is the matter? Speak! Tell me! Anything is preferable to your silence."

Madame Derblay took pity on her brother's anxiety, and making a great effort replied, "I have a sad answer to give you, my dear fellow, respecting the request you entrusted to me. It is impossible for you and Suzanne to marry."

Octave took a step back, as if he had seen an abyss open before him. He looked wildly at his sister as though he did not understand her, and repeated, "Impossible? Why so?"

Claire shook her head mournfully. "Philippe refuses," she answered.

"What reason did your husband give?" asked the Marquis.

. The young wife remained silent. Her embarrassment was very great. What answer could she give her brother? Could she confess her own painful secret to him? What pretext could she invent to impart some motive to Philippe's refusal? And it was necessary she should speak without seeming to hesitate, for Octave was looking at her most earnestly, seeking for the truth in the expression of her face, in her slightest gesture. "He gave no reason," she stammered at last, blushing with shame as she spoke. "He refused to explain himself."

"No reason?" exclaimed the Marquis, with great astonishment. "No explanation? He, Philippe, to whom I am so much attached? He didn't hesitate to inflict such a slight upon me!"

Greatly disquieted, Octave hastily wiped his eyes and then sat down. He was grievously puzzled as to the reason which Philippe had refused to give, and he asked himself what it could be, seeking for it despairingly in his own mind. Suddenly, however, he uttered an exclamation. A ray of light had dawned upon him. Money! It could only be the question of money. He had virtually no fortune and no position. That must surely be the reason why Philippe refused to give him Suzanne's hand. At this thought he hastily rose to his feet again. Claire was looking at him anxiously. But now his brow was radiant with confidence and courage, and he took a few steps forward, answering his thoughts aloud, without noticing it. "No position, it's true, but I'll make myself one," he said. "No fortune. Well, Philippe knows how a man may make one. I'll follow his example."

Suddenly he paused, stupefied and almost frightened, for Claire had sprung to her feet, and had caught hold of his arm. Two words had struck her—two only—in all that he had said, "No fortune!" And they had sufficed to agitate her strangely. Forgetful of her preoccupations, her cares and sorrows, she wished Octave to explain these words to her without delay.

"What *you*—no fortune?" she repeated; and with an imperious, almost a threatening gesture, she claimed an immediate reply.

Octave, who was greatly embarrassed and confused, tried to turn aside, but Claire, who suspected some mystery which it was urgent she should solve at any cost, caught him resolutely by the shoulders and gazed into his eyes. "What do you mean?" she asked again.

"I have imprudently spoken some words you ought never to have heard," replied Octave. "You were not aware of the loss of that lawsuit. It was intended you should never know it. But like a simpleton I have betrayed the secret which was entrusted to me."

Claire was no longer listening to the Marquis, she was thinking. The loss of that lawsuit meant ruin for them all, and if her brother had no fortune she could have no dowry. A horrible doubt came over her; she shuddered, her eyes dilated, and turning towards Octave, "But when I was married——?" she asked, finishing her phrase with a significant gesture.

"The disaster had taken place."

"And my husband—Philippe—was he aware of it?"

"He was; and he forbade us to speak of it to you. He did not wish a shadow to dim your brow. The generosity and delicacy of feeling he showed on that occasion were really admirable——"

He said no more, for a shriek resounded. Claire beat the air with her arms as if she had gone mad, and then in a husky, faltering voice exclaimed, "He did that? and I—I—Oh! the miserable woman that I am!"

As if suddenly evoked, the spacious room with the high tapestry hangings whereon the warriors smiled demurely to the goddesses appeared before her eyes, just as it looked on the night of her marriage, with the fire smouldering below the mantelshelf against which she leant, quivering from head to foot. She saw Philippe again pale and trembling almost at her feet, and yet proudly raising his brow when she haughtily bade him take her fortune. Her fortune, indeed! How disdainfully he smiled. She could understand why he had done so now, and in her despair the truth, distressing and humiliating as it was, rose to her lips. She must speak and accuse herself. She had lost all self-possession. She was seized with a mad desire to strike herself, as if to punish her flesh since she was unable to chastise her spirit.

"Oh! I lied," she stammered, "I lied when I told you that I did not know why he had refused to give you his sister's hand. It was on account of me—miserable creature that I am!—inflicting woe on all who come near me!" And then, yielding to her impulse, she made her sad confession to her brother, attenuating nothing, but insisting on her guilt, and openly displaying the horror of her conduct. "And he," she continued, "so proud, so disinterested, so good even in his anger, for he spared me. And yet with one word he might have crushed me. He did not do so, and I—I heard him supplicating me. I saw him weep, and I remained untouched. I did not understand what a wealth of deep devoted love his heart contained." Then, radiant with passion, as if her very grief had transfigured her, "Ah, if you had not spoken, my poor Octave, my life was lost for ever! What would have become of me? And it was by chance that you told me everything. Oh, I could bless you for it!" She took her brother in her arms and kissed him with passionate gratitude, while the words bubbled up to her lips like effervescence suddenly rid of restraint.

"Calm yourself, Claire, I beg of you!" exclaimed Octave, who was positively frightened.

"Fear nothing, we are saved now," she rejoined excitedly. "I will repair the wrong I have done; I will assure your happiness. Oh! I will go on my knees to Philippe; everything will now be easy and pleasant, providing I achieve success. This morning I was hardly skilful with him, but I had lost my self-possession. I love him so." A cloud passed before her brow, for she had just remembered the Duchess. "Oh! I will not have him taken from me now," she added in a husky voice. "I must win him back or I shall die!"

"Claire!" cried the Marquis.

But such was the extreme mobility of her impressions that she had already passed from sadness to joy. "Don't be frightened," she resumed, with a confident look and a gay laugh. "We have a reception to-morrow; it is my fête-day. All our friends will be there. I must be beautiful to try and please him, and I shall succeed, I am sure of it. And then I shall see him near me again, confident and loving."

Her nerves, which for some minutes already had alone been sustaining her, suddenly relaxed, and she staggered and fell into Octave's arms. He laid her gently on the grassy bank. Her bosom heaved with convulsive sobs, and for a long while she lay there utterly overcome, listening without an attempt at speaking to her brother's affectionate words of consolation. When at last she regained her self-possession, and was able to sit beside the Marquis, she remained gravely contemplating the green and peaceful valley which was stretched out before her, with the Avesnes glistening like a silver ribbon as it coursed onward through the meadows. The pointed roofs of the château sprang out of the dark clumps of lofty park trees, extending to the foot of the hill. The black smoke from the furnace chimneys trailed heavily across the sky, and the tapering steeple of the little church rose up, surmounted by its weathercock, which the sun, now sinking, burnished with its slanting rays.

This was the peaceful spot where Claire now dreamt of living. She remembered that from the same place where she at present sat she had once gazed upon it with mingled anger and disdain. Now, however, it had become her earthly paradise, for it was Philippe's home!

XVII.

The feast of Sainte Claire fell on a Sunday that year, and appropriately enough Saturday was the feast of Sainte Suzanne. Since Philippe's happiness had been wrecked he had invariably regulated his conduct in keeping with the requirements of the situation, and thus he considered he could not dispense with celebrating this double anniversary. There had been no entertainment at Pont-Avesnes since his marriage. Claire had been ill all the winter, and her convalescence had extended sufficiently far into the spring to excuse the ironmaster, even in the eyes of the most punctilious, for keeping his doors closed. However, when the moral disquietude with which Claire was afflicted openly showed itself on various occasions, Philippe decided he would make a public display of his affection for his wife by giving a fête in her honour.* Ten days had elapsed since the invitations were sent out when Claire's fruitless attempt at a reconciliation was made, with the unfortunate result that their distressing situation passed from a chronic to an acute stage.

Philippe was so discouraged that for a moment he thought of giving up the fête and sending notice of its abandonment to his guests. But it was the eve of the appointed day, and,

* Birthday festivities are not customary among Catholics on the Continent. In lieu thereof they celebrate the day set apart for their patron saint in the Roman calendar.—*Trans.*

everything considered, he determined to rely on Claire's energy. He knew that if she chose mere pride would enable her to show a smiling face to all around her. Accordingly, with an aching heart, displeased with himself and everybody else, the ironmaster made every preparation to do the honours of Pont-Avesnes with due display and gaiety.

Since morning Claire, shut up in her room with the Baroness, had been getting ready for the struggle. She was anxious to fascinate her husband, and stretched on the sofa in the subdued light, she rested at leisure with the object of enhancing the freshness of her complexion. Nor did she neglect the artifices of fashion, for she had determined to set off her beauty with a charming dress. It was white, profusely trimmed with Valenciennes lace and adorned with natural roses. The corsage, cut low in front, was somewhat higher behind, but it allowed a full view of her superb shoulders; while the whiteness of her skin was enhanced by a garland of roses, which starting from above her arm trailed downwards round her skirt, impregnating her whole person with a delicious perfume. Her lovely golden hair, caught up on the top of her head, so as to display her snowy neck, had no other adornment than a bunch of roses. But she looked so beautiful, thus attired, that Brigitte and Suzanne, who had dressed her, could not help clapping their hands with admiration. Claire glanced gratefully at the looking-glass, and then, as it was time to show herself, she went downstairs, quivering with emotion.

In the grand Louis-Quatorze reception room, which was brilliant with the light of the chandeliers, Philippe, already attired in evening dress, was talking to the Baron, who still wore a morning jacket and displayed a remarkably yellow pair of hands. As the Baroness entered the drawing-room with

Claire, and caught sight of her husband in this condition, she raised a cry of consternation. "Good heavens!" she exclaimed, "why are you in such a state at this hour? What hands you have!"

"Excuse me, my dear," replied the Baron, flushing like a schoolboy caught tripping, "but I stopped rather late in the laboratory and accidentally upset a bath of iodine, which slightly stained my fingers——"

"Slightly!" cried Madame de Préfont. "But it's horrible You are not presentable. You look like a photographer."

The Baron began to laugh. "Oh, I can assure you it will wash off easily enough." And so saying he moved towards his wife.

"Oh! don't come near me!" she exclaimed, stepping back with fright. "I've a new dress on. Make haste and go and dress, you have only just the time."

Delighted to find himself let off so easily, the Baron glided from the drawing-room like a sylph.

Philippe was looking at Claire as she approached him in all the splendour of her beauty. She was radiant, and no trace of care could be detected on her face. In the depths of his heart the ironmaster could not help admiring his wife's strength of mind. She was really valiant, he thought, and he was pleased to see her discharge her duties so brilliantly. With a smile that made her turn pale with delight he walked towards her holding a black leather jewel-case stamped with the initials C. D.

"You are not very rich in jewellery," he said, as he bowed to her. "At the time of our marriage I was not able to purchase all I wished for you. Allow me to repair this negligence." And so saying he offered her the jewel-case.

Claire was so surprised that she hesitated to take it; but

the Baroness eagerly snatched it from Philippe, opened it, and drew forth a marvellous diamond necklace which she gazed at with cries of rapture as it scintillated in the light of the chandeliers.

"Oh, my dear!" said she. "Just look at it. It is a princely present!"

Claire's brow lowered. Yes, it was a princely present. But the young wife was thinking of the forty thousand francs in gold, the assumed interest of her dowry, which were sleeping in a drawer of the handsome ebony coffer in her bedroom. She added them to the enormous sum which this necklace must have cost, and she felt profoundly humiliated. What a lesson of generosity Philippe taught her! Her supreme argument had been money, and yet he spent it with regal indifference, seemingly careless of possessing it, although he had only earned it by long and patient toil.

"Come, Philippe, it is for you to attach this badge of slavery. It is the very least you can do," said the Baroness maliciously; and then turning towards her husband, who was now entering the room clad in full evening dress, "I say, my dear," she added gaily, "you are always looking for little pebbles—well, try and find me some of the same water as these."

Meanwhile, as with trembling hands the ironmaster fastened the scintillating brilliants around his wife's neck, his fingers came in contact with her soft white skin, and he noticed that she quivered as he touched her.

"Come, come," said the Baroness, "a kiss is the rule on such a day as this——" And she maliciously pushed Claire into Philippe's arms. He turned as pale as death, and with his eye bedimmed and his throat contracted by emotion—asking himself with agony if he were going to faint—he touched his wife's forehead with his lips and imprinted on it a cold and yet a longed-for kiss. Then as if he feared he should be unable to remain master of himself, he tore himself away and abruptly left the room.

Claire had not been able, so far, to form a true estimate of her husband's important position. Wherever they went together she had seen him welcomed with marked courtesy and deference; but it was on receiving all the notabilities of the Department in her own drawing-room that she realised for the first time what weighty influence the ironmaster disposed of. Among the guests invited to the dinner one must mention M. Monicaud, the chameleon-like Republican Prefect, who was wont to tone down his opinions whenever he went into society; the Public Prosecutor, who was remarkable for the solemnity of his bearing; the Treasurer-Paymaster of the Department, an amiable *ex-viveur;* and the General commanding the division: in fact, all the civil and military authorities. In addition there was the Archbishop of Besançon, Monseigneur Fargis, to whom Philippe had presented some admirable altar-gates, and who as a rule declined all invitations. Seated on Claire's right hand, the venerable prelate smilingly affronted the presence of Monsieur le Préfet of the Doubs, who had so rigourously expelled the monks from their monasteries.

Athénaïs, who felt fairly upset with envy, was present at her rival's triumph, as encouraged for the first time by her husband's glance Claire had regained full confidence, and conversed with sparkling wit, finding the right words to flatter each of her guests in turn. She felt that Philippe admired her, and eager to please him she displayed all the attainments of her really superior mind. The Duke was struck by her radiant beauty, indeed quite fascinated, and he gazed at her with unfeigned admiration. In fact, he did not

sufficiently conceal his feelings. With his eyes fixed upon
Claire, he forgot everybody else, and such was his passionate
excitement that he abandoned all restraint. He did not notice
that Philippe was watching him with threatening attention;
and indeed, after all, what did he care for a husband? It had
long been known that he was not merely a man to rob a husband of his honour, but one to take that husband's life as
well.

Although Moulinet was mainly occupied in insinuating
himself into the good graces of the Prefect—who played such
a good knife and fork that it was easy to see he had not
always lived on the fat of the land—he was nevertheless
greatly struck by Bligny's attitude. He had already noticed
that the Duke paid far too much attention to Claire, and
although as a rule he did not attach much importance to the
flirtations of young men, he became in the present instance
extremely nervous. The fact is, the ironmaster was a power
in the Department, and it was particularly advisable for Moulinet to win at least his tacit good-will, in view of the elections.
So the chocolate-maker decided that he would have a little
private talk with his son-in-law at the first opportunity.

The Duchess, who was seated near Philippe, tried to attract
his attention by her chatter, but she found him cold, absent-
minded, and preoccupied. The Marquise de Beaulieu, who
occupied a place of honour on the ironmaster's right hand,
was greatly worried by the heat of the chandeliers, and paid
but little attention to what was going on, being mainly occupied in fanning herself. Philippe, who constantly had to
keep up the conversation, and pay attention to everybody,
suffered horribly when he noticed the manner in which the
Duke was looking at Claire. It seemed to him as if Bligny
sullied his wife's white shoulders with shameful caresses as

he gazed at them so wantonly, and he felt positively enraged. He endured, in fact, all the torments of jealousy, and gloated over the idea of killing this man, who after having already harmed him so much was still intent on torturing him. He was wearied by Athénaïs's futile prattle and her attempts to monopolise him, and he longed to be delivered of this odious couple. He remembered how his wife had entreated him to free her from the Duke and Duchess, and he realised how great her distress must be, exposed as she was to the wife's hatred and the husband's passion. He decided he would deliver her from both of them. But it was not enough to keep the Duke at a distance now; he hated him too much.

Philippe heaved a sigh of relief when the dinner came to an end, and the guests walked out on to the terrace to enjoy the fresh evening air. A charming surprise was awaiting Claire. The clumps of trees in the park were all illuminated, and festoons of flowers hung over the front of the château.

Moulinet, who had ransacked his conservatories for the occasion, now presented a basket of gilded rushwork, fully three yards across, which was full of beautiful orchids of every possible variety. Several of the guests complimented him on his lovely present, whereupon he whispered with assumed carelessness, "My gardener tore his hair when he saw the basket leave La Varenne."

Still, much as the chocolate-maker liked receiving compliments, he did not lose sight of his son-in-law, who by a skilful manœuvre had succeeded in isolating Claire and blockading her in a corner. There these two beings, who once had loved each other so sincerely, smilingly exchanged the most dangerous words. . The impassioned Duke, who was anxious to induce his cousin to look favourably on his suit, praised her beauty and expatiated on his love. Claire, on the other hand, tried to free herself from this tête-à-tête, which made her tremble, and growing more and more exasperated, she gradually raised her voice, at the risk even of attracting Philippe's attention. Thereupon Bligny changed his tactics, and becoming unctuous and gentle, merely spoke of friendship. He begged Claire to shake hands with him as a token of forgiveness, but all the while his eyes—belieing his language—sparkled with intense passion. He gradually drew nearer, and at one moment, emboldened by the obscurity, he approached so close to Claire that she exclaimed, "Take care! If you do not leave me I will call my husband, even at the risk of a scandal!"

The Duke's conduct had raised her excitement to the highest pitch, and there is no telling what might have happened if succour had not arrived appropriately enough in the form of Moulinet. With a smile on his face he walked towards Claire and Bligny, and, to the great annoyance of his son-in-law, opened a conversation with one of those commonplace remarks in which he excelled. "How lovely the sky is," he exclaimed, with an inspired air. "This is the first quarter of the moon. We shall have fine weather all the week."

The Duke looked askance at Moulinet, whilst Claire, taking advantage of the diversion, made off with a sigh of relief. Bligny turned to follow her, but with a solemn gesture his father-in-law restrained him. Taking Gaston by the arm, the chocolate-maker led him to the edge of the sheet of water, and then, as they found themselves in comparative privacy, he commenced speaking as follows: "I am sorry to see, Monsieur le Duc, that you abuse the good connection I endeavour to keep up with Monsieur Derblay, to—"

"To —?" repeated the Duke, taking Moulinet's measure in a remarkably impertinent manner.

"To begin with," exclaimed the ex-commercial judge, for the first time losing patience, "I must request you, my son-in-law," and he emphasised the expression which was so particularly distasteful to Bligny, "I must request you to abandon the mocking tone which you invariably use in speaking to me, and which I am by no means disposed to submit to any longer." .

"Monsieur Moulinet revolts, and raises the standard of commercial magistracy!" exclaimed the Duke, laughing.

"Monsieur Moulinet considers that you behave altogether improperly," rejoined the chocolate-maker in a louder tone, "both as regards himself and as regards your host, whose wife you court in the most scandalous manner."

"Has madame your daughter done me the favour to complain?" asked the Duke, with an assumption of exaggerated politeness which was even more galling than his raillery.

"Well, no," replied Moulinet. "In fact, she doesn't seem to care whether you are faithful or not, and I can't quite understand her."

"Well then?" asked the Duke ironically.

Moulinet struck an attitude, and with a crushing glance at his son-in-law, "And morality, monsieur?" he asked.

"Oh, morality! The morality of the Rue des Lombards!" rejoined the Duke with a careless gesture.

Moulinet assumed an air of self-sufficiency. "The Rue des Lombards has its merit," said he, "and you know something of it, too!"

"Oh, fie! Monsieur Moulinet," cried the Duke. "Don't jingle your ha'pence like that. We know that you are rich." And again, taking the ex-judge's measure in a contemptuous style, he added, "It's your only merit; don't abuse it."

x

"In that case," rejoined Moulinet, losing the last semblance of composure, "my merit has this advantage over yours, that it increases every day. After all, it's too much kindness to take any interest in you. Go on with your guilty enterprise. The only result can be a quarrel with the husband, and I warn you in advance that all my sympathies will be on his side."

"Much obliged," said the Duke.

"If he kills you," continued Moulinet, who grew more and more animated as he talked, "you will only have what you deserve."

"The judgment of God!"

"We will bury you, my daughter and I, and you shall have a splendid funeral service on a par with my fortune, and then we will go to Monaco, or the seaside, to weep for you during the usual twelvemonth."

"In fact, something gay in the way of mourning."

"Disgusted with your profligacy——"

"Ah, come, Monsieur Moulinet, let us finish this!" interrupted the Duke haughtily; "I don't ask advice and I don't take lessons. Your pedantic cant amused me for a few minutes, but that's quite enough."

"Very well, monsieur," said Moulinet, who was overawed by the Duke's insolence. "Do as you please. I wash my hands of the matter." And jerking his head in a dignified manner, the worthy father-in-law walked away towards the reception rooms.

A general stir had just taken place on the terrace. Whilst Philippe was talking with the Prefect and the Public Prosecutor, Suzanne had darted towards him in a state of great emotion and somewhat out of breath. "It's a deputation of the workmen!" she exclaimed. "There are ten of them, and they ask permission to come in."

"But that's capital!" cried the Prefect, whose democratic tendencies were aroused by the words "a deputation of workpeople." "A little popular demonstration, eh? Perfect!"

"Our Prefect will be asking to have the "Marseillaise" played soon," muttered the Treasurer-Paymaster with a smile.

Meanwhile Philippe had gone towards the workmen. "Ah, it's you, Gobert!" said he, as he recognised his oldest foreman, who stood waiting, rigged out in his Sunday clothes, and carrying his hat in one hand and a huge bouquet in the other. "Come along, my worthy fellow; and you, too, my friends."

But Gobert, a tall, white-haired old man, was apparently unable to set his legs in motion, and it seemed as if the sight of the elegant throng which was watching him from the terrace had turned him to stone; as though, indeed, he had come face to face with the head of Medusa. "Go on," muttered his comrades in the rear. "Go on, since it's you who've got to speak." But altogether paralyzed by emotion, he stood still there, with gaping mouth and open eyes, as motionless as if he were rooted to the spot.

It was Suzanne who broke the spell, for, taking the old workman, whom she had known ever since she was a child, by the hand, she led him towards Claire. The foreman made a deep bow, and greatly agitated, seeking for his words although he had learnt his little speech by heart, he at last began as follows: "Since the master allows it, Madame Derblay, will you condescend to accept this bouquet, which I am charged to offer you in the name of all of us, with our best wishes on your fête-day. You must know that there are eighteen hundred of us here at Pont-Avesnes who owe everything we have to your husband, who built us our houses, our schools, and our infirmary, and who cares for us as if we were his children. And, do you see, we're grateful to you for making him so happy!"

Gobert's emotion was so acute that the last words died away in his throat. However, loud shouts of applause rent the air, the Prefect giving the signal by clapping his hands as he turned, with an approving smile, towards the young husband and wife. Claire had started when she heard the old foreman speak of the happiness Philippe owed to her. Thus the same ironical praise came to her from all sides without ceasing.

The applause had finished, but Gobert, although divested of his bouquet, still stood, looking dreadfully uncomfortable, in front of Monsieur and Madame Derblay. "I've something else to say," he resumed at last. "We're about to have a general election." On hearing this Moulinet at once stepped forward, as if there were some question of his own pretensions, while the Prefect drew himself erect and cast a commanding glance around. "And we come," continued Gobert, "to ask the master to stand for the circonscription of Pont-Avesnes."

Moulinet heaved an immense sigh of relief. "The circonscription next to mine!" he cried. "Bravo!"

Meanwhile, as an echo to the old foreman's words, a storm of hurrahs and exclamations had burst forth just outside the front gates of the château. The workmen, with their wives and daughters, all decked out in their Sunday clothes, were assembled on the Place, watching the manifestation they had prepared from afar. "Open the gates," cried Philippe, "and let every one come in." A moment later a joyous throng spread through the parterres into the park, under the many-coloured Venetian lamps, which lit up the far-stretching avenues and the secluded bowers adorned with statues.

"These worthy folks have had an excellent idea," said the Prefect graciously. "Monsieur Derblay belongs to us. He is a Liberal in the most thorough meaning of the word. For all of us his name implies science, probity, work, and liberty."

"That's a candidature I'll second," repeated Moulinet. "We shall secure the whole district between us. I'll wake up my farmers. Committees, speeches, meetings—all that's my business. We shall have an easy victory."

"Upon my word, my dear Prefect, it seems to me we're exercising a little official influence on the electors," exclaimed a martial voice just behind the majestic Monicaud. The Prefect turned round as if some one had trodden on his foot, and found himself face to face with the General, who looked at him ironically. However, the representative of the Minister of the Interior contrived to smile at the representative of the Minister of War. "Eh! my dear General," said he, "after such a good dinner one can't fight one's host at dessert, you know. The stomach must be polite to its entertainer." Then, wheeling round on his heels again, he muttered between his teeth, "Dash that confounded pretorian!"

Meanwhile Philippe was speaking. "I accept the honour you do me, my friends," said he, "not out of ambition, for you know that I scarcely seek for occasions to push myself forward, but in the hope that I may be able to be of use to you."

A loud tumult followed. Acclamations rose from the crowd, and for a couple of minutes there was a frantic waving of hats and caps. Then by degrees the noise subsided. Claire had now stepped forward in her turn. "As for myself, my friends," she said, "I thank you for your kind offer from the depths of my heart. And as you are the oldest connected with the works, Gobert, come and kiss me for yourself and your comrades."

Thereupon, graceful and smiling, she offered her cheek to

the old foreman, who had flushed scarlet under his white hair, and seemed more ill at ease than ever. However, he timidly approached and kissed his master's wife with as much precaution as if her soft face had been one of the red-hot bars of iron he had so often hammered out. "Oh, madame," he said, "the Derblays were always noble folks, and you are worthy of belonging to them!"

Claire glanced at her husband triumphantly. It seemed to her as if the old foreman's words had recoupled the links that united her to Philippe.

Athénaïs was sneering, as she carried on a whispered conversation with La Brède and Du Tremblays. "Dear me," she said, "it's altogether charming; we are swimming in socialism."

A loud exclamation interrupted her. Philippe had just given orders to have several casks of wine rolled to an open space in the park, and had despatched a messenger for the village band. A platform of planks was promptly improvised, and hereupon the musicians began piping with their strident instruments. Attracted by the noise, the winegrowers of the surrounding slopes mingled with the working people, and the old feud which had long divided the district into two hostile camps seemed upon the point of subsiding. Gay and noisy was the scene in the broad avenues, lighted up with many-coloured lanterns which shone out like fantastic flowers amid the dark masses of foliage. Like a flash of lightning amid the darkness a bomb suddenly whizzed through the air, bursting with a loud report and raining golden stars upon the throng. It was the signal for a pyrotechnical display, which the Baron had privately ordered. Then the rockets began to soar through space, and the park was illuminated with the verdant and ruddy glow of Bengal lights. The musicians had ceased playing, and with their instruments on their knees they watched from their platform, as from the grand tier in a theatre, the capricious course of the flying squibs and the leaping lights of the Roman candles.

As an appropriate accompaniment young Du Tremkláys began humming in a shrill voice the opening lines of the well-known song—

"Little Peter, lift me up,
When I see the flying squib."

While the Prefect, turning towards Moulinet, enthusiastically remarked, "Do you see what a fine effect those red Bengal lights have! Ah, red is a beautiful colour!"

"I also like the green fire very much," replied the ex-judge, who had failed to grasp the allusion.

"Green's the colour of hope," said the departmental Treasurer, turning graciously to Moulinet and bowing.

This time the Duchess's father understood. He was always lucid when his own interests were concerned, and he looked benevolently at the *ex-viveur*, and decided that he was really a very well-bred man. The Treasurer, by the way, possessed the finest pair of horses in the Department.

"Well, Monsieur Moulinet," asked the Baron, who now approached, "how are you getting on? You look delighted."

"Yes, Baron," replied the ex-judge confidingly. "This luxury, these fêtes, this animation, all delight me. I was born for high life, and my tastes protest against the injustice of my birth."

"Your wit would suffice to make it forgotten," said Préfont, with imperturbable coolness.

A ruddy glow now spread over the sky. The set pieces were being illuminated, and under a flaming portico there appeared a little child—indicated in outline with rosy fire—who was crowning a woman delineated with white lights. "Love crowning Industry!" exclaimed the Baron, who thought it necessary to explain the allegory.

"An old acquaintance," muttered the majestic Monicaud to the Public Prosecutor. "Last year when I was Sub-Prefect at Neufchâtel, they served us the pink child and the white woman on the night of the national fête, and they called the group, 'The Future crowning France.'"

"And I," said the Treasurer of the Department gaily, "I saw it some years ago at a display of fireworks at Ville d'Avray, in honour of Dr. Thomson, the illustrious *accoucheur*. On that occasion the group was entitled, 'Infancy crowning Medical Science.'"

A loud noise, followed by dazzling refulgency, interrupted the conversation. The "bouquet" was mounting like a flaming sheaf towards the sky, where it stretched out over the spectators like a vault of fire. Blackened sticks then rained upon the foremost of the throng, amid shouts of laughter and alarm. At last the sky grew dark again, and the park became more obscure in the soft glow of the Venetian lamps. At the same moment, as if some invisible hand had given the signal, the musicians struck up the opening bars of a quadrille. Then, as the throng was hushed, a lad could be heard exclaiming in a mocking tone, "Take your places for the *contredanse*."

Athénaïs was suddenly seized with a grisette's fancy, with a mad longing to go and dance in the midst of all these peasants, and turning with bright eyes and glowing cheeks towards Philippe, she leant forward, exclaiming, "Oh, Monsieur Derblay, let us open this garden dance together! It will be delightful. Come, you shall dance with me!"

Philippe remained motionless, hesitating between the wish to refuse and the fear of seeming impolite. He exchanged a glance with Claire. She had turned pale on witnessing the Duchess's provoking audacity, and judged that the cup was full. Besides, she had vowed to herself that she would not allow Athénaïs to monopolise Philippe again. Still she was undecided as to the right course to take, for she feared to displease her husband. But at that moment she heard the Duke's hated voice beside her. "You see?" he muttered in a tone of raillery, at the same time calling Claire's attention to Athénaïs, who was leaning towards Philippe and looking at him coquettishly.

Claire quivered with grief and shame. Her sufferings were increased tenfold by the Duke's imprudent intervention. At this precise moment, as if their destiny were now to be decided, Philippe's eyes met hers, and she read in them so much constraint and such intense lassitude, that, impelled as it were by an irresistible power, she took a few steps forward and touched Athénaïs lightly on the arm just as she was repeating, "Come, shall we open the ball together?"

"Excuse me if I spoil your plans," exclaimed Claire, coldly. "But I should like to speak to you for a moment."

"Speak to me?" replied the Duchess with mingled surprise and annoyance. "What, now, at once?"

" Yes, at once," insisted Madame Derblay.

"It is something urgent then?"

"Very urgent."

Athénaïs gave her enemy a searching look, but Claire met her gaze with such firmness that she lowered her eyes, feeling strangely upset, and divining some serious complication. "What is the matter, dear?" she asked in a mellifluous voice, at the same time trying to take hold of Claire's hand.

"Follow me and you shall know," replied Madame Derblay sternly; and without adding a word, without turning towards Philippe, resolute if palpitating, she conducted Athénaïs to the little drawing-room, which was unoccupied.

They remained for a moment standing, like two adversaries about to close and struggle. Under the trees in the distance the improvised orchestra was just beginning to play, and the hum and buzz of the gay throng were wafted confusedly to the château. All the guests had gone into the park, and Athénaïs and Claire found themselves once more face to face, alone, and dependent on their own resources.

"Let us sit down," said Madame Derblay curtly.

"It will be long, then?" rejoined the Duchess with an impertinent yawn, which she made little pretence of repressing.

"I hope not," replied Claire.

Athénaïs installed herself in an arm-chair, and stretching out her legs, began to contemplate the jet ornaments on one of her shoes, making them scintillate in the light of the chandeliers, and apparently attaching no importance at all to what Claire might have to tell her.

"I have a favour to ask of you," resumed Madame Derblay.

"Am I so happy as to be able to oblige you?" asked Athénaïs nonchalantly.

"Yes. The other day at the paperchase in the forest, when you took my husband away with you, you asked me if I were not displeased, if I were not a little jealous——"

The Duchess tapped the floor with her heel and answered, "I was joking!"

"Well, you did wrong to think it a joke," declared Madame Derblay, "for you spoke the truth."

Athénaïs, who was greatly astonished, sat up in her chair, and put herself on her guard. "You, jealous?" she said.

"Yes."

"Jealous of me?" insisted the Duchess.

"Yes, of you," repeated Claire, and with a constrained smile she added, "You see that I am frank. It seems to me that my husband pays you more attention than is right, and so I address myself direct to you, to ask you to put a stop to a —flirtation, which you certainly attach no importance to, but which is very painful for me."

"Oh, my dear!" cried Athénaïs, turning towards Claire with a vivacity that seemed to betoken the most affectionate interest. "What! you were suffering and you said nothing about it? But do you not rather exaggerate? I don't recollect anything that could have really worried you. Monsieur Derblay is very amiable; he seems to like to talk to me, but there is nothing surprising in this sympathy between relatives and certainly nothing criminal——"

"It makes me suffer!" insisted Claire.

The little Duchess drew herself up and answered in a cutting tone, "But, my dear, you must apply to your husband for the remedy. I can't furnish it."

"Yes, you can put a stop to this intercourse."

Athénaïs sank back languidly in her arm-chair. She now realised what Claire was driving at. She wished her to disarm. Accordingly, subduing the bitterness of her voice, and speaking with an amenity which was even more exasperating than her previous arrogance, she replied, "But how can I do that? By giving your husband the cold shoulder? By being impolite to him? In the first place it would be a very disagreeable part for me to play; and besides, do you think it would be a very efficacious remedy?" She smiled as she spoke, with the bravado of a woman who is confident of her power.

"But that is not what I have to propose to you," rejoined Claire with quiet serenity.

"What have you to propose, then?"

Madame Derblay hesitated for one moment, and then boldly replied, "That you should keep away from our house for some time."

Athénaïs bounded from her chair, and, ceasing to control herself, exclaimed, "What! you think of proposing that!"

"Yes," answered Claire in a gentle voice, which was in striking contrast with her rival's bitterness. "And it is in a tone of entreaty that I make this request. Say I am mad, if you like, but do as I ask. It is a question of my happiness."

"But on what pretence would you have me keep away?" rejoined Athénaïs. "What would people say of such a sudden separation? Wouldn't it look like a quarrel, like a rupture?"

"We will find some satisfactory explanation for it."

Athénaïs was greatly embarrassed by the manner in which Claire insisted on this question. She fancied that Madame Derblay was stronger than she had believed, and she imagined that everything would be lost if she made the least concession. Accordingly she took the bull by the horns. "We might not succeed," she said; "and that would be disastrous for me. You have been frank, and now I will be frank as well. I am a new-comer in the society to which the Duc de Bligny has introduced me; I please myself in it; I wish to keep the place I have already won. But, as you know, folks are very punctilious, and, as you will understand, if my husband's family treated me coldly people would find an opportunity for disparaging remarks—there are so many who are jealous of me—and then good-bye to my dreams! If you have your love to think of, I—I have my ambition. I can understand your shielding the one, but allow me to defend the other."

Claire began to tremble with very rage. She could hardly control herself. She was seized with a longing to spring upon this miserable woman and crush her. "So, you refuse?" she asked in a muffled voice.

"Unwillingly, yes. But come, conscientiously, put yourself in my place!" And the irony of her words was so acute that Athénaïs could not restrain a smile.

Claire stepped forward, and, ceasing to control her anger, "Put myself in your place!" she fiercely said, "it is you who have put yourself in mine, and wish to do so again! Ever since I have known you you have pursued me with your envy and your hatred! As a girl you robbed me of my betrothed; as a woman you try to steal my husband from me! I did not know how to keep the former, but I shall know how to wrest the latter from you."

"Ah! So it's like that!" cried Athénaïs, turning pale with rage. "Well, let it be so! Let us raise the mask. To tell the truth, I am tired of dissimulation. Yes, since my childhood I pay you back in hatred for all the contempt which you and your friends heaped upon me. For ten years you crushed me with your name, your fortune, and your wit! Well, see! To-day I have millions of my own, I am a Duchess, and you are reduced to beg my mercy!"

"Take care!" said Claire, "I am not of a nature to allow myself to be insulted with impunity."

"And I," rejoined the Duchess, "I bear a name which sets me above the reach of your rage!"

"I will appeal against your conduct towards me."

"And to whom?" asked Athénaïs with a sneer.

"To society."

"To what society? To yours, which I have risen to? Or to mine, which you have fallen to?"

"To that society—no matter what it be—which comprises honest people who consider it a duty to respect others, and a right to insure respect for themselves. In that society, you hear me, I will repeat aloud what I have just told you. I will show you as you really are. And we shall see if the name you bear, however great it may be, will suffice to hide your baseness and your falseness."

The Duchess tried to reply, but she sought in vain for words in her envenomed heart. She could only hiss. Still, although reduced to silence, she was endeavouring at least to make an insulting gesture, when she saw Claire standing before her, looking so threatening, with ardent eyes and quivering hands, that she suddenly felt frightened. She stepped back, and in a low voice said, "So it is a scandal you are seeking to create?"

"It's an execution I mean to carry out. For the last time, will you consent to what I ask?"

"No! a hundred times, no!" answered Athénaïs, grinding her teeth.

"Then you shall see."

Footsteps were grating over the gravel, and a hum of merry voices was wafted through the open windows of the drawing-room. Suddenly Philippe appeared, coming up the steps with the Baroness on his arm. The Duke followed, laughing, with La Brède, in front of Moulinet, who had attached himself to the Baron. They perceived Claire and Athénaïs standing, pale and quivering, face to face, in so significant an attitude, that one and all stopped short in stupefaction. Then, with her head erect, sure of her conscience, strong in the suffering she had endured, Claire advanced to the centre of the room, and pointed to Athénaïs with a crushing gesture.

"Duke," she exclaimed, "take your wife away, if you do not wish me to have her turned out of the house in presence of everyone!"

Bligny remained impassive. Merely a pale smile stole over his lips. But Moulinet, who could not believe his ears, sprang forward, with a haggard face and upraised arms. "Turn my daughter, the Duchess, my daughter, out of the house!" he repeated emphatically, as if the entire aristocracy of France had been insulted in the person of Madame de Bligny.

But Athénaïs had already turned towards the Duke. "Monsieur!" she cried, in a piercing voice, "will you allow me to be insulted in this manner without defending me?"

With perfect composure Bligny took a couple of steps forward in Philippe's direction. "Do you approve, monsieur," he asked, "of what Madame Derblay has said to the Duchess? Are you disposed to apologise, or are you ready to accept the responsibility?"

These words were clear, polite, and as trenchant as steel.

Claire looked at her husband in agony. Would he disavow her, or openly take her side? For a moment she endured horrible suspense, and suffered more acutely, perhaps, than she had ever suffered before.

But on hearing Bligny the ironmaster had come forward. His stalwart form rose up in all its masculine vigour, and it could be seen that he was a full head taller than the Duke. In a grave voice, and with an energy which made everybody present start, he answered, "Monsieur le Duc, whatever Madame Derblay may do, whatever reason she may have for doing it, I consider everything she does as well done."

The Duke bowed in an incomparably elegant style, and, turning to La Brède, he made him a sign and said, "That's settled." Then offering his arm to Athénaïs, who seemed overwhelmed, he left the room followed by Moulinet, now fairly crazy, and by his faithful lieutenant, La Brède, who muttered between his teeth, "A nasty affair, and no mistake. Two cousins! Bligny is the offended one. He'll choose pistols. The ironmaster is a dead man!"

As Claire witnessed the departure of her rival, thus humiliated and vanquished, she did not think of the terrible consequences her audacity would entail. She raised a cry of triumph, and approaching her husband with passionate gratitude, "Oh, thank you Philippe!" she cried, stretching out her arms. But in a moment her ardour abandoned her, for she saw that her husband had become impassive again.

"You owe me no thanks," said he. "I defended my honour in defending you." And then perceiving that Claire remained silent and grave, he added, "Do not forget that you have guests to attend to here. No one must be allowed to suspect what has just happened."

With these words he offered his arm to the Baroness, whose nerves were so upset that she was tempted to laugh and cry at the same time. Claire wiped away a tear that was gliding down her cheek, and smiling sadly at the Baron, who had remained beside her, "Come," she said, "since it must be so, let us go and dance!"

XVIII.

Claire found the night a terribly long one. On returning to her room she realised the full gravity of the situation and felt frightened. She had certainly the right to act as she had done. Braved, threatened, outraged in her own home by a pitiless foe, she had revolted and driven her from the house. But, on the other hand, her private quarrel had become a general one. Her husband had been obliged to take her part and enter the lists against the Duke. She remembered how significantly Bligny had smiled as he said, "That's settled," and she shuddered at the recollection. She knew what a dangerous adversary the Duke was; and she realised that Philippe would find himself in imminent danger if a duel really took place. Late in the evening she had caught sight of Octave and the Baron conferring with La Brède and Moulinet. She had questioned her brother, but he had answered her evasively, with a constrained air, declaring that the negotiations would lead to an arrangement—a compromise.

Claire asked herself if any compromise were possible between these two men, who hated each other so intensely. The Duke had clearly defined the situation when he demanded either an apology or a recognition of responsibility—in other words, satisfaction. Now the young wife did not for one moment entertain the thought that her husband would apologise: hence there was but one solution possible—a duel.

Claire sprang from a brave race, and her feminine ancestors had never shrunk from the clash of arms. Her grandmother, a Bligny, had scoured the wilds of La Vendée with Stofflet's bands, using her carbine to pick off the "Blues"* whenever occasion required. When her father, the Marquis de Beaulieu, was only sixteen years old, he shut himself up at La Pénissière, and was found, three days later, under the ruins of the farm, with his arm shattered by a bullet. Now Claire was of a very similar nature to her father, but though she did not fear death herself, she was alarmed for Philippe. She felt superstitious moreover, and imagined that Fate had marked her marriage with the ironmaster with a black cross. She had a presentiment that if her husband fought he would be killed; and frightful visions passed before her eyes. She seemed to see Philippe stretched dead upon the blood-stained grass, and the Duke standing erect near by, holding his still smoking pistol, and laughing a wicked laugh. Why pistols —why use such dangerous weapons? It was in vain that she tried to persuade herself that perhaps they would fight with swords. Still and ever in her vision, she saw the two men with pistols in their hands; she heard the report of both weapons; a puff of blue smoke rose upwards, and Philippe, struck in the heart, fell heavily on to the grass.

She tried to free herself from this nightmare, which had seized hold of her although she was awake, and she went towards the window. The air was balmy, and the clear sky was radiant with stars. Among the trees of the park some of the Venetian lanterns were still alight, and fanned by the

* The Republican troops, so called by the Royalist insurgents, on account of the colour of their uniforms.—*Trans.*

breeze they stood out like red spots in the darkness. To Claire's horror, it seemed as if these red spots were stains of blood; and she hastily closed the window again, and drew the curtains so as to shut out the view of this dreadful glow. She paced round the room, pensive and absorbed, revolving her lugubrious apprehensions in her mind. "I bring woe to all who surround me," she exclaimed aloud, and the sound of her voice, breaking the silence, absolutely frightened her. She stretched herself on the sofa and tried to read, but in vain, for it seemed to her as if a bell were ringing in her ears, like some funereal knell. Then she felt anxious with regard to what Philippe was doing, and crossing the little drawing-room on tiptoe, she approached the door of her husband's bedroom. All was dark and silent —not a ray of light, not a sound. She thought that he was sleeping, and this surmise in some measure reassured her. Returning to her own room, she passed the rest of the night awake, in alternate fits of hope and despair.

Philippe was not in his room and he was not sleeping. He had shut himself up in his study, situated on the ground floor immediately under Claire's bedroom. He was aware that the duel he was about to fight with the Duke would be a serious one. A conference had taken place the same evening between the four seconds, and the situation, though grave, was so simple that an understanding had been promptly arrived at. Despite the imploring supplications of M. Moulinet, who wished to avoid a duel at any price, an appointment had been made for eight o'clock on the following morning. The chosen meeting place was situated between the woods of La Varenne and those of Pont-Avesnes, at an equal distance from the two châteaux. It was indeed that same Rond-Point des Etangs, which only a few days previously had re-echoed to the joyous cries and laughter of the hunters partaking of their sumptuous lunch. The Duke had chosen pistols, the distance was to be thirty paces, and the adversaries were to fire at will. Philippe accepted these conditions without reluctance; he had scarcely ever practised pistol shooting, but he was a first-rate shot with a rifle, and feeling sure of his *coup d'œil*, he thought to himself, with savage joy, that if he risked being killed himself, at least he would have the opportunity of killing his hated adversary. It was impossible to tell in advance which of the two opponents would prove the victor, for they were endowed with equal courage and tried calmness; but on the other hand it was well-nigh certain that one or the other of them would succumb.

Alone—having, perhaps, only a few hours to live—Philippe gave way to meditation, and passed his conduct in review. One thought sorely troubled him: he feared he had shown himself too hard towards Claire. At this supreme hour he was seized with profound pity for the poor woman who had washed her guilt away in her own tears. He saw that she was now really his. The haughty bride, who had so roughly repelled him, had become a tender, humble, devoted wife. The hard trial he had imposed upon her was completed, and he had the right to believe that if he survived she would belong to him heart and soul, and that if he died his memory would abide with her imperishably.

This was the object he had always had in view. He had attained it without going beyond, and he felt calmer as he came to this conclusion. He did not regret that he had so incessantly hammered his wife's bronze nature so as to fashion it to his liking. He considered that the result he had obtained would guarantee Claire's happiness, if Fate were propitious and he returned alive. She would surely have been unhappy had she been abandoned to herself, with her moral sense in such confusion. She was too intelligent not to understand that her life was wrecked, and too proud to confess that the fault was entirely her own; and thus she would have lived on, devoured by bitter rancour and a prey to sterile regret. The lesson he had given her was bound to be a salutary one. She had reflected, sought for the right path, and by dint of efforts conquered herself. She was now ripe for happiness. But alas! at the very moment when her regeneration was completed, when the future stretched out before her so full of smiles, adverse fate might plunge her back into despair.

The noise of footsteps resounding over Philippe's head suddenly broke the stillness of the night and made him start. He listened. It was a regular, continuous, seemingly automatic tread—the tread of the unhappy woman who was suffering such cruel agony, and who, although only separated from him by a mere flooring, was completely isolated by his implacable will. As Philippe heard the floor creak he divined how horrible Claire's agitation must be. He could picture her turning round and round the room with haggard eyes, contracted features, and trembling hands; with that wild air which, as he had often remarked, always came over her in acute moments of grief or anger. His heart began to expand, and for the first time he felt weak at the thought of his love. His temples beat precipitately, his throat tightened, and he was seized with an all-powerful desire to go and join this woman he adored and who was yet a maiden. Like a child, he gave himself all sorts of reasons to justify this resolution. Would it not be mad to risk death before taking her in his arms and covering the perfumed tresses of her golden hair with kisses? He had but to say a word, and she would fall upon his heart. Philippe took a few steps forward, and was already opening the door, when his will, returning, restrained him. Surely he was not going to give way to such degrading weakness. After all the suffering he had endured, should he be wanting in courage at the last moment? He had conquered and tamed that woman, and now should he go and lower himself for the sake of mere desire? The hour had struck when his life would be morally and materially decided. If he survived, Claire would belong to him entirely, without hesitation in the present or fear in the future. If he died, she would remember him as proud and implacable and truly great. Like a gambler, he must risk the game. All or nothing. A lifetime of pure happiness or cold and silent death. He made up his mind to this alternative, and feeling thoroughly resolute he returned and sat down at his writing-table.

Overhead Claire was still feverishly walking up and down. Suddenly he heard her open the door, and furtively cross the drawing-room towards his bed-chamber. A smile glided over his face, and he listened attentively. A moment later Claire crossed the drawing-room again, and returned to her own apartment. Thus she had had a thought similar to his own, and like himself she had abandoned it. He now realised from what a pedestal he would have fallen had he gone to her. He would have ceased to be a superior man, mastering everything by force of will; he would have seemed a vulgar being at the mercy of his passions.

The first faint light of dawn reminded him of the preparations he had to make. In the event of his death he wished to provide for his sister. He had been able to appreciate the many sterling qualities of the young Marquis de Beaulieu. He had divined that Octave was gifted with a true heart and a serious mind. If he had given a refusal when Claire asked him to bestow Suzanne's hand on her brother, it was only in view of adhering faithfully to his conjugal tactics, and striking a harder blow than all the others at his wife's heart. He had realised that the decisive crisis was approaching, and he had determined to repair the wrong he was doing Octave as soon as possible. Besides, Suzanne loved the Marquis; and Philippe's heart melted at the thought of inflicting the least grief on this dear child, who had been the happiness of his life. He determined to marry her to the Marquis, and so as to give additional solemnity to his consent, he framed it in a testamentary form. Grave and thoughtful, he took every necessary decision. He divided his fortune between Suzanne and Claire, begging "his dear wife to accept her share, in memory of the deep love he had borne her." Then he selected one of his engineers, a talented and honest man, to manage the iron works in the event of his demise; and having thus provided for everything, he thought of taking a little rest. It was necessary he should have a firm hand and perfect vision. So stretching himself on the broad leather divan, he heaved a sigh and closed his eyes.

Meanwhile there was great emotion at the Château de la Varenne. Athénaïs had returned from Pont-Avesnes in a state of perfect fury. At the moment when the woman she hated seemed finally crushed and at her mercy, a vigorous blow had enabled her to rise erect again—haughty and triumphant. It was she, the Duchesse de Bligny, who had been humiliated, vanquished, and driven from the house. And she could not hide from herself that this rupture would do her irreparable harm. All the Duke's relatives took Claire's side. The motives of the duel would be made public, and the story of how she had been expelled would be related, commented, and enlarged upon by a society that hated her. At this thought Athénaïs ground her teeth, and a longing for carnage swelled her heart. She would have liked to have been in the Duke's place, so as to have accomplished the sanguinary business herself. She longed to see Claire a widow. She pictured her, veiled, in mourning, with tears streaming down her eyes, and cursing the hour when she had insulted her. She thought to herself that by striking Madame Derblay in the person of the husband she loved she would inflict a blow on the very source of life itself. With a strident laugh she threw her gloves and her fan on the table of the drawing-room which she had just entered, and then, turning towards her father and her husband, who were watching her in silence, "As for that man," she said, "that man who defends the woman who insulted me, I must have him killed."

There was a moment's stupefaction. Moulinet was thunderstruck by his daughter's tragic exclamation; the Duke was astonished to find that his wife's hatred was as intense as his own. Still he was displeased with her for having created a scandal which had resulted, for them both, in such humiliating retirement. He blamed her for not having restrained herself. Accustomed to the graceful perfidy and smiling hatred of the aristocratic world, he considered that Athénais was horribly vulgar and clumsy. And, besides, her Borgia-like attitude thoroughly displeased him. Giving her a quiet look, he lightly exclaimed, "Kill the man! You talk of it as a settled matter, my dear. Such phrases are in their place in a melodrama, but in ordinary life they are altogether ridiculous. Rid yourself of big words and big gestures." Then with a cold smile he added, "On the other hand, you may be certain that I shall do my best to satisfy you."

"Allow me, Monsieur le Duc," exclaimed Moulinet, rousing himself from his meditation. "Allow me. You seem disposed to carry matters to such extremities——"

"Didn't you hear your daughter, my dear sir?" answered

Bligny coldly. "Do you think I am so careless of my duties as not to defend my wife?"

"That is not the question," rejoined Moulinet; "you have acted most correctly, I will admit it; but my daughter must be insane to urge you on to violence like that. On the contrary, she ought to preach conciliation. Everything may yet be arranged. A passing misunderstanding between two friends, a slight quarrel between two cousins. They will kiss each other, and it will all be settled. But a duel, a scandal, a rupture? Can't you realise the consequences it would entail? They are enormous for yourselves! And for me?—Why for me they are disastrous!—You simply kill all my chances of election!"

Despite the gravity of the situation the Duke could not help laughing; while Athénaïs, who was couched, like a coiling viper, in her arm-chair, gave a disdainful hiss.

"Excuse me, Monsieur le Duc," resumed Moulinet in a tone of authority. "I think I have done enough for you to insist on my wishes being carried out in the present instance. This deplorable affair must be arranged. Every day there are similar matters which result in pacification. The task is an easy one. We will draw up a little *procès verbal* by which Madame Derblay will declare that she withdraws what she said. My daughter will withdraw what she replied. You, my son-in-law, you must withdraw your challenge, and something being withdrawn on all sides it will only remain——"

"For us to withdraw ourselves," said the Duke.

"But it is done every day——"

"Not when such men as Monsieur Derblay and myself are in presence. Believe me, Monsieur Moulinet, silence your excellent heart. Stifle the candidate's alarm and let matters proceed as it has been decided—I wish you good night. I have to talk to La Brède before going to bed." Thereupon, quietly bowing to his wife and his father-in-law, the Duke left the room.

Moulinet approached Athénaïs. "Come, my dear child," he stammered.

But without even looking at him the Duchess, who was extremely pale, rose from her seat, opened the door of her room, and disappeared. Moulinet sadly jerked his head, and confessed to himself for the first time that there were really some difficulties which could not be surmounted by money. "Night gives advice," he muttered. "To-morrow it will be daylight; we shall see matters more clearly." And clinging as it were to a vague hope, he went to stretch himself in the bed of the Emperor Charles V.

The ironmaster had been sleeping calmly for a couple of hours when a touch on his shoulder woke him up. He opened his eyes; and on seeing that the Marquis de Beaulieu was standing before him, he sprang eagerly to his feet. It was already broad daylight, half-past six by the clock. "We have the time," murmured Philippe.

Never had he felt stronger or more composed, and he realised this with pride. This man of will was always secretly delighted when he obtained some such proof of his own moral force. He went to the window and opened it. The air was fresh and pure, impregnated with the scent of flowers moist with dew. He let his eyes wander over the park. A light transparent blue haze was hanging like a veil over the trees, and the sun, already high in the heavens, was scintillating on the calm surface of the sheet of water. Nature seemed to have adorned herself in his honour. "A splendid day!" he gaily cried, just as though he had been going out on some mere sporting expedition.

But as he spoke his eyes met the Marquis's, and he seemed to read mute reproach in Octave's saddened gaze. He at once went towards his brother-in-law and affectionately took hold of his hand. "Do not be astonished to find me so careless and almost joyful this morning," he said. "I have a presentiment that everything will finish to my advantage." Then becoming grave again, he added, "Still, as misfortune may happen, I have taken all necessary decisions, and you will find them recorded in this letter." So saying, he pointed to an envelope addressed to Maitre Bachelin, which was lying on his writing-table. "I have chosen you and my old friend to be my executors, and what I have bequeathed to you, my dear Octave, is very dear to me indeed——"

A ray of joy lighted up the Marquis's face. He tried to speak, but his voice died away in his throat, and catching Philippe by the arms he began to sob on his shoulder.

"Come, Octave, be firm," resumed Philippe. "I hope that I shall be present at your wedding to give my sister away myself. But if I were no longer there, my friend, love her dearly when you are married, for she deserves it. She has a tender heart, which the least grief would break." It was with infinite softness of tone that he spoke of the child whom he had reared and cherished with a father's love; but passing his hand across his forehead, he speedily became calm and smiling again. "I must go and dress," he said. "Will you come up-stairs with me? You will keep me company. And then we will seek the Baron. I should like to leave the house without attracting notice."

Octave lowered his head without answering. But at last, making a great effort, he exclaimed, "Before coming to you this morning, Philippe, I saw my sister. Will you promise me not to start without seeing her?"

Philippe looked questioningly at the Marquis.

"It is not admissible," resumed Octave, "that you should leave her without giving her the opportunity of justifying herself in your eyes, if such indeed be possible." And as the ironmaster made a sudden gesture of surprise, the Marquis added gravely, "Three days ago I learned what had occurred between Claire and you. She confessed everything to me. I know how guilty she was, Philippe, and believe me, I pity you for having endured such bitter grief as much as I admire you for having known how to hide it. But come, I beg you be indulgent and generous. It would be noble on your part not to crush this poor woman in despair. You are a brave and an energetic man, and one has a right to say everything to you. Reflect that she may never see you alive again. Do not leave her crushed with remorse at the thought that she has not merely desolated your life, but led you perhaps to death itself."

The ironmaster turned ashy pale and averted his face. He took a few steps in the direction of the window, and then returning towards Octave, "I will do what you ask of me," he said. "But this interview will be a horribly painful one, both for your sister and myself. Do all you can to shorten it and facilitate my departure by coming to fetch me."

The Marquis acquiesced with a gesture, and having pressed Philippe's hand affectionately, followed him to the bedroom on the floor above.

XIX.

The Baroness joined her cousin very early in the morning. She found her in a state of torpor after the horrible agitation of the night, and when she spoke to her she was unable to obtain any reply. With a contracted mouth and fixedly staring eyes, the young wife crouched on the sofa as if she were absolutely crushed. All her life seemed to be centred in her wild dark stare, which appeared to be fixed on some frightful vision. Several hours elapsed without a change. Each time the clock struck, indicating the flight of time, Claire started; but if it had not been for this spasmodic motion and for the fierce glow in her eyes, one might have imagined her to have been asleep.

At last, however, her brother's arrival roused her. She clung passionately to the hope of seeing Philippe before he started. Fever mounted to her face, and her cheeks glowed with fire, as in an exhausted voice she begged Octave to try and induce her husband to grant her this supreme favour. Agitation then seized hold of her again, and she became extremely restless, constantly going to the window and raising the blind to see if she had been deceived, if Philippe were really starting, and then hastening to the door and listening, in hopes that she might hear his approach. The Baroness was frightened as she beheld Claire more anxious and enervated each moment, and displaying every sign of growing madness.

Suddenly a noise of footsteps made the young wife shrink into a corner, as if she were afraid of finding herself face to face with the man whom she called upon with all the strength of her soul. She turned deadly pale, a black circle encompassed her eyes, and she made a gesture to the Baroness as a request for her to withdraw. Then, trembling in every limb, dumb with emotion, she remained standing in the centre of the room, which Philippe had just entered. They remained in presence of each other without exchanging a word. He noticed with grief the traces of frightful anguish on her face; whilst she, on her side, tried to collect her thoughts, finding only emptiness in her agonising brain, though but a moment before she had had so much to say. She was soon unable to endure this weighty silence any longer, and approaching Philippe, she took his hand in hers; then, with a heartrending sob, she began to cover it with tears and kisses.

The ironmaster had expected an explanation; he was prepared for entreaties; but this sudden explosion of grief, which he knew was sincere, came upon him unawares, and fairly unmanned him. He wished to withdraw his hand, on which the scalding tears of the woman he loved were falling rapidly, but he was unable to do so, and he quivered, feeling as if all his strength were leaving him. "Claire," said he, in a low tone, "come, you trouble me greatly. I so need to be calm; and calm yourself, I beg of you. Be stronger; spare me, if you care for my life."

On hearing these words Claire raised her head. The expression of her face was no longer the same. She seemed to have come to some sudden resolution. "Your life!" she said. "Ah! rather mine, a hundred times! Miserable woman that I am! It is I who have exposed you to this danger by my violence. But I ought to have borne everything. In suffering I expiated my conduct towards you. And yet, in a moment's rage, I forgot everything. But this duel is senseless. It shall not take place. I know how it can be prevented.

"And how?" asked Philippe already frowning.

"By sacrificing my pride to your security," answered Claire. "Oh, nothing shall hinder me since it is a question of your life. I will humiliate myself before the Duchess if needs be. I will speak to the Duke. There is still time!"

"I forbid your doing it," replied the ironmaster with contracted features. "Do not forget that you bear my name. Any humiliation you suffered would reflect upon myself. And besides, understand that I hate him, this man who is the cause of all my woe! For the last year I have been longing to find myself face to face with him. Ah, believe me, this day is welcome!"

Claire bowed her head. She had long been accustomed to obey when Philippe ordered. Calmed, as it were, by this outburst, he now resumed more softly. "I appreciate the feeling that guided you in this proposal, and I am grateful to you for it. At the outset of our married life there was a misunderstanding which has caused us both to suffer grievously. I do not hold you entirely responsible. It was partly my fault as well. I did not know how to understand you, how to sacrifice myself; I loved you too much. But I cannot now go away, leaving you with the thought that I still harbour rancour against you. You may be at peace, Claire, and in your turn forgive me the sufferings I have caused you, and bid me good-bye."

As Claire heard this, her face became radiant, and raising her arms to heaven in an impulse of passionate gratitude, "Forgive you? I?" she cried. "But can you not see that I worship you? Have you never detected it in my eyes or my voice?" Whilst speaking she came close to Philippe, and now throwing her beautiful arms round his neck, she laid her fair head on his shoulder, intoxicating him with the perfume of her person and inflaming him with her passionate glances. She spoke as in a dream, "Ah! do not go. If you knew how much I love you. Stay here with me and be mine. We are so young, we have so many years to be happy. Why care about that man and that woman who hate us so? We will forget them. Let us fly from them, afar. There we shall find happiness, life, and love."

Philippe gently parted the arms that clung around him and freed himself from Claire's embrace. "Here," said he quietly, "'tis a question of honour and duty."

The young wife heaved a heartrending sigh. She became conscious again of the frightful reality, and her vision rose before her once more—the Duke, his pistol in his hand, laughing his wicked laugh. She wished to spring forward, make a final effort, and detain Philippe despite himself. "No! no!" she cried; but at the same moment the door opened, and Octave appeared on the threshold. He made a sign to Philippe, and then immediately withdrew. Claire realised that the time for her husband to start had now arrived. A veil seemed to be torn away from before her eyes, she understood that it was all over, and, falling on her husband's breast again, she embraced him for the last time with convulsive earnestness.

"Good-bye," murmured the ironmaster.

"Oh, don't leave me like that! Not with that icy word. Tell me that you love me! Do not go without having told me so."

But Philippe remained inflexible. He had confessed that he forgave her, but he would not acknowledge that he loved her. Freeing himself from her again, he walked towards the door. Then, on the threshold, turning round, "Pray God that I may come back alive," he said, as if to give her a supreme hope.

That was all. The young wife gave vent to a shriek which made the Baroness hasten to the spot. The vehicle in which the ironmaster, Octave, and the Baron took their places at once started down the avenue. Careless of the Baroness's presence, Claire threw herself on to the sofa and hid her head among the cushions, as though she wished neither to see nor hear anything, as if she longed to be able to suspend her life during the terrible hour that was about to ensue. But a gentle voice suddenly aroused her. Suzanne was knocking at the door and asking, "Can I come in?"

Claire and the Baroness exchanged a painful glance. It was again necessary to dissimulate, to try and deceive this child, who knew nothing of the truth. Setting the door ajar, Suzanne popped her head into the room. She looked fresh and gay. "Come in, my dear," said Claire, and, making a prodigious effort, she tried to smile.

"What! you are not dressed yet," cried the young girl, seeing that her sister-in-law still wore her dressing-gown. "Why, I've already been round the park in the little chaise." Whilst speaking, Suzanne moved about the room, foraging like a young cat. "Ah, do you know," she suddenly exclaimed, "I have just met Philippe with the Baron and Monsieur Octave. They were in a closed carriage, and looked rather strange. Where can they have gone like that, all three of them?"

Claire flushed and turned pale alternately, and drops of perspiration overspread her forehead. Each word that Suzanne spoke seemed to torture her.

"Oh, if my husband were there," said the Baroness,

"they must have gone for some experiments, some visit to the pits."

"Which way were they going?" asked Claire in a trembling voice.

"Towards the meres," said Suzanne; "perhaps they were going to La Varenne."

"Oh, no!" replied the Baroness. "The Duc de Bligny is not a man to get up before ten o'clock."

Claire no longer listened. "Towards the meres," Suzanne had said. And at once there rose before her eyes a vision of the forest glade, with its grassy lawn, its white fence, and the still water shaded by the drooping branches of the trees. This quiet, lonely spot was just the place for a duel. Its desolate aspect seemed to destine it for some tragic scene. It was there that the Duke and Philippe would fight; she felt sure of it; she seemed to see them. She was seized again with frightful agitation, and became extremely restless. Suddenly she divested herself of her dressing-gown and donned a morning costume. She had formed a plan, and was intent upon accomplishing it. "You used the little chaise," she said to Suzanne; "where did you leave it?"

"In the courtyard of the stables," replied the young girl. "They must be unharnessing the horses."

"No matter; I shall take it. I have something to do in the neighbourhood," rejoined Claire; and without waiting she hastily threw a lace *fichu* over her head and hurried from the room.

Alone, handling the reins excitedly, she started off at a rapid pace. Motion, instead of calming her fever, only excited her the more. She felt frenzied by the speed of the horse, and urged him into a yet faster gallop, careless of the ruts of the forest, and seemingly courting an accident.

Nothing stopped her; on and on she went with distended nerves, biting her lips with vexation at not being able to go faster, envying the birds their wings, and listening, with a palpitating heart, as if she feared that in the silence of the wood she might suddenly hear the fatal report of firearms.

But the forest remained silent. On the high road, in the distance, the bells of passing vehicles could be heard merrily jingling. The mossy avenue stretched before her, deadening the clatter of the horse's hoofs. His flanks were steaming, and he was surrounded with a vapoury cloud. Impelled frantically on and on, he suddenly stumbled and fell. Claire sprang from the vehicle, and darted on foot through the forest. Instinct warned her that she was reaching the goal, and as she listened she suddenly heard some one talking near her.

She glanced rapidly around. Some twenty paces distant, above the meres, M. Moulinet's Chinese kiosk mirrored its porcelain tiles in the sleeping water. By installing herself there Claire would be able to see everything that happened, without being seen herself. Lightly, like some hunted hind, she glided through the trees and climbed the steps leading to the kiosk. Suddenly she paused, with a feeling of mingled anxiety and alarm.

In the centre of the clearing the Baron was striding along, counting the thirty paces that were to intervene between the two adversaries. La Brède was loading the weapons, with the assistance of Moulinet, who looked extremely pale and wild. At the farther end of the glade Philippe walked slowly to and fro, conversing with the doctor and Octave. Near the kiosk stood the Duke, munching a cigar, and carelessly decapitating the forest-flowers with a cane which he held in his hand. With a pang at her heart Claire recalled the aspect of the Rond-Point on the day when it was full of horsemen and elegantly attired women, with the luncheon-tables sumptuously set out, and served by footmen from La Varenne. Everything had then been gay and brilliant. No doubt she had felt jealous, but what was her jealousy in comparison with her present tortures? Below her stood the two men who were bent on killing each other for her sake, and in a moment one or the other of them would be stretched on the grass. A cloud passed before her eyes, and she had to cling to the balustrade to avoid falling. However, her weakness did not last long. She looked again, breathing heavily, and seized with horrible curiosity.

The two adversaries were now in position, and M. Moulinet had just cried out in a supplicating tone, "Gentlemen, for heaven's sake, gentlemen!" But La Brède had drawn him aside, and was severely lecturing him in a corner. Octave now handed Philippe his weapon and at once drew aside.

"Are you ready, gentlemen?" asked La Brède in a firm voice.

"Yes," replied the Duke and Philippe simultaneously.

La Brède at once resumed, counting slowly, "One—two—three—fire!"

Claire saw the two pistols lowered threateningly. At this supreme moment she lost all self-control. An invincible impulse urged her forward, and with a shriek she bounded down the steps, and eager to save Philippe, clapped her hand upon the muzzle of Bligny's pistol. A loud report was heard, and Claire turned as pale as death itself. Excitedly waving her gashed and bleeding hand, she shook it in Bligny's face, covering him with blood. Then, heaving a deep sigh, she tottered and fainted away.

There was a moment of indescribable confusion. The Duke

had retreated, horror-stricken, when he felt this warm rain of blood fall upon his face. Philippe had darted forward, caught hold of Claire, and taking her in his arms, as if she had been a child, carried her to the carriage which was waiting hard by. Her eyes were closed. Assisted by the doctor, the ironmaster anxiously raised the poor mutilated hand and passionately kissed it.

With a gloomy face and almost feminine delicacy of touch the doctor anxiously examined the wound. "Nothing broken," he exclaimed at last in a tone of relief. "We have got off on cheaper terms than I expected. It is true that the hand will be badly damaged, but Madame Derblay will only have to keep her glove on." He began to laugh, regaining at once all his customary surgical self-possession, and then he settled the cushions of the vehicle so as to make Claire comfortable.

Philippe, who was still grievously upset, stood looking at his wife, feeling frightened by her prolonged fainting-fit. However, he was roused to consciousness of the situation on hearing the Baron call him. La Brède, who seemed greatly disturbed, approached at M. de Préfont's side.

"I am charged by the Duc de Bligny, monsieur," said he, "to express to you how deeply he regrets the misfortune he has involuntarily caused. The accident that has happened to Madame Derblay has greatly afflicted him, and his ideas are altogether modified. It seems to him that it is now quite impossible to follow up this affair. My friend's courage is above all question, yours also, monsieur. We are all men of honour, and you may be sure that what has happened will be faithfully kept secret."

The ironmaster glanced at the Duke. Trembling and livid, he was leaning against the paling wiping his face, and each time that he removed his handkerchief he noted with a painful shudder a fresh stain of blood. He reflected to himself that his bullet might have mortally wounded Claire, pierced her fair brow or her white bosom; and at the thought he judged himself severely, was horrified at his conduct, and determined he would never more interfere with the woman who had suffered so much on his account.

La Brède was still talking to Philippe with unusual emotion. The ironmaster vaguely heard the young man express his personal regrets, and let him shake his hand. Then perceiving that the Duke was going off with Moulinet, he pushed the doctor into his own carriage, climbed on to the box, caught up the reins, and started off at a rapid pace.

In the spacious room, hung with old tapestry whereon the young goddesses replenished the warriors' goblets, Philippe sat in silence beside Claire's bed as in the days of her long illness. Fever had seized hold of the young wife, an hour had elapsed without her regaining consciousness, but she was now stirring on her pillows. Suddenly her eyes opened, and it seemed as if she were looking for Philippe. The ironmaster immediately rose and leant towards her. A smile passed over her lips, and throwing her bare arms round her husband's neck she tenderly drew him towards her. Her brain was so disturbed that she was only in a state of semi-consciousness. It seemed to her as if she were floating like a spirit in the celestial ether. She felt no pain, for a delightful sensation of languor had come over her. Then, so low that Philippe scarcely heard her, she murmured, "I am dead, am I not, my love, and dead for you? How happy I feel! You are smiling at me—you love me. I am in your arms. How sweet is death! And what an adorable eternity!"

Suddenly she was awoke by the sound of her own voice.

An acute pain passed through her hand and she remembered everything—her despair, her anguish, and her sacrifice. "No! I live," she cried; and then repulsing Philippe and looking wildly at him, as though her life or death depended on his answer, "One word?" she asked. "Tell me—do you love me?"

Philippe showed her a radiant face. "Yes, I love you," he replied. "There were two women in you. She who caused me so much suffering no longer lives; but you—you are the one I have never ceased to love."

A cry escaped Claire; her eyes filled with tears, she clung frantically to Philippe, their lips met, and in inexpressible ecstasy they exchanged their first kiss of love.

THE END.

42, CATHERINE STREET, STRAND,
SEPTEMBER, 1884.

VIZETELLY & CO.'S NEW BOOKS, AND NEW EDITIONS.

In Demy 8vo, cloth gilt, price 12s. 6d.

A JOURNEY DUE SOUTH;

TRAVELS IN SEARCH OF SUNSHINE.

By GEORGE AUGUSTUS SALA.

ILLUSTRATED WITH FULL-PAGE ENGRAVINGS BY VARIOUS ARTISTS.

CONTENTS :—

- I.—A Few Hours in the Delightful City.
- II.—Life at Marseilles.
- III.—Southern Fare and Bouillabaisse.
- IV.—Nice and its Nefarious Neighbour.
- V.—Quite Another Nice.
- VI.—From Nice to Bastia.
- VII.—On Shore at Bastia.
- VIII.—The Diligence come to Life again.
- IX.—Sunday at Ajaccio.
- X.—The Hotel too soon.
- XI.—The House in St. Charles Street, Ajaccio.
- XII.—A Winter City.
- XIII.—Genoa the Superb: the City of the Leaning Tower.
- XIV.—Austere Bologna.
- XV.—A Day of the Dead.
- XVI.—Venice Preserved.
- XVII.—The Two Romes. I. The Old.
- XVIII.—The Two Romes. II. The New.
- XIX.—The Two Romes. II. The New (*cont.*).
- XX.—The Roman Season.
- XXI.—In the Vatican : Mosaics.
- XXII.—With the Trappists in the Campagna.
- XXIII.—From Naples to Pompeii.
- XXIV.—The Show of a Long-Buried Past.
- XXV.—The "Movimento" of Naples.
- XXVI.—In the Shade.
- XXVII.—Spring Time in Paris.
- XXVIII.—"To All the Glories of France."
- XXIX.—Le Roi Soleil and La Belle Bourbonnaise.
- XXX.—A Queen's Plaything.

IMPORTANT NEW WORK BY THE AUTHOR OF "SIDE LIGHTS ON ENGLISH SOCIETY."

Two Vols. large Post 8vo, attractively bound, price 25s.

UNDER THE LENS:
SOCIAL PHOTOGRAPHS.
By E. C. GRENVILLE-MURRAY.

ILLUSTRATED WITH ABOUT 300 ENGRAVINGS BY WELL-KNOWN ARTISTS.

CONTENTS OF VOL. I.

JILTS:—Mrs. Pinkerton—A Western County Belle—Zoe, Lady Tryon—An Inconsol< Jilt—A Jilted Drysalter—Love and Pickles—An Entr'acte—Mrs. Prago and Miss Daisy Caunt< A Widow with a Nice Little Estate—An Unmercenary Pair of Jilts.

ADVENTURERS AND ADVENTURESSES:—Of the Genus Generally—M< monial Adventurers—The Joint Stock Company Chairman—A Financial Adventurer—A fessional Greek—The Countess D'Orenbarre—Lady Goldsworth—Mirabel Hildacourse—Lily —Bella Martingale—Pious Mrs. Palmhold—Mrs. Decoy—Mrs. Lawkins.

PUBLIC SCHOOLBOYS AND UNDERGRADUATES:—Drawbacks of —Of Various Eton Boys—Rugby and Rugbeians—Harrow, Winchester, Westminster—Ox Undergraduates — University Discipline—Sporting and Athletic Undergraduates—Reading Religious Undergraduates.

CONTENTS OF VOL. II.

SPENDTHRIFTS:—Prefatory—The Gambletons—Lord Charles Innynges—Lord L Poor—Lord Rottenham — Lord Barker—The Marquis of Malplaquet—The Lords Lumber-Calling Earley—Tommy Dabble—Dicky Duff.

HONORABLE GENTLEMEN (M.P.'s):— Preliminary — Erudite Membe< Crotchety Members — Free Lances — The Irish Contingent—Very Noble M.P.'s—Moncy Ba Beery M.P.'s—Workingmen M.P.'s—Party Leaders—A Seatless Member.

SOME WOMEN I HAVE KNOWN:—An Ex-Beauty—Miss Jenny—Mademoi Sylvie—Miss Rose—Madame de l'Esbrouffe-Tourbillon.

ROUGHS OF HIGH AND LOW DEGREE:—How Roughs are Made—The N< man Rough—The Foreign Garrison Rough—The Clerical Rough—The Legal Rough—M< Roughs—The Rough Flirt—The Wife-Beating Rough—Vandal Roughs—The Tourist Rough—Nautical Rough—The Professional Bruiser—The Low-Class Rough—Women Roughs.

VIZETELLY'S ONE-VOLUME NOVELS.

BY ENGLISH AND FOREIGN AUTHORS OF REPUTE.

In Crown 8vo, good readable type, and attractive binding, price 6s. each.

NEW VOLUMES.

A MUMMER'S WIFE.
By GEORGE MOORE,
AUTHOR OF "A MODERN LOVER."

PRINCE SERGE PANINE.
By GEORGES OHNET,
AUTHOR OF "THE IRONMASTER."

TRANSLATED, WITHOUT ABRIDGMENT, from the 110TH FRENCH EDITION.

Third Edition.

THE IRONMASTER; OR, LOVE AND PRIDE.
By GEORGES OHNET.

TRANSLATED WITHOUT ABRIDGMENT FROM THE 146TH FRENCH EDITION.

"'Le Maître de Forges' of M. Georges Ohnet, of which the above is a close translation, has proved the greatest literary success in any language of recent times, one hundred and forty-six editions having been already sold in France. It is a story of admirably sustained interest, skilfully told in graceful yet forcible language. The strongly-marked characters develop themselves naturally, both in their language and their actions. The book, moreover, unlike the general run of French novels, conveys a sound moral. It chastises the malice which is born of envy, and establishes the folly of that selfish pride which blinds its possessor to all consideration for the commoner clay of humanity. It shows anew how needful it is that husbands and wives alike should study each other's characters before marriage, and it enforces in convincing language the oft-repeated lesson, that a woman should never trifle with the affection of the man to whom she is mated for life.

NUMA ROUMESTAN; OR, JOY ABROAD AND GRIEF AT HOME.
By ALPHONSE DAUDET.

TRANSLATED BY MRS. J. G. LAYARD.

"'Numa Roumestan' is a masterpiece; it is really a perfect work; it has no fault, no weakness. It is a compact and harmonious whole. Daudet's other works have their inequalities, their anomalies, certain places where, if you tapped them, they sounded hollow .... The beauty of 'Numa Roumestan' is that it has no hollow places; the logic and the image melt everywhere into one .... Alphonse Daudet was born in Provence. His style is impregnated with the southern sunshine, and his talent has the sweetness of a fruit that has grown in the warm open air. 'Joy abroad and grief at home'—that proverb, says Alphonse Daudet, describes and formulates a whole race. It has given him the subject of an admirable story in which he has depicted with equal force and tenderness the amiable weaknesses, the mingled violence and levity of the children of the clime of the fig and olive .... I will only repeat that I delight in 'Numa Roumestan.'"—MR. HENRY JAMES.

"Of all Daudet's productions 'Numa Roumestan' is the one that I regard as most personal to himself. He has put his whole nature into it, helped by his southern temperament, having only to make large drafts upon his most intimate recollections and sensations. I do not think that he has hitherto reached such an intensity either of irony or of geniality.... Happy the books which arrive in this way at the hour of the complete maturity of a talent! They are simply the widest unfolding of an artist's nature; they have in happy equilibrium the qualities of observation and the qualities of style."—M. EMILE ZOLA.

Other Works of this Series are in preparation.

In Large Crown 8vo, beautifully printed on toned paper, and handsomely bound, with gilt edges, price 7s. 6d., suitable in every way for a present,

AN ILLUSTRATED EDITION OF

M. GEORGES OHNET'S CELEBRATED NOVEL,

THE IRONMASTER; OR, LOVE AND PRIDE.

CONTAINING 40 FULL-PAGE ENGRAVINGS BY FRENCH ARTISTS,
PRINTED SEPARATE FROM THE TEXT.

Second Edition. In Large Post 8vo, with Frontispiece and Vignette, cloth gilt, price 9s.

HIGH LIFE IN FRANCE UNDER THE REPUBLIC:

A SERIES OF SOCIAL AND SATIRICAL SKETCHES IN PARIS AND THE PROVINCES.

BY E. C. GRENVILLE-MURRAY,

AUTHOR OF "SIDE LIGHTS ON ENGLISH SOCIETY," &c.

"Take this book as it stands, with the limitations imposed upon its author by circumstances, and it will be found very enjoyable.... The volume is studded with shrewd observations on French life at the present day."—*Spectator.*

"A very clever and entertaining series of social and satirical sketches, almost French in their point and vivacity."—*Contemporary Review.*

"Mr. Grenville-Murray's Pistache is capital, and so is Gredon, who gets adopted and befooled, despite his Yankee training, by the *soi-disant* Duke of Pontbrizé . . The whole story of Timoleon Turtine, winding up with the commission agent's episode, is excellent."—*Graphic.*

"Mr. Grenville-Murray's sketches are light and pointed, and are full of that particular humour in which Frenchmen are supposed to be such adepts."—*Scotsman.*

In Large Post 8vo, cloth gilt, price 9s.

IMPRISONED IN A SPANISH CONVENT:

AN ENGLISH GIRL'S EXPERIENCES.

BY E. C. GRENVILLE-MURRAY.

ILLUSTRATED WITH PAGE AND OTHER ENGRAVINGS.

Fourth Edition, in Post 8vo, handsomely bound, price 7s. 6d.

SIDE-LIGHTS ON ENGLISH SOCIETY:

Sketches from Life, Social and Satirical.

By E. C. GRENVILLE-MURRAY.

ILLUSTRATED WITH NEARLY 300 CHARACTERISTIC ENGRAVINGS.

CONTENTS:

I. **FLIRTS:**—Born Flirts—The Flirt who has Plain Sisters—The Flirt in the London Season—The Ecclesiastical Flirt—The Regimental Flirt on Home and Foreign Service—The Town and Country House Flirt—The Seaside Flirt—The Flirt on her Travels—The Sentimental Flirt—The Studious Flirt.

II. **ON HER BRITANNIC MAJESTY'S SERVICE:**—Ambassadors—Envoys Extraordinary—Secretaries of Embassy—Secretaries of Legation—Attachés—Consuls-General—Consuls—Vice-Consuls—Queen's Messengers—Interpreters—Ambassadresses.

III. **SEMI-DETACHED WIVES:**—Authoresses and Actresses—Separated by Mutual Consent—Candidates for a Decree Nisi—A very virtuous Semi-Detached Wife—Ulysses and Penelope.

IV. **NOBLE LORDS:**—The Millionnaire Duke—Political Peers—Noble Old Fogies—Spiritual Peers—The Sabbatarian Peer—The Philanthropist Peer—Coaching Peers—Sporting Peers—Spendthrift Peers—Peers without Rent-rolls—Virtuoso Lords—Mad and Miserly Peers—Stock Exchange and Literary Lords.

V. **YOUNG WIDOWS:**—Interesting Widows—Gay Young Widows—Young Widows of Good Estate—Young Widows who take Boarders—Young Widows who want Situations—Great Men's Young Widows—Widows under a Cloud.

VI. **OUR SILVERED YOUTH, OR NOBLE OLD BOYS:**—Political Old Boys—Horsey Old Boys—An M. F. H.—Theatrical Old Boys—The Old Boy Cricketer—The Agricultural Old Boy—The Wicked Old Boy—The Shabby Old Boy—The Recluse Old Boy—The Clerical Old Boy—A Curiosity—An Old Courtier.

"This is a startling book. The volume is expensively and elaborately got up; the writing is bitter, unsparing, and extremely clever."—*Vanity Fair.*

"Mr. Grenville-Murray sparkles very steadily throughout the present volume, and puts to excellent use his incomparable knowledge of life and manners, of men and cities, of appearances and facts. Of his several descants upon English types, I shall only remark that they are brilliantly and dashingly written, curious as to their matter, and admirably readable."—*Truth.*

"No one can question the brilliancy of the sketches, nor affirm that 'Side-Lights' is aught but a fascinating book ...... The book is destined to make a great noise in the world."—*Whitehall Review.*

THE RICH WIDOW (reduced from the original engraving).

Second Edition, in large 8vo, handsomely bound, with gilt edges, price 10s. 6d.

PEOPLE I HAVE MET.

By E. C. GRENVILLE-MURRAY.

Illustrated with 54 tinted Page Engravings, from Designs by FRED. BARNARD.

CONTENTS :—

The Old Earl.	The Rector.	The Doctor.	The Bachelor.
The Dowager.	The Curate.	The Retired Colonel.	The Younger Son.
The Family Solicitor.	The Governess.	The Chaperon.	The Grandmother.
The College Don.	The Tutor.	The Usurer.	The Newspaper Editor.
The Rich Widow.	The Promising Son.	The Spendthrift.	The Butler.
The Ornamental Director.	The Favourite Daughter.	Le Nouveau Riche.	The Devotee.
The Old Maid.	The Squire.	The Maiden Aunt.	

"Mr. Grenville-Murray's pages sparkle with cleverness and with a shrewd wit, caustic or cynical at times, but by no means excluding a due appreciation of the softer virtues of women and the sterner excellences of men. The talent of the artist (Mr. Barnard) is akin to that of the author, and the result of the combination is a book that, once taken up, can hardly be laid down until the last page is perused."—*Spectator.*

"All are strongly accentuated portraits. 'The Promising Son' is perhaps the best, though the most melancholy of the series. From first to last, as might be expected, the book is well written."—*Standard.*

"Mr. Grenville-Murray's sketches are genuine studies, and are the best things of the kind that have been published since 'Sketches by Boz,' to which they are superior in the sense in which artistically executed character-portraits are superior to caricatures."—*St. James's Gazette.*

"All of Mr. Grenville-Murray's portraits are clever and life-like, and some of them are not unworthy of a model who was more before the author's eyes than Addison—namely Thackeray."—*Truth.*

An Edition of "PEOPLE I HAVE MET" is published in small 8vo without Mr. Barnard's Illustrations, price 6s.

A BUCK OF THE REGENCY: *from "DUTCH PICTURES."*

"Mr. Sala's best work has in it something of Montaigne, a great deal of Charles Lamb—made deeper and broader—and not a little of Lamb's model, the accomplished and quaint Sir Thomas Brown. These 'Dutch Pictures' and 'Pictures Done With a Quill' should be placed alongside Oliver Wendell Holmes's inimitable budgets of friendly gossip and Thackeray's 'Roundabout Papers.' They display to perfection the quick eye, good taste, and ready hand of the born essayist—they are never tiresome."—*Daily Telegraph.*

In Crown 8vo, price 5s.

DUTCH PICTURES, and PICTURES DONE WITH A QUILL.

Illustrated with a Frontispiece and other Page Engravings.

FORMING THE FIRST VOLUME OF THE

CHOICER MISCELLANEOUS WORKS OF GEORGE AUGUSTUS SALA.

A SMALL NUMBER OF COPIES OF THE ABOVE WORK HAVE BEEN PRINTED IN DEMY OCTAVO, ON HAND-MADE PAPER, WITH THE ILLUSTRATIONS ON INDIA PAPER MOUNTED.

The Graphic remarks: "We have received a sumptuous new edition of Mr. G. A. Sala's well-known 'Dutch Pictures.' It is printed on rough paper, and is enriched with many admirable illustrations."

In preparation, uniform with the above Volume,

UNDER THE SUN.

ESSAYS MAINLY WRITTEN IN HOT COUNTRIES.

BY GEORGE AUGUSTUS SALA.

Illustrated with an etched Portrait of the Author, and various Page Engravings.

In One Volume, Demy 8vo, 560 pages, price 12s., the FIFTH EDITION *of*

AMERICA REVISITED,

From the Bay of New York to the Gulf of Mexico, and from Lake Michigan to the Pacific;

INCLUDING A SOJOURN AMONG THE MORMONS IN SALT LAKE CITY.

BY GEORGE AUGUSTUS SALA.

ILLUSTRATED WITH NEARLY 400 ENGRAVINGS.

CONTENTS.

Outward Bound.
Thanksgiving Day in New York.
Transformation of New York.
All the Fun of the Fair.
A Morning with Justice.
On the Cars.
Fashion and Food in New York.
The Monumental City.
Baltimore come to Life again.
The Great Grant "Boom."
A Philadelphian Babel.
At the Continental.
Christmas and the New Year.
On to Richmond.
Still on to Richmond.

In Richmond.
Genial Richmond.
In the Tombs—and out of them.
Prosperous Augusta.
The City of many Cows.
A Pantomime in the South.
Arrogant Atlanta.
The Crescent City.
On Canal Street.
In Jackson Square.
A Southern Parliament.
Sunday in New Orleans.
The Carnival Booming.
The Carnival Booms.
Going West.

The Wonderful Prairie City.
The Home of the Setting Sun.
At Omaha.
The Road to Eldorado.
Still on the Road to Eldorado.
At Last.
Aspects of 'Frisco.
China Town.
The Drama in China Town.
Scenes in China Town.
China Town by Night.
From 'Frisco to Salt Lake City.
Down among the Mormons.
The Stock-yards of Chicago.

"It was like your imperence to come smouchin' round here, looking after de white folks' washin."

"In 'America Revisited' Mr. Sala is seen at his very best; better even than in his Paris book, more evenly genial and gay, and with a fresher subject to handle."—*World.*

"Mr. Sala's good stories lie thick as plums in a pudding throughout this handsome work."—*Pall Mall Gazette.*

"A new book of travel by Mr. Sala is sure to be welcome. He possesses the happy knack of adorning whatever he touches, and of finding something worth telling when traversing beaten ground."—*Athenæum.*

"A pleasant day may be spent with this book. Open where you will you find kindly chat and pleasant description. The illustrations are admirable."—*Vanity Fair.*

"As for the style of this entertaining and lively book, it is exactly what we should have expected. The writer is full of life, observation, and swiftness to seize upon salient and characteristic points. His description of the Chinese quarter of San Francisco may be strongly commended."—*Saturday Review.*

"This brilliant work possesses an irresistible charm, difficult to define indeed, but none the less delightful. Reading it is like listening to a good talker—the usual slightly wearisome sense of reading is effaced by the vivaciousness of the style in which the cleverest *feuilletoniste* of the day has narrated his experiences on the occasion of his last visit to America."—*Morning Post.*

"'America Revisited' is bright, lively, and amusing. We doubt whether Mr. Sala could be dull even if he tried."—*Globe.*

Seventh Edition, in Crown 8vo, 558 pages, attractively bound, price 3s. 6d., or gilt at the side and with gilt edges, 5s.

PARIS HERSELF AGAIN.

By GEORGE AUGUSTUS SALA.

WITH 350 CHARACTERISTIC ILLUSTRATIONS BY FRENCH ARTISTS.

"The author's 'round-about' chapters are as animated as they are varied and sympathetic, for few Englishmen have the French *verve* like Mr. Sala, or so light a touch on congenial subjects. He has stores of out-of-the-way information, a very many-sided gift of appreciation, with a singularly tenacious memory, and on subjects like those in his present work he is at his best."—*The Times.*

"Most amusing letters they are, with clever little pictures scattered so profusely through the solid volume that it would be difficult to prick the edges with a pin at any point without coming upon one or more. Few writers can rival Mr. Sala's fertility of illustration and ever ready command of lively comment."—*Daily News.*

"'Paris Herself Again' furnishes a happy illustration of the attractiveness of Mr. Sala's style and the fertility of his resources. For those who do and those who do not know Paris these volumes contain a fund of instruction and amusement."—*Saturday Review.*

"This book is one of the most readable that has appeared for many a day. Few Englishmen know so much of old and modern Paris as Mr. Sala. Endowed with a facility to extract humour from every phase of the world's stage, and blessed with a wondrous store of recondite lore, he outdoes himself when he deals with a city like Paris that he knows so well, and that affords such an opportunity for his pen."—*Truth.*

"'Paris Herself Again' is infinitely more amusing than most novels, and will give you information which you can turn to advantage, and innumerable anecdotes for the dinner-table and the smoking-room. There is no style so chatty and so unwearying as that of which Mr. Sala is a master."—*The World.*

VIZETELLY & CO.'S RECENT PUBLICATIONS.

ZOLA'S POWERFUL REALISTIC NOVELS.

Uniform with NANA *and* THE "ASSOMMOIR." *In Crown 8vo, price 6s.*

PIPING HOT!
("POT-BOUILLE.")
BY EMILE ZOLA.

Unabridged Translation from the 63rd French edition. Illustrated with Sixteen Tinted Page Engravings by French Artists.

In Crown 8vo, handsomely bound, price 6s.

NANA:
A REALISTIC NOVEL. BY EMILE ZOLA.
TRANSLATED WITHOUT ABRIDGMENT FROM THE 127TH FRENCH EDITION.

A New Edition. Illustrated with Twenty-Four Tinted Page Engravings, from Designs by Bellenger, Clairin, and André Gill.

Mr. HENRY JAMES on "NANA."

"A novelist with a system, a passionate conviction, a great plan—incontestable attributes of M. Zola—is not now to be easily found in England or the United States, where the story-teller's art is almost exclusively feminine, is mainly in the hands of timid (even when very accomplished) women, whose acquaintance with life is severely restricted, and who are not conspicuous for general views. The novel, moreover, among ourselves, is almost always addressed to young unmarried ladies, or at least always assumes them to be a large part of the novelist's public.

"This fact, to a French story-teller, appears, of course, a damnable restriction, and M. Zola would probably decline to take *au serieux* any work produced under such unnatural conditions. Half of life is a sealed book to young unmarried ladies, and how can a novel be worth anything that deals only with half of life? How can a portrait be painted (in any way to be recognizable) of half a face? It is not in one eye, but in the two eyes together that the expression resides, and it is the combination of features that constitutes the human identity. These objections are perfectly valid, and it may be said that our English system is a good thing for virgins and boys, and a bad thing for the novel itself, when the novel is regarded as something more than a simple *jeu d'esprit*, and considered as a composition that treats of life at large and helps us to *know*."

*** An Edition of "NANA" is published without the Illustrations, price 5s.

In Crown 8vo, uniform with "NANA," *price 6s.*

THE "ASSOMMOIR;"
(The Prelude to "NANA.")
A REALISTIC NOVEL. BY EMILE ZOLA.
TRANSLATED WITHOUT ABRIDGMENT FROM THE 97TH FRENCH EDITION.

Illustrated with Sixteen Tinted Page Engravings, by Bellenger, Clairin, André Gill, Leloir, Rosé and Vierge.

"After reading Zola's novels it seems as if in all others, even in the truest, there were a veil between the reader and the things described, and there is present to our minds the same difference as exists between the representations of human faces on canvas and the reflection of the same faces in a mirror. It is like finding truth for the first time.

"Zola is one of the most moral novelists in France, and it is really astonishing how anyone can doubt this. He makes us note the smell of vice, not its perfume: his nude figures are those of the anatomical table, which do not inspire the slightest immoral thought; there is not one of his books, not even the crudest, that does not leave behind it pure, firm, and unmistakable aversion, or scorn, for the base passions of which he treats. Brutally, pitilessly, and without hypocrisy he strips vice naked and holds it up to ridicule. Forced by his hand it is vice itself that says, 'Detest me and pass by!' His novels, as he himself says, are really 'morals in action.'"—*Signor de Amicis on the "Assommoir."*

TO BE FOLLOWED BY THE MORE POPULAR OF EMILE ZOLA'S REMARKABLE WORKS.

THE ARRIVAL OF THE ELEVEN YOUNG MEN AT NANA'S EVENING PARTY.

In Crown 8vo, handsomely bound and gilt, price 6s., the Third and Completely Revised Edition of

THE STORY OF
THE DIAMOND NECKLACE,

COMPRISING A SKETCH OF THE LIFE OF THE COUNTESS DE LA MOTTE, PRETENDED CONFIDANTE OF MARIE-ANTOINETTE, WITH PARTICULARS OF THE CAREERS OF THE OTHER ACTORS IN THIS REMARKABLE DRAMA.

By HENRY VIZETELLY.

Illustrated with an Exact Representation of the Diamond Necklace, from a contemporary Drawing, and a Portrait of the Countess de la Motte, engraved on Steel.

"Mr. Vizetelly's tale has all the interest of a romance which is too strange not to be true. . . . . . His summing up of the evidence, both negative and positive, which exculpates Marie-Antoinette from any complicity whatever with the scandalous intrigue in which she was represented as bearing a part, is admirable."—*Saturday Review.*

"We can, without fear of contradiction, describe Mr. Henry Vizetelly's 'Story of the Diamond Necklace' as a book of thrilling interest. He has not only executed his task with skill and faithfulness, but also with tact and delicacy."—*Standard.*

"Had the most daring of our sensational novelists put forth the present plain unvarnished statement of facts as a work of fiction, it would have been denounced as so violating all probabilities as to be a positive insult to the common sense of the reader. Yet strange, startling, incomprehensible as is the narrative which the author has here evolved, every word of it is true."—*Notes and Queries.*

In Large Crown 8vo, handsomely printed and bound, price 6s.

THE AMUSING
ADVENTURES OF GUZMAN OF ALFARAQUE.

A SPANISH NOVEL. TRANSLATED BY EDWARD LOWDELL.

ILLUSTRATED WITH HIGHLY-FINISHED ENGRAVINGS ON STEEL FROM DESIGNS BY STAHL.

"The wit, vivacity and variety of this masterpiece cannot be over-estimated."—*Morning Post.*
"A very well executed translation of a famous, 'Rogue's Progress.'"—*Spectator.*
"The story is infinitely amusing, and illustrated as it is with several excellent designs on steel, it will be acceptable to a good many readers."—*Scotsman.*

In Post 8vo, price 2s. 6d.

THE CHILDISHNESS AND BRUTALITY OF THE TIME:

SOME PLAIN TRUTHS IN PLAIN LANGUAGE.

Supplemented by sundry discursive Essays and Narratives.

By HARGRAVE JENNINGS, Author of "The Rosicrucians," &c.

"Mr. Jennings has a knack of writing in good, racy, trenchant style. His sketch of behind the scenes of the Opera, and his story of a mutiny on board an Indiaman of the old time, are penned with surprising freshness and spirit."—*Daily News.*

"A chatty and extremely interesting discourse upon the great factors that compose and regulate the social life of the present day."—*Newcastle Chronicle.*

In Crown 8vo, attractively bound, price 3s. 6d.

THE RED CROSS, AND OTHER STORIES.
By LUIGI.

" The short stories are the best—Luigi is in places tender and pathetic."—*Athenæum.*

" The plans of the tales are excellent. Many of the incidents are admirable, and there is a good deal of pathos in the writing."—*Scotsman.*

" Pleasant and bright if somewhat sensational, dealing with the old world and the new, and offering a welcome variety of style, these tales may be recommended to the lovers of fiction."—*Literary World.*

In Two Volumes, post 8vo, price 10s. 6d.

SOCIETY NOVELETTES.
By F. C. BURNAND, H. SAVILE CLARKE, R. E. FRANCILLON, JOSEPH HATTON, RICHARD JEFFERIES, the Author of "A French Heiress in her own Château," &c. &c.

ILLUSTRATED WITH NUMEROUS PAGE AND OTHER ENGRAVINGS,

FROM DESIGNS BY R. CALDECOTT, LINLEY SAMBOURNE, M. E. EDWARDS, F. DADD, &c.

"The reader will not be disappointed in the hopes raised by Messrs. Vizetelly's pleasing volumes. . . . There is much that is original and clever in these 'Society' tales."—*Athenæum.*

" Many of the stories are of the greatest merit; and indeed with such contributors, the reader might be sure of the unusual interest and amusement which these volumes supply."—*Daily Telegraph.*

" We strongly advise the reader to begin with 'How one Ghost was laid,' and to follow it up with 'Jack's Wife,' with whom, by the way, as portrayed both by artist and author, he cannot fail to fall in love. These two graceful little extravaganzas will put him into so excellent a temper that he will thoroughly enjoy the good things that follow."—*Life.*

" The two volumes contain a large amount of capital reading. The stories are of all kinds excepting unpleasant kinds."—*Scotsman.*

In Crown 8vo, price 3s. 6d.

A NEW EDITION, COMPRISING MUCH ADDITIONAL MATTER, OF

IN STRANGE COMPANY.
By JAMES GREENWOOD (the "Amateur Casual").

ILLUSTRATED WITH A PORTRAIT OF THE AUTHOR, ENGRAVED ON STEEL.

In square 8vo, cloth gilt, price 3s. 6d.

LAYS OF THE SAINTLY;
OR, THE NEW GOLDEN LEGEND.

By the LONDON HERMIT (W. PARKE),
Author of "Les Manteaux Noirs."

WITH HUMOROUS ILLUSTRATIONS BY J. LEITCH.

"Shows much facility in turning a verse, and some talent for parody. The burlesque of Dolores is clever in its way."—*Graphic.*

"The stories are told in bright and luminous verses in which are dexterously wrought parodies of a good many present and some past poets."—*Scotsman.*

"Lovers of laughter, raillery, and things ludicrous would do well to become possessed of this volume of humorous poems levelled against the absurd though amusing superstitions of the Middle Ages."—*Newcastle Chronicle.*

"Mr. Walter Parke's versatility is marvellous."—*Life.*

"We have had no such imitations of the idiosyncrasies of modern poets since the days of the gifted brothers James and Horace Smith."—*Lady's Pictorial.*

In Demy 4to, handsomely printed and bound, with gilt edges, price 12s.

A HISTORY OF CHAMPAGNE;
WITH NOTES ON THE OTHER SPARKLING WINES OF FRANCE.

By HENRY VIZETELLY,
WINE JUROR FOR GREAT BRITAIN AT THE VIENNA AND PARIS EXHIBITIONS OF 1873 AND 1878.

Illustrated with 350 Engravings,
FROM ORIGINAL SKETCHES AND PHOTOGRAPHS, ANCIENT MSS., EARLY PRINTED BOOKS, RARE PRINTS, CARICATURES, ETC.

"A very agreeable medley of history, anecdote, geographical description, and such like matter, distinguished by an accuracy not often found in such medleys, and illustrated in the most abundant and pleasingly miscellaneous fashion."—*Daily News.*

"Mr. Henry Vizetelly's handsome book about Champagne and other sparkling wines of France is full of curious information and amusement. It should be widely read and appreciated."—*Saturday Review.*

"Mr. Henry Vizetelly has written a quarto volume on the 'History of Champagne,' in which he has collected a large number of facts, many of them very curious and interesting. Many of the woodcuts are excellent."—*Athenæum.*

"In the handsome volume before us Mr. Henry Vizetelly has quite eclipsed all his former efforts."—*Morning Advertiser.*

"How competent the author was for his task is to be inferred from the functions he has discharged, and from the exceptional opportunities he enjoyed."—*Illustrated London News.*

In ornamental covers, price One Shilling each.

GABORIAU'S SENSATIONAL NOVELS.

THE FAVOURITE READING OF PRINCE BISMARCK.

> "Ah, friend, how many and many a while
> They've made the slow time fleetly flow,
> And solaced pain and charmed exile,
> Miss Braddon and Gaboriau!"
> *Ballads of Railway Novels in "Longman's Magazine."*

IN PERIL OF HIS LIFE.
"A story of thrilling interest and admirably translated."—*Sunday Times.*

"Hardly ever has a more ingenious circumstantial case been imagined than that which puts the hero in peril of his life, and the manner in which the proof of his innocence is finally brought about is scarcely less skilful."—*Illustrated Sporting and Dramatic News.*

THE LEROUGE CASE.
"M. Gaboriau is a skilful and brilliant writer, capable of so diverting the attention and interest of his readers that not one word or line in his book will be skipped or read carelessly."—*Hampshire Advertiser.*

OTHER PEOPLE'S MONEY.
"The interest is kept up throughout, and the story is told graphically and with a good deal of art."—*London Figaro.*

LECOQ THE DETECTIVE. Two vols.
"In the art of forging a tangled chain of complicated incidents involved and inexplicable until the last link is reached and the whole made clear, Mr. Wilkie Collins is equalled, if not excelled, by M. Gaboriau. The same skill in constructing a story is shown by both, as likewise the same ability to build up a superstructure of facts on a foundation which, sound enough in appearance, is shattered when the long-concealed touchstone of truth is at length applied to it."—*Brighton Herald.*

THE GILDED CLIQUE.
"Full of incident and instinct with life and action. Altogether this is a most fascinating book."—*Hampshire Advertiser.*

THE MYSTERY OF ORCIVAL.
"The Author keeps the interest of the reader at fever heat, and by a succession of unexpected turns and incidents, the drama is ultimately worked out to a very pleasant result. The ability displayed is unquestionable."—*Sheffield Independent.*

DOSSIER NO. 113.
"The plot is worked out with great skill, and from first to last the reader's interest is never allowed to flag."—*Dumbarton Herald.*

THE LITTLE OLD MAN OF BATIGNOLLES.

THE SLAVES OF PARIS. Two vols.
"Sensational, full of interest, cleverly conceived and wrought out with consummate skill."—*Oxford and Cambridge Journal.*

THE COUNT'S MILLIONS. Two vols.

INTRIGUES OF A FEMALE POISONER.

THE CATASTROPHE. Two vols.

In Small Post 8vo, ornamental covers, 1s. each ; in cloth, 1s. 6d.

VIZETELLY'S POPULAR FRENCH NOVELS.
TRANSLATIONS OF THE BEST EXAMPLES OF RECENT FRENCH FICTION OF AN UNOBJECTIONABLE CHARACTER.

"*They are books that may be safely left lying about where the ladies of the family can pick them up and read them. The interest they create is happily not of the vicious sort at all.*"
— SHEFFIELD INDEPENDENT.

FROMONT THE YOUNGER & RISLER THE ELDER. By A. DAUDET.
"The series starts well with M. Alphonse Daudet's masterpiece."—*Athenæum*.
"A terrible story, powerful after a sledge-hammer fashion in some parts, and wonderfully tender, touching, and pathetic in others, the extraordinary popularity whereof may be inferred from the fact that this English version is said to be 'translated from the fiftieth French edition.'"—*Illustrated London News*.

SAMUEL BROHL AND PARTNER. By V. CHERBULIEZ.
"M. Cherbuliez's novels are read by everybody and offend nobody. They are excellent studies of character, well constructed, peopled with interesting men and women, and the style in which they are written is admirable."—*The Times*.
"Those who have read this singular story in the original need not be reminded of that supremely dramatic study of the man who lived two lives at once, even within himself. The reader's discovery of his double nature is one of the most cleverly managed of surprises, and Samuel Brohl's final dissolution of partnership with himself is a remarkable stroke of almost pathetic comedy."—*The Graphic*.

THE DRAMA OF THE RUE DE LA PAIX. By A. BELOT.
"A highly ingenious plot is developed in 'The Drama of the Rue de la Paix,' in which a decidedly interesting and thrilling narrative is told with great force and passion, relieved by sprightliness and tenderness."—*Illustrated London News*.

MAUGARS JUNIOR. By A. THEURIET.
"One of the most charming novelettes we have read for a long time."—*Literary World*.

WAYWARD DOSIA, & THE GENEROUS DIPLOMATIST. HENRY GRÉVILLE.
"As epigrammatic as anything Lord Beaconsfield has ever written."—*Hampshire Telegraph*.

A NEW LEASE OF LIFE, & SAVING A DAUGHTER'S DOWRY. By E. ABOUT.
"'A New Lease of Life' is an absorbing story, the interest of which is kept up to the very end."—*Dublin Evening Mail*.
"The story, as a flight of brilliant and eccentric imagination, is unequalled in its peculiar way."—*The Graphic*.

COLOMBA, & CARMEN. By P. MÉRIMÉE.
"The freshness and raciness of 'Colomba' is quite cheering after the stereotyped three-volume novels with which our circulating libraries are crammed."—*Halifax Times*.
"'Carmen' will be welcomed by the lovers of the sprightly and tuneful opera the heroine of which Minnie Hauk made so popular. It is a bright and vivacious story."—*Life*.

A WOMAN'S DIARY, & THE LITTLE COUNTESS. By O. FEUILLET.
"Is wrought out with masterly skill and affords reading which, although of a slightly sensational kind, cannot be said to be hurtful either mentally or morally."—*Dumbarton Herald*.

BLUE-EYED META HOLDENIS, & A STROKE OF DIPLOMACY. By V. CHERBULIEZ.
"'Blue-eyed Meta Holdenis' is a delightful tale."—*Civil Service Gazette.*
"'A Stroke of Diplomacy' is a bright vivacious story pleasantly told."—*Hampshire Advertiser.*

THE GODSON OF A MARQUIS. By A. THEURIET.
"The rustic personages, the rural scenery and life in the forest country of Argonne, are painted with the hand of a master. From the beginning to the close the interest of the story never flags."—*Life.*

THE TOWER OF PERCEMONT AND MARIANNE. By GEORGE SAND.
"George Sand has a great name, and the 'Tower of Percemont' is not unworthy of it."—*Illustrated London News.*

THE LOW-BORN LOVER'S REVENGE. By V. CHERBULIEZ.
"'The Low-born Lover's Revenge' is one of M. Cherbuliez's many exquisitely written productions. The studies of human nature under various influences, especially in the cases of the unhappy heroine and her low-born lover, are wonderfully effective."—*Illustrated London News.*

THE NOTARY'S NOSE, AND OTHER AMUSING STORIES. By E. ABOUT.
"Crisp and bright, full of movement and interest."—*Brighton Herald.*

DOCTOR CLAUDE; OR, LOVE RENDERED DESPERATE. By H. MALOT. Two vols.
"We have to appeal to our very first flight of novelists to find anything so artistic in English romance as these books."—*Dublin Evening Mail.*

THE THREE RED KNIGHTS; OR, THE BROTHERS' VENGEANCE. By P. FÉVAL.
"The one thing that strikes us in these stories is the marvellous dramatic skill of the writers."—*Sheffield Independent.*

In large imperial 8vo, price 6d.

THE SOCIAL ZOO;

SATIRICAL, SOCIAL, AND HUMOROUS SKETCHES BY THE BEST WRITERS.

Copiously Illustrated in Many Styles by well-known Artists.

NOW READY.

OUR GILDED YOUTH. By E. C. GRENVILLE-MURRAY——NICE GIRLS. By R. MOUNTENEY JEPHSON——NOBLE LORDS. By E. C. GRENVILLE-MURRAY.——FLIRTS. By E. C. GRENVILLE-MURRAY——OUR SILVERED YOUTH. By E. C. GRENVILLE-MURRAY——MILITARY MEN AS THEY WERE. By E. DYNE FENTON.

TO BE FOLLOWED BY YOUNG WIDOWS—CLUB MEN—BEHIND THE SCENES—JILTS—OUR YOUNG MEN—THE TUNEFUL QUIRE—ON H.B.M.'S SERVICE.

A Volume containing the First Five Numbers of the "SOCIAL ZOO" is now ready, in an attractive binding, price 3s. 6d.

2c VIZETELLY & CO.'S RECENT PUBLICATIONS.

MR. HENRY VIZETELLY'S POPULAR BOOKS ON WINE.

"Mr. Vizetelly discourses brightly and discriminatingly on crus and bouquets and the different European vineyards, most of which he has evidently visited."—*The Times.*

"Mr. Henry Vizetelly's books about different wines have an importance and a value far greater than will be assigned them by those who look merely at the price at which they are published."—*Sunday Times.*

Price 1s. 6d. ornamental cover; or 2s. 6d. in elegant cloth binding.

FACTS ABOUT PORT AND MADEIRA,

GLEANED DURING A TOUR IN THE AUTUMN OF 1877.

By HENRY VIZETELLY,

WINE JUROR FOR GREAT BRITAIN AT THE VIENNA AND PARIS EXHIBITIONS OF 1873 AND 1878.

With 100 Illustrations from Original Sketches and Photographs.

BY THE SAME AUTHOR.

Price 1s. 6d. ornamental cover; or 2s. 6d. in elegant cloth binding.

FACTS ABOUT CHAMPAGNE
AND OTHER SPARKLING WINES,

COLLECTED DURING NUMEROUS VISITS TO THE CHAMPAGNE AND OTHER VITICULTURAL DISTRICTS OF FRANCE AND THE PRINCIPAL REMAINING WINE-PRODUCING COUNTRIES OF EUROPE.

Illustrated with 112 Engravings from Sketches and Photographs.

Price 1s. ornamental cover; or 1s. 6d. cloth gilt.

FACTS ABOUT SHERRY,

GLEANED IN THE VINEYARDS AND BODEGAS OF THE JEREZ, & OTHER DISTRICTS.

Illustrated with numerous Engravings from Original Sketches.

Price 1s. in ornamental cover; or 1s. 6d. cloth gilt.

THE WINES OF THE WORLD,
CHARACTERIZED AND CLASSED.

VIZETELLY & CO., 42, CATHERINE STREET, STRAND.

www.ingramcontent.com/pod-product-compliance
Lightning Source LLC
Chambersburg PA
CBHW032044220426
43664CB00008B/861